The Journal of the
Hannah Arendt Center for
Politics and Humanities
at Bard College

The Journal of the Hannah Arendt Center for
Politics and Humanities at Bard College

hac.bard.edu

©2020 Bard College

Published by
The Hannah Arendt Center for Politics and Humanities at Bard College
Roger Berkowitz, Editor
Samantha Rose Hill, Managing Editor

Editorial Board
Jerome Kohn
Patchen Markell
Wyatt Mason
Thomas Wild

Produced by
Bard College Publications Office
Mary Smith, Director
Barbara Ross, Copy Editor
Kenneth Treadway, Designer

Cover: ©Estate of Fred Stein, fredstein.com

ISSN: 2168-6572
ISBN: 978-1-936192-65-6
Bard College, PO Box 5000
Annandale-on-Hudson, NY 12504-5000
bard.edu

Foreword

In what seems like another world—a world from before the COVID-19 pandemic and the Black Lives Matter revolutionary moment—the Hannah Arendt Center Annual Fall Conference 2019 addressed the intersection of racism and antisemitism. The premise of bringing together the two most deadly twentieth-century ideologies of racialized slavery and racialized genocide was as simple as it was, and still is, provocative. We sought to ask what could be learned from thinking about the similarities and differences between the two most destructive racisms in human history.

When Hannah Arendt sat down to write *The Origins of Totalitarianism* after spending over ten years in exile, she began with a history of antisemitism. In order to understand the horrific emergence of totalitarianism, she had to confront the question of why the Jewish people had been targeted. She found the commonsense explanation—that Jews were scapegoats—to be wrong. The scapegoat explanation, she writes, was "one of the principal attempts to escape the seriousness of antisemitism and the significance of the fact that the Jews were driven into the storm of the center of events." For Arendt, antisemitism chose the Jews as the key to the world's ills for very specific reasons, and those reasons needed to be understood and confronted.

Arendt argued that political antisemitism is more than Jew hatred; rather, it is a pseudoscientific ideology seeking to prove that Jews are responsible for all the evils of the world. In its social form, antisemitism unleashed the fantasy of "the Jew" in general as the foreigner. The social fantasy of "the Jew" forced upon Jews a terrible choice, between being a parvenu who rejects their Jewishness and assimilates or a pariah defined by their Jewishness. In its political form, antisemitism is a form of racial ideology that justifies oppression and even annihilation of Jews as foreigners who are the key to the problems of the world.

Although Arendt is often accused of ignoring her Jewish identity, her work is consistently attentive to the Jewish question, beginning with her early writing on Rahel Varnhagen, where she argues that Jews were faced with the cruel choice of becoming parvenus or pariahs. Captured by Nazis twice, forced to flee first to Germany and then to Occupied France, Arendt thought about how one could live in the world as a refugee and foreigner. One could either try to assimilate and cast off their history, or they could choose to carry their identity with them through the world and embrace their otherness. The former, she wrote in "We Refugees," were destined to become Ulysses-like wanderers, while the later had a chance at finding a form of peace in an unsettled world. Arendt's sharp distinction between pariahs and parvenus reflects her understanding of antisemitism and totalitarianism; ideologically, antisemitism had in part been so successful because Jewish people were already freely shedding their Jewish identity, and she refused to do this.

When Arendt came to the United States as a stateless refugee, she began writing for small Jewish journals, and reflected upon the similarities and differences between racism in American and antisemitism in Europe. She called slavery the original sin of America and called for a constitutional amendment explicitly recognizing African Americans as full members of the American Republic. Arendt argued that racism is an ideology like antisemitism. It offers a pseudoscientific justification for violence that elevates one group at the expense of another. And imagining that racial differences must lead to a race war means that "racism may indeed carry out the doom of the Western world, and, for that matter, of the whole of human civilization."

In writing about racism in America, however, Arendt consistently made arguments that rubbed many in the civil rights community the wrong way. She distinguishes *racism* from *race thinking*, which is a form of prejudice. Racial prejudice exists, like all prejudices, as "an integral part of those human affairs that are the context in which we go about our daily lives." She said clearly that racial prejudices are "probably wrong" and "certainly pernicious," but she also argued that they must be taken seriously as opinions. Racism, on the other hand, is an ideology that justifies political oppression and "differs from a simple opinion in that it claims to possess either the key to history, or the solution for all the 'riddles of the universe.'"

From *The Origins of Totalitarianism* to "Reflections on Little Rock," Arendt's thinking on race is controversial, and has often led many to quickly dismiss her thoughts on race and antisemitism entirely. The opening essays by Eric K. Ward, John McWhorter, Eric Kaufmann, Marc Weitzmann, Adam Shatz, Thomas Chatterton Williams, Nacira Guénif-Souilamas, Marwan Mohammed, Etienne Balibar, Peter Baehr, and myself are adapted from talks given at the Arendt Center Conference and explore these oft-shunned concepts in the context of our contemporary political moment, which is marked by antisemitic and racist violence.

In addition, we reprint here a series of essays and responses to an original essay by Raymond Geuss on the occasion of Jürgen Habermas's 90th birthday. In his original essay, Geuss questions a core Habermasian assumption that conversation is fundamental to freedom and democracy. Against Habermas, Geuss argues that speech is not governed by an ideal that leads to moral or political agreement. On the contrary, most discussions, "even discussions that take place under reasonably favorable conditions, are not necessarily enlightening, clarifying or conducive to fostering consensus." Seyla Benhabib responded to Geuss, and this led to a series of rejoinders by Geuss, Benhabib, and Martin E. Jay. As a whole, the exchange represents an important inquiry into the claim that communication and discourse in political and social life can bring about more rational opinions.

We also include essays that offer essential takes on core issues of profound concern to Hannah Arendt and our world. Natan Sznaider writes about the famous interview between Arendt and Günter Gaus. Jana Marlene Madar explores the close connection between Arendt and the German poet Friedrich Hölderlin. Peter Brown mines Arendt's brief letter to James Baldwin to examine the varying ways these two thinkers imagine love to play a role in politics. Samantha Hill reflects on Arendt from her experience reading Arendt's Notebooks in the German Literature Archive in Marbach. Antonia Grunenberg brings Arendt into conversation with her friend Walter Benjamin. Philippe Nonet looks closely at the work of Arendt's first teacher, Martin Heidegger, and argues that, beginning in the 1950s, Heidegger came to see his philosophical project to think the Being of beings as a dead end. Jana V. Schmidt looks to Arendt to think again about the question of woman as different and a new beginning. And finally, Ellen Rigsby reviews David Arndt's book *Arendt on the Political*.

—Roger Berkowitz

About the Hannah Arendt Center

The Hannah Arendt Center for Politics and Humanities at Bard College is an expansive home for thinking in the spirit of Hannah Arendt. The Arendt Center's double mission is first, to sponsor and support the highest-quality scholarship on Hannah Arendt and her work, and second, to be an intellectual incubator for engaged humanities thinking at Bard College and beyond, thinking that elevates and deepens the public argument that is the bedrock of our democracy. The Arendt Center cares for and makes available the Hannah Arendt Library, with nearly 5,000 books from Hannah Arendt's personal library, many with marginalia and notes. Visit hac.bard.edu for more information.

VOLUME 8   *HA*

Racism and   Introduction: Racism and Antisemitism   10
Antisemitism   *Roger Berkowitz*

                   How Antisemitism Animates White Nationalism   17
                   Eric K. Ward

                   What Is Racism?   24
                   John McWhorter

                   Whiteshift: Immigration, Populism, and the   30
                   Future of White Majorities
                   Eric Kaufmann

                   Discussion: The Great Replacement   45
                   Marc Weitzmann, Adam Shatz, Thomas Chatterton Williams,
                   Nacira Guénif-Souilamas, and Marwan Mohammed

                   The New Racism?   61
                   Etienne Balibar

                   Are "They" Us? The Intellectuals' Role in   66
                   Creating Division
                   Peter Baehr

                   Reflections on Hannah Arendt's "Reflections on   73
                   Little Rock"
                   Roger Berkowitz

Dialogue   A Republic of Discussion: Habermas at 90   81
                   Raymond Geuss

                   Jürgen Habermas's 90th birthday   89
                   Seyla Benhabib

                   Professor Benhabib and Jürgen Habermas   92
                   Raymond Geuss

                   Contra Geuss: A Second Rejoinder   97
                   Seyla Benhabib

"The Liberal Idea Has Become Obsolete":   100
Putin, Geuss, and Habermas
Martin E. Jay

Presuppositions: A Reply to Benhabib and Jay   106
Raymond Geuss

Geuss, Habermas, and the Rose of Unreason   110
Martin E. Jay

Essays   Introduction to the Arendt-Gaus Interview   116
Natan Sznaider

Arendt, Hölderlin, and Their Perception of Schicksal: 122
Hölderlinian Elements in Arendt's Thinking and the
Messianic Notion of Revolution
Jana Marlene Madar

Toward a Poetic Reading of Arendt and Baldwin   139
on Love
Peter Brown

In the Archive with Hannah Arendt   147
Samantha Hill

Twilight of the Gods: Walter Benjamin's Project of a   153
Political Metaphysics in Secular Times—and
Hannah Arendt's Answer
Antonia Grunenberg

"*Der Holzweg*": Heidegger's Dead End   165
Philippe Nonet

Woman as Witness, Beginner, Philosopher   175
Jana V. Schmidt

Book Review   *Arendt on the Political* by David Arndt   182
Ellen M. Rigsby

Contributors   187

Racism and Antisemitism

Introduction: Racism and Antisemitism

Roger Berkowitz

One day before the 2019 Hannah Arendt Center Conference on "Racism and Antisemitism," a gunman in Germany tried to storm a synagogue where Jews were praying. It was Yom Kippur, the Day of Atonement, the holiest day of the year for Jews. Foiled by security, he killed two people outside. Like the gunman who attacked two mosques in Christchurch, New Zealand, the German gunman livestreamed his attack. He "identified himself as Anon, denied the Holocaust, denounced feminists and immigrants, then declared: 'The root of all these problems is the Jew.'"[1]

The shooting of Jews in Germany on Yom Kippur barely registered. And no wonder. Hateful attacks on Jews, Muslims, blacks, gays, trans people, refugees, and other minorities are rising. The list of unarmed black men and women killed by police continues to grow, including Michael Brown, Dontre Hamilton, Eric Garner, John Crawford, Ezell Ford, Dante Parker, Tanisha Anderson, Tamir Rice, and Botham Jean, who was killed in his own apartment by an allegedly confused off-duty white police officer in Dallas. Here is a partial list of targeted racist mass killings in the last few years:

- Twenty-two people were killed and twenty-four injured in a mass shooting in El Paso targeting Mexicans and the so-called Hispanic invasion of Texas.[2]
- One woman and three others were injured at the shooting inside the Chabad Synagogue in Poway, California, by a gunman who blamed Jews for a white genocide, a common conspiracy theory; he published a rant in which he wrote, "Every Jew is responsible for the meticulously planned genocide of the European race."[3]
- Fifty-one people were killed and forty-nine injured in attacks at the Al Noor Mosque and the Linwood Islamic Center in Christchurch, New Zealand. The gunman streamed his attack on Facebook after issuing a 74-page manifesto titled "The Great Replacement," a reference to the "Great Replacement" conspiracy theory discussed in the essays by Adam Shatz, Marc Weitzmann, and Thomas Chatterton Williams in this volume.
- Two people were killed and five wounded at an attack on a yoga studio in Tallahassee, Florida, by a gunman who openly expressed his hatred of women and wrote about rape, torture, and murder in his journals.
- Eleven people were killed and seven injured inside the Tree of Life synagogue in Pittsburgh during Shabbat services. The gunman blamed immigrants and migrant caravans from Central America; he posted

online shortly before the attack that "HIAS [a Jewish American non-profit that provides humanitarian aid and assistance to refugees] likes to bring invaders in that kill our people. I can't sit by and watch my people get slaughtered. Screw your optics, I'm going in." He later told police, "All these Jews need to die."

- Six worshippers were killed and nineteen others injured in the Quebec City mosque shooting by a gunman with white nationalist and anti-Muslim beliefs.
- Forty-nine people were killed at a Latino gay nightclub, Pulse, in Orlando in 2016.[4]
- A counterprotester at the 2017 Unite the Right rally in Charlottesville was killed when a former teacher "fascinated by Nazism and Hitler" accelerated his car into a crowd of marchers.[5]
- Nine African American parishioners were murdered in 2015 by white supremacist Dylann Roof in the Charleston church massacre.[6]

The FBI Hate Crimes Report for 2017 lists 900 crimes targeting Jews and Jewish institutions, which is a 37 percent increase in antisemitic hate crimes. There were 2,013 hate crimes against African Americans, representing a 16 percent increase.[7] Closer to home in New York City, in the week leading up to the Arendt Center Conference, the NYPD published a report showing the city recorded 323 hate crimes from 1 January 2019 through 6 October 2019, up 33 percent from 243 incidents in the same period in 2018.

In New York City, antisemitic incidents are the most common hate crimes, having increased 53 percent in 2019, to 170 from 111 incidents in the same period in 2018. Hate crimes against black people rose 7 percent, to 31 incidents so far this year, compared with 29 incidents in the same period in 2018. And hate crimes motivated by victims' sexual orientation rose 8 percent, to 42 incidents so far in 2019, compared with 39 incidents in the same period last year. There were also 25 crimes motivated by animus against white people, a 92 percent increase from 13 incidents in the same period last year.[8]

How are we to make sense of these atrocities? Are these simply the latest in a never-ending string of hateful acts? History is filled with examples of religiously and racially motivated killings, expulsions, and mass murders. The hatred of foreigners is nothing new. And yet we must not become numb to these racially and religiously motivated killings. As Hannah Arendt wrote,

> The conviction that everything that happens on earth must be comprehensible to man can lead to interpreting history by commonplaces. Comprehension does not mean denying the outrageous, deducing the unprecedented by precedents, or by explaining phenomena by such analogies and generalities that the impact of realty and the shock of experience are no longer felt.[9]

We must allow ourselves to be shocked by our current moment. But being shocked does not leave us helpless. Shocked and awed by the outrageousness of our present, we must nevertheless seek to understand the present on its own terms. Such an understanding means "the unpremeditated, attentive facing up, and resisting of, reality."[10]

The Arendt Center Conference in fall 2019 happened on the heels of a string of racist, antisemitic, and homophobic incidents at Bard College and its sister school Simon's Rock. In September, antisemitic and racist graffiti was found at Simon's Rock after an African American woman claimed to have been attacked. Members of the Patriot Front, a white nationalist group, were found on campus at Bard placing stickers on campus buildings, and some people from a neighboring community were apprehended after driving though campus shouting racial and homophobic slurs at students. Thankfully, they were apprehended.

We know now that the alleged racial attack at Simon's Rock did not happen. After multiple investigations by Simon's Rock, Bard College, and the Berkshire County District Attorney, and a second independent investigation by outside attorneys, the investigators all agreed that, in the words of the outside investigative report, the claim of a racist attack against a female student was probably "staged in order to provoke further conversation on campus about racism."[11] In other words, the young woman who claimed she was attacked and beaten in a racist assault fabricated the assault in order to push the campus to address problems of racism on campus.

"Why would anyone fake a hate crime?"[12]

That is the question Wilfred Reilly asks in his book *Hate Crime Hoax*. Reilly, who is a professor of political science at Kentucky State University and who calls himself a "proud Black man,"[13] compiled a data set of what he labels "409 confirmed cases of fake hate crimes."[14] Reilly argues that in the period of his study from 2013 to 2017, "literally hundreds of major hate crime hoaxes have taken place on American university campuses."[15] While most of these fake hate crimes are like the one at Simon's Rock—where minority students fabricate a racial attack to provoke discussion of racism—it is also a "fact that hate crime hoaxes are increasingly being perpetrated by white members of the alt-right, with the explicit goal of making Black people and leftist causes look bad."[16] For Reilly, fake claims of hate crimes are dangerous. They foster "real hostility between the races, which could lead to violence in the future."[17] Fake hate crimes can make racial violence appear normal, and can become a "precursor to real atrocities."[18] And yet, Reilly argues that "false hate crime allegations have value because they provide support for the metanarrative of majority group bigotry."[19]

What is more, even fake claims of racist attacks can work. At Simon's Rock, the response by the college went out of its way to acknowledge that even if the specific incident was made up, the atmosphere of racism it sought to publicize was real:

> This outcome will impact people in different ways. Even as we bring this matter and investigation to a close, we cannot close our eyes or minds to the reality of racial injustice or our responsibility to those most vulnerable to hate. We want to assure you that our commitment to building a more equitable, inclusive, and safe community remains steadfast and ongoing.
>
> Our Council for Equity and Inclusion will be working with colleagues at Bard's Council for Inclusive Excellence to develop departmental strategic plans for diversity, equity, and inclusion.[20]

It is understandable for the college to want to downplay the fact of the fake report. We are living through a boorish and polarized political climate. The messages of intolerance and prejudice by political leaders has given license to expressions of hostility and hate on social media and spread fear that reaches to undergraduate campuses such as Simon's Rock and Bard.

The Arendt Center Conference is one way to respond to and resist that atmosphere of fear. It is an effort to do what we in the liberal arts do best, to think deeply, meaningfully, and provocatively about the most important issues facing our world. The inspiration for this conference was Hannah Arendt's work on racism and antisemitism.

Most people think that antisemitism and racism are rooted in the hatred of Jews and blacks. But the key insight in Arendt's unorthodox approach to thinking about antisemitism and racism is her original distinction between Jew hatred and antisemitism, that the hatred of Jews and blacks is not the same as antisemitism and racism. It is the intense dislike of Jews that underlies the long and painful history of anti-Jewish sentiments and medieval superstitions. When such hatred presented Jews as eyesores, rootless foreigners, traitors, or dirty animals, it was hard for Jews to maintain their dignity, and it was easy to see Jews as vermin. Such hatred can lead to conflicts, discrimination, ghettoization, dehumanization, crusades, and pogroms.

Radical in Arendt's approach is her argument that Jew hatred is not the sole cause of antisemitism or the Holocaust. Antisemitism is largely divorced from the concrete experience of and dislike of Jews. Instead, it is a secular ideology. Ideologies treat a complicated historical process according to a simplified idea; literally, an ideology is "the logic of an idea."[21]

The main ideologies Arendt discusses are antisemitism, racism, Darwinism, and Communism. Communism is the simplified idea that all of world history can be understood according to laws of class struggle; the coming victory of the proletariat is an expression of pseudoscientific historical laws. Similarly, antisemitism and Darwinism are variants of racist ideologies. As an ideology, racism makes the "logical" claim that race is the key to our social problems. It asserts that one group of people is the cause of all that is wrong in the world: if the Jews could simply be eliminated or African Americans enslaved, economic and political difficulties would fade away. For racists, the "struggle between the races for world domination" dominates world history.[22] The Darwinist idea that society is a struggle between the weaker and the stronger in which the stronger and more fit win out—"survival of the fittest"—is what connects some versions of ideological Darwinism to racist ideologies.[23]

That antisemitism is a racism and is distinguished from the hatred of Jews has always struck me as capturing something right. In his book *Stamped from the Beginning: The Definitive History of Racism in America*," Ibram Kendi makes a similar point: he argues that racism does not begin in hate and ignorance but in the need to rationalize economic and political policies that lead to racial discrimination.[24] Fed by the need to justify discrimination, racist ideas have led to a racial imaginary that leads all people to think something is wrong with black people. And these racialized ideas and justifications are then mobilized repeatedly in political projects of racial hegemony.

Kendi agrees with Arendt is his view that racism does not emerge from hatred. Just as Arendt thinks Jew Hatred is distinct from antisemitism, Kendi argues that racial hatred is not the source of racism. For both Arendt and Kendi, racism emerges in the ideologies and justifications that seek to rationalize political and economic oppression.

While Kendi agrees with Arendt that racism is a political use of an ideological fantasy, he offers a program of antiracism that, I believe, would differ from Arendt's. Since racism will only end when racial discrimination ends, antiracism requires that we stamp out racial discrimination and create racial equality as a fact. Antiracism means taking seriously the root of racism as an ideology produced to justify the fact of politically enforced discrimination.

Arendt's thinking on antisemitism and racism is valuable because she insists that we understand that bigotry and racial prejudices, while they are often ugly and harmful and can in certain circumstances lead to horrific political acts of racism, are in the end deeply human and part of life. This does not mean we should simply give in to prejudice. But it does mean that the goal of antiracism cannot be to eradicate all prejudice and discrimination.

Arendt argues that all humans hold prejudices, which are simply prejudgments that we share and take to be self-evident. For Arendt, "whole battalions of enlightened orators and entire libraries of brochures will achieve nothing" in the fight to end prejudice. She argues that prejudice can be fought only through politics, the effort over time to reveal the truth and the falsity that lies within the prejudice. "That is why in all times and places it is the task of politics to shed light upon and dispel prejudices, which is not to say that its task is to train people to be unprejudiced or that those who work toward such enlightenment are themselves free of prejudice."[25]

What Arendt has taught me about racism is that racism has many different meanings, and that resisting racism must begin with trying to understand it. There is ideological racism like antisemitism and antiblack racism used to justify slavery in the United States, where racism is a system of thought "based upon a single opinion that proved strong enough to attract and persuade a majority of people."[26]

Racism can also mean racial prejudice, understood as a deeply held attitude or belief about people based on their race, ethnicity, religion, or gender. If we can acknowledge our prejudices and inform them with considered judgments, we have a chance, as individuals and as a society, to grow, and through that growth make society more ample, more possible: a shared world in which "tolerance" can be replaced by community, and hate by mutual respect. It is when prejudices coalesce into rigid ideologies—when we insist, in spite of evidence to the contrary, that prejudice is more true than the present moment—that prejudices come to justify other manifestations of racism, discrimination, and systematic racism; that we lose ourselves, and we lose the ambitions of democracy in the reality of demagoguery.

The actuality of a racist society begins with the passivity of individuals unwilling to see the roots of this failure in themselves. And it is here that racism risks becoming ideological and even systematic racism, the measurable differential discrimination based on racial criteria but not observably or measurably traceable to intentional racial prejudices.

In other words, Arendt has made me see racism as much more complicated and hydra like. Her work has not offered me answers to the question of how to respond to racism and antisemitism, but it has made me rethink the questions I ask.

The essays in this collection, like the talks at the Arendt Center Conference, profess many different ideas of what it means to be an antiracist or to oppose antisemitism or other racisms. Many of these opinions will be new. Some will provoke you and others may shock you. But I hope they will make you think.

Hannah Arendt says that thinking has no worldly usefulness. Thinking is a conversation with yourself; as a dialogue with oneself, thinking generally has no impact on the world. There is, however, one exception; thinking matters in the world, Arendt argues, when the thinker stands opposed to the mob. In times of crisis, when everyone else is swept away and caught up with movements and ideologies, doing what everyone else is doing, the thinker, insofar as he or she thinks, separates herself from the crowd, stops, holds herself apart. Thinking—by that very act of asking questions, and being different, and being thoughtful—serves as an example to other people that they too can and should reflect critically and independently on what they are doing.

1. Melissa Eddy, Rick Gladstone, and Tiffany Hsu, "Assailant Live-Streamed Attempted Attack on German Synagogue," *New York Times*, 21 February 2020.

2. Ed Lavandera and Jason Hannam, "El Paso Suspect Told Police He Was Targeting Mexicans, Affadavit Says," CNN, 9 August 2019.

3. Allison Kaplan Sommer and Danielle Ziri, "Gunman Opens Fire at San Diego Synagogue; One Killed, Three Wounded," Associated Press, 28 April 2019.

4. Ashley Frantz, Faith Karimi, and Eliott C. McLaughlin, "Orlando Shooting: 49 Killed, Shooter Pledged ISIS Allegiance," CNN, 13 June 2016.

5. Minyvonne Burke and Marianna Sotomayor, "James Alex Fields Found Guilty of Killing Heather Heyer during Violent Charlottesville White Nationalist Rally," *NBC News*, 7 December 2018.

6. Emily Shapiro, "Key Moments in Charleston Church Shooting Case as Dylann Roof Pleads Guilty to State Charges," *ABC News*, 10 April 2017.

7. US Department of Justice, "2017 Hate Crime Statistics"; available at ucr.fbi.gov/hate-crime/2017.

8. Ben Chapman and Katie Honan, "New York City Sees Surge in Hate Crimes," *Wall Street Journal*, 8 October 2019.

9. Hannah Arendt, *The Origins of Totalitarianism* (New York: Harcourt Brace Jovanovich, 1976), viii.

10. Ibid.

11. Letter from Simon's Rock to the Campus Community, 23 December 2019; available at docs.google.com/document/d/1C31eaOomQOtPV_eJ-6x-jCgIv8_8BoqllLPOy5eahdA/edit.

12. Wilfred Reilly, *Hate Crime Hoax: How the Left Is Selling a Fake Race War* (Washington, D.C.: Regnery Publishing, 2019), 1.

13. Ibid., xiii.

14. Ibid., xxii.

15. Ibid., 7.

16. Ibid.

17. Ibid.

18. Ibid., 6.

19. Ibid., 5.

20. Letter, Simon's Rock to the Campus Community.

21. Arendt, *Origins of Totalitarianism*, 469.

22. Ibid., 470.

23. Ibid., 463.

24. Ibram Kendi, *Stamped from the Beginning: The Definitive History of Racism* (New York: Bold Type Books, 2016).

25. Hannah Arendt, *The Promise of Politics*, ed. Jerome Kohn (Schocken: United States, 2005), 99–100.

26. Arendt, *Origins of Totalitarianism,* 159.

How Antisemitism Animates White Nationalism

Eric K. Ward

On a red-eye from Los Angeles, looking through social media, I realized it was forty years ago this month that I snuck out the window of my house to go to my first punk show, the Germs, in Orange County. I think about that night now, not only because it was a great show but also because it shaped my life in really significant ways.

I am a child of Los Angeles. I grew up there. I'm part of four generations of Los Angeleans; my family came to LA in the early 1900s. We often don't talk about it in this context, but my family were refugees. They were fleeing Shepherdsville, Kentucky, for their lives. My aunt, my great-great aunt, was coming around a bend one day in—I always think of it as a carriage with horses, but it was likely a cart and a mule. She came around the bend and came across a lynching that was happening in Shepherdsville. This was the story in our family. About six or seven years ago I started searching around— because I didn't know how true this was, right? Memory is a strange thing. Myth is a strange thing. But I did find the story of Marie L. Thompson—the lynching of Marie L. Thompson.

Marie L. Thompson was a sharecropper. She and her son were working a portion of property that was owned by a white man who one day accused her son of stealing tools and started to beat him. She intervened and began to fight this man and ended up killing him. She was arrested and put into jail. Later that night a lynch mob came, and they lynched her. The official newspaper story went on to say that somehow she was able to wrap her legs around the neck of one of the lynch-mob persons. Somehow she was able to pull him toward her and somehow it knocked her off the tree. She grabbed his knife, and she held off the lynch-mob crew. They ended up killing her by shooting her to death. That was the story in the newspaper.

Then, two years ago, I found another story, the lynching not of Marie L. Thompson of Shepherdsville but of Mary L. Thompson of Shepherdsville, Kentucky. And in this story, Mary L. Thompson actually survived her lynching and died at an old age.

These stories together tell the cautionary tale I'm trying to convey: often we perceive that we know exactly what is happening, particularly those of us who are human rights activists or academics. We believe that we *actually know* what is happening in the world, often relying on conventional wisdom rather than research to understand phenomena.

I'll relay this in a different story, one that will tell you how I came to this work.

Back to being a kid in Long Beach, California: I'm in the punk rock scene. Eventually, with a bunch of friends, we form a band. Some folks may have heard of the band. It went on to be known as Sublime. One day, I decide I'm getting out of LA. I have two friends who are moving up to Eugene, Oregon. I want to leave LA because I cannot see myself beyond the age of 23. For an 18-year-old, a 19-year-old, 20-year-old, 21-year-old, 22-year-old black male in Los Angeles, that was pretty common.

I wanted to live past my twenties, and I was trying to figure myself out. I'd like to tell you that it was as simple as my friends were moving up there so I decided to move up, but that's not always how stories go.

What really happened is, my two friends asked me, "Do you want to move to Eugene, Oregon?" They were going to the University of Oregon. And my first response to these two friends who I grew up with and loved and spent a lot of time with was, "Why in the hell would I ever leave LA?" And then, "Why would I leave it and move to Eugene, Oregon?" And if you could have opened the back of my head to look in, what you would have seen was San Francisco, a lot of trees, and the Space Needle, which wasn't even in Oregon! I had no conception of what Oregon looked like. I'd only left Southern California once in my life, and it wasn't to go to Oregon.

So, because I didn't have an understanding, I began to fill in the blanks. The ways that I began to fill in the blanks were by things that *I thought* I knew. I knew *Little House on the Prairie*. I remember asking my friends, "Do they have electricity in Eugene, Oregon? Do they have running water? Was there McDonald's? Do you think that they have cable, and do they have MTV on it?" These were real questions that I had. These were stereotypes. As we know, there are rural parts of Oregon, but there are also urban parts. There are highways; there's an electrical system. All those things existed. But because I hadn't spent time experiencing it or learning, I filled in with stereotypes. That's often how we understand race in America, and it is certainly how we have come to understand the white nationalist movement in America today. We think we understand these social movements, but we don't.

I want to spend some time on white nationalism and why it's important. If you work on issues of immigration, issues of climate justice, issues around supporting the rights of the LGBTQ community, issues around racial justice, policing—and the list goes on—you need to understand white nationalism. White nationalism is one of the most significant threats to democracy that we have faced from a social movement in decades. Left unchallenged, it can rescript how we understand America.

When I talk about white nationalism, what do I mean? I want to talk about it by first talking about something else: white supremacy. America was founded on white supremacy. White supremacy is a system based on disparity, on the idea that some people are superior, and some people are inferior based on skin color. Most of us are familiar with the term. White supremacy was built off of three core pillars: The first was the genocide and stolen resources of the native population. The second was the exploitation of black labor through a system called chattel slavery. And the third, not often acknowledged, was the control of sexuality, primarily women's sexuality. These were the three core pillars of white supremacy. It functioned by convincing people who had lighter skin that they were superior simply because they had lighter skin. Now, it's important for me to say (everyone take a big deep breath, breathe it out), none of us are responsible for that system. None of us were around hundreds of years ago as it was being constructed. But it is part of the society that we live in today.

White supremacy and white nationalism are often conflated. We treat them as the same thing. Often my friends in the racial justice sphere of the human rights movement say to me, "We've seen this before. This is just the same as the Klan of the 1920s. We have survived this before, we'll survive it again." That's similar to how I thought about Oregon before I went there. That is based off of a perception, not reality.

If white supremacy is a system, white nationalism is a social movement. White supremacy is built on exploitation; white nationalism seeks the full removal of people of color and Jews from the United States. To say it again: White supremacy seeks to exploit people of color and women. White nationalism is committed to a form of ethnic cleansing to create a white-only ethnostate. To conflate white supremacy and white nationalism, I often tell my friends, would be like conflating a Big Mac and a cow because they're both made out of beef. When you drop your Big Mac you do not call a veterinarian. In the same way, the tools we have developed to challenge white supremacy are not the tools that we need to effectively challenge white nationalism.

So if white nationalism is different, where does it come from? Ironically, white nationalism comes from the victory of the civil rights movement. When I worked in philanthropy, I spent my time supporting Black Lives Matter and the Movement for Black Lives. I did it by marching in the streets and supporting the movement's leaders, but also by raising dollars. One of my favorite shirts that folks used to wear said on the front, NOT MY MAMA'S CIVIL RIGHTS MOVEMENT. I loved that shirt. I love it in the same way that I love how I used to think about Oregon: it's cute.

But the truth is, that shirt was actually honest. We weren't our mothers' civil rights movement. Our mothers' civil rights movement was really badass, and they were badass because they had to organize at a time when white supremacy was the actual rule of law. It wasn't contested, it wasn't debated; it was the way things were. People did not wake up wondering if they were superior simply because they were white. The majority of people in this country thought they were superior as white people in the same that they knew if they breathed in, they would breathe out. It was just the way it was.

Then comes along the civil rights movement, and the civil rights movement organizes and defeats Jim Crow in the South. It is actually the largest defeat that white supremacy ever faced. Now, please don't come away from this saying, "Eric Ward said white supremacy doesn't exist in America anymore." I can tell you as an African American, it certainly does. And if you talk to folks in the Muslim community, if you talk to immigrants, if you talk to other black folks and indigenous folks and people of color, they will tell you that white supremacy still exists. But it's different now. It's not the rule of law. It's de facto, not de jure. While we don't like to celebrate victories, the civil rights movement was a real victory.

Now imagine, for a second, that you're a person who believes in a Jim Crow America. You believe separate is equal. You don't see it as cruel; it's just the way it is. Black people are inferior. How do you then explain that you just lost to black people? Not only just lost, but lost the largest possible political defeat. Do you just say, "I guess I got it wrong"?

Think about any tests that you failed. One time I failed a test, and I spent a lot of time trying to figure out what went wrong—and the answers I came up with always pointed the finger at someone else.

In the same way, if you were a person who believed in Jim Crow, you were never going to accept that black people were equals. So you had to construct another idea. It was in that construction that antisemitism took a new ideological form in America. It went like this: Our segregationists decided they didn't lose to black people, because it would be impossible to lose to people who were inferior. So it had to be someone else. They began to borrow from something they had learned in Europe as World War II veterans and things they had learned from a man by the name of Henry Ford.

Most of us know Henry Ford as the inventor of the automobile. What most of us don't know is that Henry Ford was an incredible anti-Semite, so much so that he received one of the highest civilian honors from Nazi Germany. But he also did something else that softened the landscape for antisemitism in America as an ideological force. He came across a book called *The Protocols of the Elders of Zion*. The *Protocols* were a forged document—not real—that purported to tell the story of a global Jewish conspiracy to destroy European Christendom. It started with the idea that a group of Jewish elders met in the cemetery at midnight—where all conspiracies are hatched—and conspired to control the media, to control the economy, to control culture, etc. World War II veterans were exposed to that narrative. It was a powerful narrative. How powerful? During the lifespan of Nazi Europe, the National Socialist Movement published over a dozen editions of the *Protocols*. For a while in the early 2000s, *Protocols* was one of the most popular books on Amazon. It was a such a powerful narrative that even if you haven't read it, you all probably know the story.

Let me give you an example: have you ever watched or heard of *The X-Files*? It was a very popular TV show, one of the most watched, from 1993 to 2018. I watched a lot of *The X-Files*. The story is this: There's an FBI agent who thinks that there is a conspiracy. The conspiracy is, aliens have infiltrated all aspects of society—economic, government, etc.—and they are slowly trying to take over the world and infuse humans with alien blood. That is the plotline of *The X-Files*. And that is also the plotline of *The Protocols of the Elders of Zion*. (Now, please don't take away that Eric Ward is saying *The X-Files* is antisemitic. I'll let the folks who are doing cultural studies figure that out.)

The X-Files was popular because that narrative is very compelling. It makes a complex world very simple. And if you don't think the world is complex, take a trip to the store and try to find a toothbrush or a toothpaste. I can find myself standing in the aisle for 25 minutes trying to figure out which toothpaste to get. All I really want is some toothpaste, not all those choices.

Antisemitism simplifies a world that is complex. It simplifies by scapegoating a marginalized and vulnerable community, a community that we don't see as vulnerable and marginalized. In fact, antisemitism takes the Jewish community and endows it with almost supernatural attributes. This is what seeped into the segregationist movement in the post–civil rights movement. The answer to the question of "How did we lose?" became "We didn't lose to black people; we lost to this Jewish conspiracy." That became the answer when women began to advocate for their own rights, when immigrants began to advocate for their own rights, when LGBTQ folks began to advocate for their own rights. It was never that these marginalized and vulnerable communities were exerting their own agency; it was merely that they were puppets of a larger conspiracy.

It is possible that, in the United States, antisemitism may be more of a threat to communities of color, to the LGBTQ community, to other vulnerable communities, than to the Jewish community itself. Antisemitism strikes at the heart of democratic practice. Democracy is hard. Democracy is challenging. And the white nationalist movement has organized in very significant ways to undercut democracy by simplifying it.

Is everyone in the white nationalist movement a hardcore anti-Semite? Probably not. It is likely that a large percentage have never even heard this conspiracy theory. You would have to go back to the core of white nationalist theorists, like William Pierce of the National Alliance, to the pages of *Spotlight Magazine* and the Liberty Lobby of Willis Carto, and Tom Metzger of White Aryan Resistance. It is in their foundational works that I came to understand the importance of antisemitism to white nationalism.

I'm not aiming to persuade you that the white nationalist movement is a threat. If you have not understood the threat after Pittsburgh, South Carolina, Charlottesville, El Paso, Poway, Gilroy, and the dozens of other hate crimes and murders that have happened in the United States, there is nothing that

I can say that will convince you otherwise. But I will share this about why it's important:

First, let's go back to David Duke. David Duke, former grand wizard of the Ku Klux Klan, who ran for elected office as a Democrat—didn't just run as a Republican; he ran as a Republican, an Independent, and a Democrat. When he first started running, people could not believe that a former Klansman had the gall to run for political office. It was the '80s. People mobilized and they marched, and he lost. He turned around and ran again. People were outraged. Then he turned around and he ran again, and people were outraged, but he won his seat in the Louisiana State Legislature and got a standing ovation when he was sworn in. He ran twice for the US Senate from Louisiana, once for the US House, twice as a presidential candidate, and once to be governor of Louisiana. He lost all of those. But what we often don't talk about is that in 1991 when he ran for governor, David Duke won the 55 percent of the white vote in Louisiana—what he called "my constituency." That means that if people of color couldn't vote, David Duke would have been the governor of Louisiana.

That freaked people out. So we did what we do in the human rights movement when we panic. We like to do a lot of polling and focus groups, right? The answer someone could have told us over a cup of coffee was this: what happened was that David Duke had bombarded the public for so long with his ideas that they no longer seemed so extreme. I liken it to fashion shows. I used to love *The Fashion Minute* on CNN when it first started. They would go to London and Rio de Janeiro and Tokyo and show off the latest fashions. I had this love-hate thing with watching these fashions come down the runway. They're so extreme, they're so out there. I would say, "Oh my God, I hate that! Who's going to wear that? No one's going to wear that! So out there! They've gone too far this time!" But sure enough, after not too long, less extreme versions of those styles would end up on the streets.

In the same way that the fashion industry seeks to influence what happens in the cultural mainstream, the white nationalist movement has influenced what has happened in the political mainstream. And like many social movements, they have been very effective.

Those of us in the human rights movement can be very arrogant. We think we're the only ones who can effect change in society, that we're the only social movements worth paying attention to. The truth is that *all* social movements can affect society. They can shift the terrain upon which we understand issues. If you don't believe this, consider: when was the last time we had a serious conversation in this country on the environment and on universal health care and access? Who was the president who championed those two things along with ending racial discrimination in employment? No, it wasn't Obama. No, it was not Clinton. It was Richard Nixon.

Society and social movements shift, and this is why we need to be vigilant around the white nationalist movement today. To understand this movement, we need to understand antisemitism and the world that it exists in. It is not merely one of the items on the laundry list of white nationalism; it is the paper upon which white nationalism is written. If we are to defeat white nationalism and open up the political space once again to advocate against Islamophobia, against xenophobia, against antiblack racism, we need to defeat the narrative of white nationalism. This is why confronting antisemitism is important. It is why in the academy, professors and students need to take antisemitism seriously, to understand the ideological role that it plays in America today. That is the task before us.

What Is Racism?

John McWhorter

What is racism? If I sit here and I tell you that racism is discriminatory feelings or actions against an individual who you feel is inferior, I'm not telling you anything new. I don't think we need to have a conference about that.

I think I want to jump right to what's considered step 2 in this discussion, which is that racism is not only a matter of personal racism but is also a matter of what was once called *societal racism*. After that, the renewal of the term was *institutional racism*. Today we're encouraged to call it *white supremacy*. All three of those terms mean the same thing—societal racism, institutional racism, white supremacy—the idea being that it's not only a matter of somebody drawing something on a wall or somebody calling someone a dirty name, or not allowing someone to become a lawyer; but that we have a system in this country where there are disparities in the achievements of people that correlate with race, and that the reason for that is racism, and that that's the kind of racism that we need to be focusing on.

Now, Racism 101, as in discrimination, hatred of others: I think we all agree we don't need to think about whether or not that's a bad thing, and it needs to be battled most certainly, including the sorts of things that have happened on this campus recently, including what happened to Tamir Rice, including that if a black person is in a doctor's office, often a doctor subconsciously thinks that black people tolerate pain more easily than white people. These things need to be not just talked about but battled.

However, if we're talking about racism in a broader sense, if we're anxious to say, as many people are, that no, it's not just that kind of racism, which frankly is kind of easy, but also institutional racism that we need battle. I'm really worried about how we use that term these days. I think that our use of the term *institutional racism* is counterproductive, and I don't just mean that it makes people angry; I mean that it ends up denying people who've been left behind the help they need, and this is why: institutional racism refers to the fact that there are disparities in society, that black people have less of various things than white people. I'm oversimplifying in saying that it's only about black and white, but I'm sure you understand why.

Now, I'll say that to call person-to-person racism and institutional racism variations on the same thing is very dangerous. It's counterproductive in the way that I mentioned. When we say "institutional racism" it's an extended use of the word *racism*, and what we're referring to is the disparities. That's different from something being written on a wall. So it's a different kind of racism. Maybe we're calling it racism, but we know that it's not the same thing. But no, you don't. You don't. That's actually not true, because the issue is that there are these disparities in society because of racism ultimately of the person-to-person kind. The idea isn't that the disparities in society are by chance, and if it's not that it's by chance, what else is it supposed to be? It's racism. The idea is that institutional racist disparities are due in some way, either in the past or the present, but mostly the present, to racist discrimination against human beings that has some kind of aggregate effect.

What that means is that when we say "institutional racism" it triggers the same brain responses as saying just "racism." If you want an analogy, think about implicit association tests, where we learn that someone shown a black face is more likely to think of words like *angry* and *ignorant* than if they're shown a white face. These things are often subconscious, such as racist bias; same thing with the terms *societal racism* and *institutional racism*. What we think of is just racism.

And so this is why that's a problem: if we hear those terms and we think, therefore, that our job is to respond with the same gut, with the same parts of the brain, with same sometimes almost unconstructed indignation as we respond to one-to-one racist discrimination—this is the problem with it. It's not just that it's messy or that I don't like it for some random reason; it means that poor black people don't get less poor.

There are two things: There's battling racist discrimination, which is one of the evils of the human condition, and we should lessen it as much as we can. But then there's also political activism. There's helping people who've been left behind. And you're often taught that battling this is the same thing as battling that—and it's not. And I'm going to put it in a very specific way.

Unequal outcomes do not always stem from unequal opportunity. They don't. I almost wish they did, because then our job as people interested in changing society would be easier. But life is almost never easy. I'll add that unequal outcomes do not always stem from unequal opportunity due to racism. In fact, they usually don't. I know a lot of you don't want to hear it, but I'm sorry, it's true. And that means that we need to get rid of that simplistic sense that if there are disparities, they're due to something we would call racism and deserve the same kind of response that we would give to a swastika on the wall. And the reason we don't want that is because it leaves people poor.

Let's say that there is a lousy inner-city school. Most of the students in it are black or Latina. Nobody does much learning. Now, we're conditioned today to say that that's racism that's creating the conditions of that school, and so what we're going to do is, we're going to eliminate racism, and that will make the school better. No, that's not why that school is such a lousy place.

Now, starting in the 1960s, that school started to become lousy after having been a good one for a long time because of white flight from the neighborhood, which ended up eating the property tax base. That was racism. But it was sixty years ago. If we're talking about now, here in 2019, the question is whether eliminating racism will fix that school. We can't go back to 1959. So what's doing in the school now? It's much more complicated than racism. I wish it weren't. But it is. And if we want to help the children in that school we've got to think more largely than being an antiracist, the reason being not that Ibram Kendi's book [*Stamped from the Beginning: The Definitive History of Racism*, 2016] isn't interesting, but because we want to help those children in the school and their parents.

So what's wrong with the school? One thing that's wrong with the school, which today is run by black people—which is another chink in the idea that racism is the issue—but it's run by black people, and education schools are what taught most of the teachers there. And since about 1960 most education schools in the United States don't teach teachers how to teach. Instead, they often teach teachers about liberal and leftist ideology, and they explicitly tell teachers that their job is to teach children how to see the world as a good-hearted political activist. Now, that comes from a good place in the heart, but a lot of those teachers, through no fault of their own, have been grievously undertrained by an education school orthodoxy that is extremely antiracist. The people who run these schools think of themselves as fighting the good fight, but it means that there are teachers who forget that they don't know how to keep order, they don't know how to teach anybody how to read, they don't know how to teach anybody math. I have a very snooty voice. I am not criticizing the teachers; they can't help it, the schools let them down. But that is a much larger percentage of why that school doesn't work than that some-body doesn't like black people.

Or, another reason that school doesn't work is because most of the kids come from homes where they only have one parent. Now, that can work, but it's pretty clear that it's better for there to be two parents around in some way. But really, with most of those kids there's no dad. Where's Dad? Dad's in jail. Why is Dad in jail? Probably because of something having to do with drugs. Why is he in jail because of something having to do with drugs? Because there's a ridiculous war on drugs that puts people up the river for long peri-ods of time for reasons that don't make any sense. All of that started in the late '60s and was reinforced in the early '90s, this war on drugs.

Now, your impulse is to say, "Racism!" Especially with this whole business of Kamala Harris dumping on Joe Biden, etc., lately. No. In the late '60s and especially in the early '90s those drug laws were heartily espoused by very black people, including the ones living in communities where these sorts of activities were going on and making life difficult, including many members of the congressional black caucus who don't know what to say about it now. We don't have crystal balls, we can't know what's going to happen; but these draconian drug laws, which are a terrible thing, were something that a lot of serious race people were behind. You're not told that very much, and I understand why, so I'm telling you. And what that means is that the war on drugs that has helped make it so hard to keep order in a school like that is not something you can simply dismiss as racist even if some of the people who formulated were somewhat. You can find some evidence of that. Black people liked the war on drugs.

So I think that if you're going to make black people less poor, then one thing you need to do is devote all of your heart and soul to eliminating the war on drugs. For those of you who are under a certain age, if you haven't done it yet, watch *The Wire*. Watch especially the first and third seasons of *The Wire*, and watch what the war on drugs does to black communities, and see what you need to fight. And it is not how white people feel about black people; it's that law.

Now, let's pull the camera back out. I'm talking about that school. So you look at that school, and you see all these black people being screwed over by a bad education, and you think, *That's racist*. No. That's oversimplified. It's so oversimplified that you end up not being in a position to help the kids in the school. That's why we need to be careful of the way we think about institutional racism and the usage of that term.

There are a couple of quick examples: You can have a grand old time—this has been the fashion since about 2013—of teaching white people to acknowledge their privilege, because yeah, you whites in the audience, you are privileged. You certainly are, and I hope you know it. But this business of white people with their hands up in the air as if they're in church talking about how privileged they are—what that creates is *that*. I've been watching that happening for six years, and I don't see anything changing. It creates that.

And in the meantime, talk about that school, what a lot of those kids need is to be taught—you're going to be bored for a second—they need to be taught to read via phonics instead of the whole-word method. I'm sorry, that sounds so inconsequential, but that is something that's being done especially to kids from bookless homes, who are disproportionately children of color, every day. They're being taught to read by just looking at the whole word and guessing, which is something that really doesn't work if you're not raised in a print-rich environment. That is something that schools are taught, and they're taught it as a kind of social justice, because it's better for dark-skinned kids to learn to be creative. But if you agitate for that school to use phonics instead of the whole-word method to teach kids to read, it's available for you to see online how that turns a school upside down within two or three years right there. If you can't read, then you're not going to be good at math, and next thing you know you're in jail, to be rhetorical. You need to espouse phonics.

But that doesn't get as much attention as being an antiracist, etc., because it lacks the drama. But we're not supposed to be interested in drama; we're supposed to be interested in changing people's lives. So we have people attesting to their white privilege while kids are being taught to read badly. That's injustice right there.

Or, we have the latest celebrity who says something tacky about race. Sometimes it's the president. And we have to talk about that for two weeks, and we have to talk about how racism always rears its ugly head. In the meantime, there are long-acting reversible contraceptive devices. They should be available free to any woman who wants them, especially poor women. Poor women are disproportionately black. No, I'm not talking about eugenics. Black women like these devices; they actually agitate for more. There are three thorough academic studies that demonstrate that. Five years, you don't have to worry about anything that you're doing, but you have a child when you want one. A lot of entrenched poverty is based on issues of family planning. They're called LARCs.

Not exciting, I know. That's not as exciting as talking about racism, but more LARCs would mean happier and more successful black people. We should talk about that. Phonics. LARCs. If you want some excitement, battle the war on drugs. That's exciting. Battle that. It can be done. It's already melting. The attitudes about marijuana are changing. The idea is for attitudes about, yes, cocaine and heroin and everything else to change. It would turn black America upside down.

But instead we are taught that our job is to think about institutional racism, and to be upset about it, and to battle racism as if this kind of racism were the same thing as inequities in society. Societal inequities that are based on race do not usually trace to racism in the sense that we know it, and anybody who tells you that is oversimplifying.

Now, quick sidebar: talking about this kind of racism, this kind of open discrimination—it must be battled. But to an extent, depending on what kind we mean, I would like to say that there is an extent to which, if somebody calls you a dirty name or scrawls something on a wall, your job is to look down on that person. Your job is not to look at that and pretend injury. I've been called a nigger a couple of times, and as far as I was concerned it meant that I was superior. The minute it came out of that person's mouth, I thought, *I'm better*, and I walked away. As I got a little older I realized that I was supposed to fall down on the bed and cry, and start talking about slavery. No. That would make me a weak person, and I'm a person of ordinary strength. Notice, I'm not telling you, "Be strong!" I'm telling you, "Be yourselves." You're being taught to pretend that you're weaker than you are.

Now, if somebody is hurting you, it's different. I'm not talking about somebody abusing you physically. Of course there's a [the issue of] where do you draw the line in terms of how often this sort of abuse is going to come. But if we're talking about those past passes, quiet sorts of things every now and then— When I was in college, which was not that long ago at this point, well, if somebody scrawled something on the wall, you just thought, *Bastard!* and you moved on. That did not make it a different time. There was color then. It was just like now. Everything was in color. There was sex. It was not 1917.

And yet that is the way we thought of it, and it is the way people should think of it now. Don't let anybody, adult or child, lower you to pretending to be hurt. That's a sidebar.

Now I'm going to wrap up. I want you to take away three things, because three is the magic number: Unequal outcomes are not always due to unequal opportunity due to race. I think all of you understand what I mean on a gut level, but we're taught that when it comes to the descendants of African slaves we're supposed to suspend our sense of judgment and logic. I think that that's a terrible idea, and I know that a lot of black people have learned to hear something like that and take it as a compliment, the idea being that it's somehow advanced to think of a cry of weakness as a form of strength. That starts roughly with Stokely Carmichael in 1966. It is not the way race activism has to be. It wasn't the way race activism was before then. And it's a detour. Weakness is not strength.

Second thing: I have oversimplified nothing. I know that that will be one of the criticisms, that I'm oversimplifying. But what do you mean? Do you mean that I haven't done a recitation of the horrors of racism, because I can do it—I can say Tamir Rice, I can say the hospital office, I can talk about car insurance discrepancies with the same sorts of people. I can give you a whole recitation of all of those things. But I'm not here to give you a liturgy; this isn't church. I'm here to tell you how I think we might go about making life better for poor black people, not to mention poor Latino people. My recitation of those horrors does not create that; we are not in church. So if I've "oversimplified," then you need to think back to what I said about that inner-city school, and whether you agree with what I said. I wasn't oversimplifying. I was trying for a bit of detail and nuance. So make sure that "oversimplify" isn't really a synonym for just that you don't agree. I'm not being simplistic.

And third: This is something I want you to remember, because it's true. If you pretend to accept that unequal outcomes are always due to unequal opportunity, and you let that kind of reasoning pass when you wouldn't let it pass in any other discipline or endeavor that you're engaged in; if you think that that kind of reasoning is somehow plausible and permissible when it comes to black people; then quite unintentionally you're being racist. I mean it. I'm going to finish by saying it one more time, because I'm not pulling that back, I mean exactly what I said: if you accept that unequal outcomes are always due to unequal opportunity based on racism, knowing full well on some level that that's a kind of reasoning that you wouldn't apply anywhere else in your life, whatever color you are, you're being a racist.

Thank you.

Whiteshift: Immigration, Populism, and the Future of White Majorities

Eric Kaufmann

Thanks very much for welcoming me to such a beautiful campus and to the Arendt Center. Three sort of apologies to begin with: First, that I don't have a British accent, despite teaching at a British university; so you don't get to have that. Second, PowerPoint: yes, I'm sorry, I'm using it; but I won't, hopefully, hit you over the head with it too much. And third, I am a social scientist, so I guess I'm breaking with that humanities thrust of most of today. But hopefully I can keep you entertained at least a little bit for the next 20 minutes.

My book *Whiteshift* is very much about the rise of right-wing populism and also connecting this to the idea of white identity. The title *Whiteshift* is because my agent said we need to have a one-word title, but it has two real meanings. The first is, in our lifetimes, the decline of white majorities in Western societies, North America and Western Europe—you're familiar with the idea that whites, non-Hispanic whites, will decline to roughly 50 percent of the US population around 2050. That's also going to happen in New Zealand and Canada. In Western Europe it will happen by the end of the century. That's a major, *major* change in these societies. I'm arguing that it is this demographic shift that ultimately underlies what we're seeing in terms of the upsurge of right-wing populism, and it's very much connected to the immigration issue, which I'm going to talk about a fair bit.

The second meaning of *whiteshift* is really a much longer-term development. I'm arguing that white majorities will ultimately give way to mixed-race majorities, but that's not going to happen for quite some time. So if you take England and Wales, some work I've done with a demographer there suggests that the mixed-race share, which is only 2 percent of the population now, is still only going to be about 7 percent by midcentury. It's not till we get to the end of the century that we start to see a jump—it's up to 30 percent based on existing intermarriage rates. Immigration doesn't affect the picture much. And then very quickly after that, 50 years later, it's 75 percent of the population.

That's the sort of second, more longer-term meaning of *whiteshift*: that the meaning of *white* is going to change substantially to become what Mike Lind talks about as being a "beige" ethnic majority.

There [are] two real entities that I'm talking about in this book: one is ethnicity and the other is nationhood. By ethnicity I'm referring to a community that believes itself to be of shared ancestry. We heard about the Jews and descent back to Abraham, for example. This idea of having a myth of origin is central to the meaning of ethnicity. That means ethnicity is not just a minority thing but a majority thing as well. Roughly 70 percent of the world's countries have an ethnic majority of at least 50 percent of the population, so this is a fairly widespread phenomenon in the world. The decline of white ethnic majorities in the West is sort of [the] first problematic of the book.

The second, however, has to do with national identity. *Nation* refers to the territorial political unit. So the United States would be the nation; the ethnic majority would be white American, for example, even though "white American" is kind of a blend of different European groups that have intermarried together.

When it comes to the nation, it's not just about the American creed, for example; but it is also about a whole set of secondary symbols—landscape, history, the ethnic makeup of the population, sports—all these sorts of what are known as everyday symbols are also part of the national identity of many people; and it's there that we're seeing more of the divisions emerging around what is the nation, and people who are attached to a particular ethnic composition of the country, even if they accept that everybody, regardless of ethnicity, is an equal member of the nation. They may have a view of the nation [they] knew growing up, how fast that nation is changing, etc. So the nation is the second category I'll look at: ethnic majorities and also nations and what I call ethnotraditional nationalism, which is attachment to a conception of the country that embodies a particular historic ethnic composition—not the same thing as ethnic nationalism, which is, for example, what white nationalism is about, which says you must be white to be a member of the nation and everyone else is outside of that. So it's partly moving to another category, which is not quite about ethnic nationalism and it's not quite civic nationalism. I'm interested in particular in how white ethnic majorities in this decline phase that they're in, in this century, how they are responding to these demographic changes; and immigration is really the central one if we want to explain the shift in politics that's taking place, the populism and the polarization.

Now, if you look at this [chart] from the American National Election Survey—sorry, political scientists love these sorts of charts, and I work mainly with survey data—what this really tells us is that Donald Trump's vote, for example, is not about the economy. This [*pointing*] is white Americans. If you look at this chart, you can see that down here we have your view on immigration, from "increase it a lot," to "reduce it a lot"; and here we have your probability of having voted Trump in the 2016 elections. You can see that if you want immigration reduced a lot, it's more or less an eight-in-ten chance that you voted Trump; and if you wanted it increased a lot, it's sort of less than a one-in-ten chance. That's an absolutely massive statistical effect.

All these different colored lines are income bands, how much money you make: under $15,000, or $90,000, or $150K. That doesn't make any difference at all in this model. In some cases, with the Brexit vote in Britain, for example, poorer people were more likely to vote to leave the European Union. That is a significant effect. So I'm not saying the economy doesn't matter at all, but the vote for Trump is really about immigration. And there's a consensus in the political science literature that immigration attitudes are not related to personal economic circumstances on the whole, to income, job share, etc. This idea anti immigrant views are really about competition in the labor market is, I think, an extremely weak argument.

So then, it begs the question, where do attitudes to immigration come from? This is where I want to get into a discussion of things like white identity and also psychological factors, because these psychological factors are becoming increasingly important for our politics. The so-called open-closed cultural dimension is taking over—not taking over, but it is increasing in importance compared to the old left-right economic dimension around redistribution of wealth versus free markets, which was a big issue in the second half of the twentieth century. It's still there—I'm not claiming that issue's gone away. But this new cultural issue is really reconfiguring politics in a big way. If you think of Britain, where I've lived for over twenty years, the Labour Party and the Conservative Party have almost an identical class makeup now, which would have been unthinkable in 1950, when the Tories were the middle-class party and the Labour Party was the working-class party. But that's completely shifting, and it's shifting in all Western countries, because these cultural issues—Brexit is reflecting that—are leading to a realignment in politics.

What on earth does this picture [*pointing at the next slide*] have to do with immigration attitudes? Anybody's workspace look like that? It turns out there is an important statistical relationship. What is that relationship? Well, this is some data from the United Kingdom, and what this really shows is that if you are in favor of much tighter restrictions on immigration, then of the people who are in favor of much tighter immigration restrictions 70 percent say their workspace is neat and tidy; 30 percent, that it's messy; whereas if you're in favor of much looser restrictions it's sort of 50–50. That's a statistically significant relationship, and it has really to do with perceptions of difference, difference as disorder. This is the orientation that some—well, political psychology would refer to this as psychological authoritarianism, this idea of seeing difference as disorder and wanting to limit the degree of difference in society.

Here's another one: I'm Canadian, and so if we go about seven hours northwest of here we'd see a lot of this kind of scene of cabins on a lake. The kind of person who goes to this would probably tend to return each year and go there on holiday. So the question for you really is, do you go to the same place on holiday each year or do you go somewhere different—again, a very powerful link to use on immigration. I should, by the way, preface this by saying that this is restricted to 18-to-24-year-old upper-middle-class white British people. We screened out, to a large extent, age, class, and ethnicity as influences on where you go on holiday or how neat your desk is. What you see here is those who are in favor of much tighter restrictions: almost 50 percent say they go to the same place on holiday each year—about 10 points higher than those who go somewhere different; whereas amongst those who want much looser restriction, it's more or less three-to-one saying they go somewhere different on holiday each year.

What has that actually got to do with politics? Because these are not political issues—messiness of desks, going on holidays somewhere different each year. What they are is a clue to a particular psychological makeup which twin studies tell us is actually 50 percent genetic. So we have a very strong genetic input through psychology into political attitudes. Jonathan Haidt has looked into this quite a bit, and in his TED Talk he says, well, what kind of person would want to "join a global community . . . welcoming people from every discipline and culture," etc., etc.[1] Well, that's going to be somebody with a particular psychological makeup: high in openness, which is one of the big five personality traits, and low in this desire for order, which is known as authoritarianism in the literature, or this desire for the present to be like the past, which is known as status quo conservatism by writers like Karen Stenner. This idea of seeing differences as disorder and change as loss is key to understanding the psychology, this conservative psychology which animates those who have a lower tolerance for demographic change coming through immigration, and therefore tend to be more anti-immigration.

That tends to feed in also into other forms of identification. You may have come across these people, the British royal family? So the question becomes, what kinds of people are very attached to family and rate family as being extremely important? It's important to preface this by saying, in the UK, family is not a political issue; that is, not an issue that has been politicized. It has been in the US to some degree.

Quite striking, actually, is, if the question here is "family over everything," how much you agree with that statement, again the people who want much tighter restrictions, it's sort of 70 percent—something like 75 percent are agreeing with that, and maybe only about under 20 percent disagree; whereas amongst those who want much looser restrictions, only 35 percent would agree with this statement and 50 percent would disagree. So again, another massive difference around the attachment to family.

Jonathan Haidt has a recent paper, a coauthored paper, that looks at this and actually shows that conservatives are more attached to family, and liberals, more attached to friends.[2] This is partly to do with being attached to ascribed identities that come through birth, which tend to root you in time and place, versus chosen voluntary identities, which appeal more to a different type of psychology. So this sort of psychological basis is becoming more important for ordering our politics, and especially around the issue of immigration.

I want to segue here into talking about ethnicity and race, because there's a connection, I believe—from family, attachment to family, to being attached to ancestry and then being attached to race. I don't expect you to understand this right away, but what I've done here is, I've asked a question which is asked on the US Census. This is from the United States, and this is something that was asked only a few weeks ago; I did a survey on this. There's a question that says, "What is your main ancestry?" Is it Haitian, German, Irish, Jewish, whatever? And second, how important is your ancestry to who you are, your sense of who you are?

It turns out that the importance of your ancestry to your sense of who you are is [an] incredibly strong predictor of the importance of your racial identity to your sense of who you are. So, whether we're talking about minorities or whites, if you say that your ancestry really isn't important; and, as a Salvadorean, or a Filipino, or an Irish—yes, that's my ancestry; it doesn't mean much to me—the chance that your racial identity as Hispanic, Asian, black, white, is going to mean something to you is quite low, less than 2-in-10, whether we're talking about whites or minorities.

However, if you say that ancestry is, say, German, Irish, or "American," which is a major ancestry, particularly in the Southern United States, if you say that that's very important to your sense of who you are—amongst whites—then you've about a 6-in-10 chance of saying that white identity is an important component of who you are. Likewise, for minorities it's even higher, and there are various reasons for that; but if you take Hispanics and Asians, if you're strongly attached to being Cuban or Puerto Rican, you're going to be strongly attached to being Hispanic.

Part of the point of this is to say that there are, I think, very similar dynamics going on between whites and nonwhites; that is, the attachment to white identity is driven largely through this attachment to ancestry. It is not principally about wanting to get more resources and power. . . . The other point behind this is that people are more attached to their ancestry, their ethnicity, than to the racial group, which is a kind of supra-ethnic umbrella group.

That also doesn't make a whole lot of sense from a power-driven perspective. If you see the world in power terms, you should be more attached to the larger, more powerful entity, which is the racial group rather than the ethnic group, which is about ancestry. However, if this is about cultural attachment to symbols, myths, and memories, then the attachment to ancestry makes more sense because this is where the richness of the narrative and the collective memory comes from. So, I really think that this is evidence that whites are really not that different from nonwhites. Their attachment to race is very much driven through cultural attachment—attachment to symbols, stories, memories, etc.

That then complicates, I think, an analysis that would tend to see whiteness as all about power and domination and would tend to stigmatize it as essentially about white supremacy and racism. Not to say that there aren't bad things that can happen from identifying positively with a particular ancestry:

you can be nepotistic, you can favor your group and discriminate against others. So, I'm not claiming this is all fine. However, it does sort of raise a question mark around some of the interpretations of white identity that put it down largely to domination and power dynamics.

This is sort of a segue into some earlier research I did in 2017, in eighteen countries. This [*pointing to chart*] is just from the United States, where, if you extrapolate from this idea of racial identity as coming from that conservative orientation which focuses on family and ancestry, then what you see is a big split between those who value their white identity and those who don't. We know from work by Ashley Jardina—for example, in her book *White Identity Politics*[3]—that the degree of attachment to white identity is both a major predictor of immigration attitudes, but also [of] support for Donald Trump. And what we see coming in addition to that is that there's a divide over whether this is seen as legitimate. Is it legitimate to defend your group's interest?

In other words, a white American who identifies with her group and its history wants to reduce immigration and the motivation is to maintain her group's share in America's population. The question that I put here to people is: Is this person a) acting in her group's racial self-interest, which is not racist, or b) being racist? We'll leave the don't-knows to one side. Now, I have to confess, I got this notion of racial self-interest from Shadi Hamid over at Brookings, who wrote a quite interesting piece in the *Washington Post* on this.[4]

So the question really is, is somebody who wants to reduce immigration simply doing something that is rationally going to maximize her group's self-interest because very few European or Canadian or Australian people are going to come to the United States for demographic and economic reasons; or is this actually a racist thing? And what you see is a very sharp split between, particularly, white liberals and white conservatives. Amongst white Clinton voters with postgraduate degrees, 91 percent say this woman is being racist. For Trump voters without degrees, it's about 6 percent. In Britain, "Leave" voters—people who voted to leave the European Union—without a degree, the percentage is zero. These are incredibly sharp splits, but they're not splits specifically about immigration; they're splits over the morality of immigration.

What we have is two things going on. We have a polarization around how you respond to demographic change in immigration: are you a person who sees change as interesting and exciting, or are you a person who sees change as loss? That leads to one set of divisions. But the second, overlaid on top of this, is an interlocking polarization over the legitimacy of immigration restrictions. Is it even legitimate to want to restrict immigration, particularly for ethnocultural reasons? That is a second and perhaps even more burning split—it's sharpest in the United States, but it's there in all Western countries. If you look at non-Western countries, the split is not anywhere near as strong on this ideological measure.

So we have two sets of interlocking polarization layered one on top of the other. And that then results in something quite interesting.

This is a chart that looks at the share of white Americans who want to reduce immigration, beginning in 1992 and moving forward to 2016, which is when Trump comes into office. The blue is Democrats and the red is Republicans, and you can see that actually about half of white Americans wanted to reduce immigration. But the differences by party were very small—5 points maybe, expanding a little bit as we get out into the Obama era, but nothing really that dramatic until we hit 2016, and then all of a sudden there's this 50-point gap in opinion between [white] Republicans and Democrats. Now, part of that is because Obama voters who wanted less immigration switched to voting for Trump. But in addition, and what's often not focused on, is that a lot of Democrats actually became a lot more liberal on immigration; and in fact, some of the most recent data we have for 2018, from the American National Elections Study, suggests almost 60 percent of white Democratic voters want increased immigration, which is really unprecedented in the data that we have.

So you're getting this polarization—first of all, because you get conservatives who want immigration reduced, but also then you get liberals who are reacting against, in this case, the increased conservatism on immigration. So, you get this ratcheting effect, and you see that polarization. That's starting to happen in Europe as well, by the way. You can see it in the latest European elections, where both the cosmopolitan liberal side and the right-wing populist side both did better at the expense of mainstream parties—and that's, again, this cultural axis, the so-called open-closed cultural axis, overlaying and taking over to some extent from the economic left-right axis.

What I've been talking about here is that the orientation toward diversity and change, which is deeply psychological, has a strong hereditary component. It determines—or in many ways governs—whether somebody processes immigration as a nice thing and an interesting thing, as a stimulating thing; or as something that is causing insecurity of their identity and is leading them to think things were better in the past.

Second, as we've seen, the orientation toward white identity and the defense of group interests is very different. Conservatives see it as quite natural and normal to defend groups' demographic interests by, for example, restricting immigration. Liberals see that as racism, and this is again a misunderstanding, which I think is leading to a second level of polarization.

What I argue in the book is that we need to be able to have a conversation on this open-closed dimension, because really, it's not about open-closed. There are very few people who want an open door, and very few people who want zero immigration. What it really is— or what it should be — is a debate about how fast immigration should happen, what is the level. We shouldn't have people saying, on one side, anyone who wants a higher level is a globalist traitor; and on the other side, anyone who wants a lower level is in some way a deplorable racist. We need to be able to get past that binary black-white kind of thinking to saying, okay, let's negotiate, let's reach an accommodation that satisfies as best we can both sides in this debate, just as we have on the tax debate, between people who want lower taxes and less welfare spending, and those who want more welfare spending. We can reach an accommodation. I know it's not perfect, but we should be able to talk about the immigration and cultural issues the same way we do the economic issues; because otherwise, if we just turn it into " you're either a good person or a bad person, open or you're closed," then we get this pitched battle and this increasing polarization.

The second thing is the social psychology literature, [which] tells us that attachment to the in-group and hatred of the out-group are different disposi-tions. You know, . . . if I'm a professor and I'm attached to being a professor, it doesn't mean I hate lawyers. I may hate lawyers anyway, but that's a separate question.

Attachment to your in-group is not correlated with hatred of the out-group except in situations of violent conflict. In the American National Election Study we know that white Americans who are attached to being white are no more likely to feel cool toward blacks and Hispanics than white Americans who are not particularly attached to being white, because partly, as we saw from those slides, the attachment to being white stems as a sort of emergent property out of attachment to, for example, family and ancestry.

So, it's important to disentangle "attachment to" and "hatred of." There's an important paper by Marilyn Brewer called "In-group Love and Out-group Hate," which sort of goes through this literature, and it's got thousands of citations and this really decades-long psychology literature that establishes that these are quite different dispositions.[5] Whereas if we conflate them and think that any white person who actually identifies with their group must hate blacks and Hispanics or all members of out-groups, I think we're backing people into a corner. Again, citing more research here: in experiments where you get people to read about a policy and then you add, "And this is racist" to it, there's a certain chunk of the particularly conservative electorate that will react very negatively to that and increase their support—for example, for Donald Trump and for conservative policies as a sort of reactance. There are about three or four studies that show this effect, so it's really not a good strat-egy, I think, to be pursuing. What we should be pursuing is a kind of middle ground, a kind of accommodation. I do believe there is a way of finding an accommodation on these tricky cultural issues that are increasingly dividing Western societies.

Part of the book, really, looking long-term, is to say ideally conservatives would be able to see in the rising mixed-race population a continuation of their ancestry, of their collective memories—see it as a positive thing. And liberals, too, can see this as a positive thing. A message that is saying, "More diversity is great, and if you don't like it, you're a racist," is guaranteed to go down badly with people who aren't psychologically wired to prefer diversity. Everyone has to tolerate diversity; that's the hallmark of a liberal society. But to say people must celebrate and prefer [it] is actually kind of not particularly realistic and, I think, is not a particularly sharp political strategy.

Discussion and Audience Q&A

Samantha Hill: Eric, you're going to have to forgive me, because I took off my political science hat a number of years ago and have been reading mostly Hannah Arendt; so my questions might seem a little naïve. And I want to start with a pretty straightforward question to kind of fill out the narrative that you're creating around all of this political, sociological research that you've done and all these numbers that you've just shared with us.

The first question is in two parts: 1) What *is* whiteness in the way that you're talking about it; and, 2) if there is whiteness as an ethnic group in the way that you're describing it, is it legitimate to advocate for white identity, and what does that mean?

EK: Great—some really good questions. So, I'm not a huge fan of the term *whiteness* because I'm a fan of talking about white, whites as a racial group or an ethnic group—which are not the same thing. If you think about the United States, American history, you had a dominant ethnic group in the United States prior to, let's say, Kennedy's election, which was defined by being Protestant and white, often descended from early settlers to the United States. Catholics and Jews were outside of that, but they were still white. The meaning of whiteness, I guess, racially has to do with phenotype and appearance, and I kind of think of it more, you know, like the color. So we can't necessarily tell when blue becomes green—that's a fuzzy boundary—but it's very much about physical appearance; whereas ethnicity, which is about myths of origin and the cultural markers that [were] a boundary between the ethnic majority group—in this case Protestants—and other groups. So I think talking about whiteness obscures that nuance.

But as with any identity, anything taken to an extreme is going to be negative, absolutely. And that could be true of ideology, like religion, or socialism, or whatever—or liberalism. So it's very important that any identity be moderate. . . . There are some people who say, "Ah, identity politics is just the worst thing in the world!" Or there are people who say, "No, it's a great thing." Going back to Jonathan Haidt's distinction between a "common enemy" version of identity that says we define ourselves as Irish because we hate the English, that kind of identity is, I think, not a particularly good form of identity because it's premised on hating an out-group. Now, maybe they deserve it, and okay, fine. But if that's what you hang your identity on, then I think that's a problem. But then there's what Haidt calls "common humanity" identity, which says, "No, we're attached to our traditions and myths and memories, but we don't hate anybody, and this is just our culture that we want." I think I would be in favor very much of that second form of identity, and also that it doesn't transcend liberal principles. So, this idea of equal treatment has to be maintained. You're not going to just hire members of your own group because you're really attached to your own group: you've actually got to moderate that in line with liberal principles.

SH: One of the topics that came up in your talk was immigration, and what kind of role immigration is playing in our current electoral politics, and thinking about perceptions of disorder, and immigration attitudes. And one of the things that you talked about for quite a bit in your book is the need for long-term refugee camps to deal with the current refugee crisis that we're facing. So one of the things I was thinking about as I was reading your book and thinking about the current immigration crisis in the United States and the concentration camps along the border that have been set up for migrant children is, how are you thinking about that in the context of the upcoming presidential election? . . . I'm assuming, given your talk, you don't desire to have Donald Trump reelected in 2020. How can we, as not–Donald Trump voters—I'll just throw the political net, cast it wide there—how can we talk about immigration in a way that will lessen these attitudes?

EK: Well, I do think that the sort of liberal side needs to have an answer on immigration. And certainly in the case of Brexit the Remain side just were told, change the subject, whenever immigration came up, to the economy. That didn't work in the Brexit case, and I don't know in the US case whether that will work. There needs to be an answer. So I think taking the border seriously, how are you going to control unauthorized immigration? The Democrats would have to have some answer to that question, I would say.

SH: Do you have an answer?

EK: Yes. I mean, I think that there has to be border security. If you go back to the Obama period, Obama did take that issue seriously. And I would have thought that the Democrats today should kind of do what—I think there are lessons from the Obama period. Now, you may not like what he did, but I actually think you have to reassure [voters]. There's a chunk of voters who want to see something done about illegal immigration, and it's not unreasonable. If we take other countries in the West, if anything like the numbers of illegal immigrants that exist in the US existed in Britain or France or anywhere else—I mean, there would be hue and cry. So actually, the US is extremely tolerant on this issue if we compare to other Western [countries]—even Canada, quite frankly. So I think there has to be some policy. So one of the things would be, okay, better not stigmatizing Mexico—the way Trump talks about Mexico is very counterproductive. What you want to do is cooperate with Central American countries, with Mexico, in a way that will help solve the problem. You want to have enough resources to provide better facilities on the border, so you're not putting people in cages. These are all ways in which the Democrats could distinguish themselves from Trump, but yet have a message on the border. I think that would be sensible.

Q: I thought your statistics were interesting, but I wonder, have you considered the possibility that those second-order effects that have resulted, really come from the neoliberal policies that have eliminated many of the institutions of social solidarity and economic security in our country, so that people have to find a way in which to deal with the fact that they now live much less connected and more insecure lives as a result of our government's policies?

EK: I think there's no question that neoliberal economics is important—I think it's an upstream factor that matters. But I guess I'm more analyzing the proximate determinants. I would agree with you that, particularly in Europe—maybe in the United States it's harder to see, and the reason I say that is, we would expect people who have more job insecurity or lower incomes to therefore be more likely to vote for Trump, which they're not. Now, it could be that they're cross-pressured between the sort of economic insecurities and other cultural issues. But we haven't seen, honestly haven't seen, a huge amount of evidence that people's economic precariousness per se is a factor in right-wing populism. It is a factor in left-wing populism—Jeremy Corbin in Britain, for example, or Bernie Sanders. But in terms of right-wing populism, I haven't seen very compelling evidence that this is a major factor. Of course it is a factor—I'm not saying it means nothing; but I just don't think it's as important a proximate factor as these sort of cultural-psychological forces that are more closely connected to the immigration issue.

SH: I just want to jump in there from the American perspective, because you know since the 1970s in the United States we've been dealing with economic stagnation. We're essentially experiencing an existential crisis in this country right now—suicides in record numbers, drug epidemic deaths in record numbers—so I'm thinking of, like, Arlie Hochschild's book *Strangers in Their Own Land*, where we get a portrait of a low-income community in Louisiana that's voting for Trump, that has a very right-wing populist agenda, even though we, from a liberal perspective, might think that it's counterproductive to their own immediate interests. I'm not sure how we separate economics from at least racial identity, especially in the history of the United States, when we're talking about what's motivating voters.

EK: Well, . . . I tend to stick with what the data tells me, and it's not actually telling me that the economic position of individuals is really that big a factor. And I know Hochschild's book, but I think there's a risk, particularly, taking a geographic lens on a problem, so places outside the big cities that maybe are struggling.

Geography can be very distorting, so the main reason, for example, that cities tend to have a low Trump vote or a low Brexit vote is because they have three types of demographics, which are young people in their 20s, people with degrees, and ethnic minorities—all groups that have very low populist voting. When you strip that out, actually you take a white working-class Londoner and a white working-class person anywhere else in the country, they are as likely to vote Leave as in London. So I'm not so convinced.

SH: So here's my fear. Here's my fear with that: if you try to strip out the other—I'll call them identity markers, like class, and sex or gender, and talk about whiteness as an ethnic identity—it feels l like you're crystalizing whiteness into an identity that you're advocating people stake their political claim in. I'm not sure how that is going to move either the needle on the left or the right when it comes to trying to defeat Trump in 2020, or to, you know, perhaps push against the kind of identity politics that is motivating a lot of the very-left political agenda right now, because you're still advocating for identity politics, just based upon whiteness, which does have a history of class and oppression in the United States.

EK: I'm not advocating for identity politics. What I'm sort of saying is—

SH: So white ethnic identity is not an identity. White people shouldn't take meaning from their identity as whites.

EK: No, I'm not saying that. What I'm saying is, let's treat all groups equally. That if you try and suppress even a common humanity-based moderate white identity while encouraging a sort of common enemy-type identity amongst other groups, that's not a good formula. What you want to do is say, identity is fine, and that will influence your politics—it's not the case that all politics is identity politics, but identities are going to affect politics. But it's got to be moderate, and it's got to be this common humanity-based identity.

SH: But how can you talk about white identity in the United States without talking about the history of racism?

EK: Because, again, there's a history of racism, *but*. Okay, look. I think there's a difference between, again, hostility to out-groups and attachment to in-groups. Now, again, there is a distinction there to be made. I think to just say this identity is toxic because of a history, and it's forever going to be toxic, is simply a bad strategy, regardless of whether you think that's an ethical stance to take. I just really think it's not a good strategy for progressives to take to actually toxify that [white] identity, which, as I've argued, is coming largely out of identification with ancestry and cultural attachments simply because there may be an association in the past [that] is very real. But I just think to hang that forever—

SH: But in your imagination, what are the material elements of that attachment to one's family? I mean, are we actually talking about apple pie and baseball? Because I meant that as a metaphor.

EK: Right. Well, people are attached to these identities. If you take ancestry, there are kinds of collective memories associated with that. There are symbols and traditions, family background. I think to sort of rule that out of bounds on the basis of drawing a connection back to, you know, very real sins that were committed in the past, and to say that that forever means that this identity is something that has to be repressed and others to be celebrated—even though, actually, if we scratch the surface of a lot of these other identities we would find similar histories of going back to colonialism or whatever—I just think it's not a productive way to go. I think you want to have a moderation of these identities, subordinate to liberal principles of equal treatment, for example.

SH: So what's the story white people should tell themselves?

EK: I don't think that white guilt is the right story. I think, acknowledge the sins, by all means, that were committed by white groups who may or may not have been your ancestors, that's absolutely right; but I think to actually make that the definition of whiteness is just sort of terrible. I just think that's not productive. I think it's important to acknowledge, absolutely, but actually to make that the defining feature is strategically just a bad move.

SH: Yeah, yeah. So I was reading your book at a bar the other night, and an African American woman sat down next to me, and she said, "What's that about?" I told her, and she put her hand on my arm and she said, "Please go tell your people to chill the fuck out." So, you know, as one of our speakers said earlier, I think there's a bit of agreement that people are tired of white people saying, "Yes, I feel so bad," because it's still been making the narrative all about white people. That's not quite your point, but I think it follows the same line of thinking. But you still haven't answered my question: what is the good story, then, that white people should be telling themselves in your view so that they still feel like they have meaning in their lives?

EK: Well. Wow. Part of the story is that particularly identification with her ancestral group is fine, but not with the white group—I mean, sure, they've done bad things and they've done good things, and for most groups, you'll find that if you go through their past far enough. I just think that they can take pride in building a civilization that, by world historical standards, is quite advanced, has flaws—the same story that any other group can tell, a similar story about the good things they did, and that that should be defining the identity while not denying. Many groups deny, you know. In Turkey they haven't come to terms with the Armenian genocide. Yeah, you don't want to be doing suppression, but you don't want to necessarily have to wallow in the sins every morning. All I'm saying is, that's the balance that I'm kind of looking for.

Q: I feel like there's a big contradiction in your argument, which is that, on one hand, you have like a very kind of accepting view of whiteness as an identity, you kind of frame it as a relatively innocent thing, right. There's a difference between solidarity with your own group and hatred of another. But then the whole argument of your book is that, because of this solidarity, white people don't want nonwhite people coming into their country. I know, it's just about immigration. But I think if you look at the history of American immigration and all the legislation, even the existence of immigration debates as a matter of public policy, it's always been about nonwhite people coming into the country and attempts to restrict that. I mean, if you look at Ellis Island, for example, white people were flooding into the country. There was never a question of documentation. You came in, and if you were disease-free they would let you in. This existence now of an immigration debate, where people are upset about immigrants coming in, and they want to restrict it, it's rooted in race, and I have no doubt—and I would be surprised if anyone did—that if it were white people flying across the southern border right now instead of brown people, the debate would not exist.

EK: some really good points—I actually think what's happening now is not that different from what happened in the 1920s, for example, or other periods in other countries—in Scotland in the interwar period, with Irish migration. That essentially, whenever you get these large-scale migrations and demographic changes you tend to get populist movements pushing back on that, which you had in this country when it was white people. In Britain, the Brexit vote, a big chunk of that was about East European white immigrants, right? So now of course we can again play around with white and what that means. This is essentially people who are outside the ethnic majority population.

Of course, over time you have assimilation and you have redefinition of the boundaries of what it means to be part of the ethnic majority. So I'm saying in the book, for example, that the definition of the ethnic majority will eventually encompass people who don't look white but have some European heritage. So, there's going to be this continual expansion of the meaning.

I don't know if I've fully answered your question. I probably haven't. I'm happy to continue it later.

---

1. Jonathan Haidt, "The Moral Roots of Liberals and Conservatives," TED Talk, March 2008; available at ted.com/talks/jonathan_haidt_the_moral_roots_of_liberals_and_conservatives/transcript?language=en.

2. See Marilyn B. Brewer, "In-group Identification and Intergroup Conflict: When Does In-group Love Become Out-group Hate?," in Richard D. Ashmore, Lee Jussim, and David Wilder, eds., *Social Identity, Intergroup Conflict, and Conflict Resolution* (Oxford: Oxford University Press, 2000), 17–41.

Discussion: The Great Replacement

Marc Weitzmann, Adam Shatz, Thomas Chatterton Williams,
Nacira Guénif-Souilamas, and Marwan Mohammed

Ian Buruma: In 1996, I believe it was, the French writer Renaud Camus had an epiphany, and the epiphany was we—I suppose I could say *we* in this case—white Europeans were going to be replaced very soon by Muslims who would then destroy our civilization in the process. So this will be the sort of call of the discussion of the next panel, what all this means, etc.

I'll introduce the speakers very briefly starting with the first speaker, Marc Weitzmann, who's a very prolific writer, journalist, novelist. His book *Hate*, I believe, is being published in the United States as we speak. Then there's Adam Shatz, who's written a great deal about France, about culture, about jazz, and so on, has taught at Bard, and writes for the *London Review of Books*. Thomas Chatterton Williams, best known for his book *Losing My Cool*. He's the last person to lose his cool in my acquaintance. And then there's Nacira Guénif-Souilamas, sociologist, who's written on Muslim affairs and teaches sociology and anthropology at the University of Paris 8. And finally there is Marwan Mohammed, a sociologist, visiting scholar at the John J. College of Criminal Justice, and I believe he's written a great deal about the prison system and related affairs.

Marc, why don't you start?

Marc Weitzmann: Talking with some students last night I realized that the Great Replacement theory, even though it made front page in most of American media after the Charlottesville demonstration of white supremacists in 2017, and even more after the Christchurch killings in New Zealand that made forty-nine Muslim victims, is a notion pretty much unknown in the US. No one really knows what it's about. And it's a shame, really, because once you begin to grasp what it's about, you realize that the Great Replacement theory actually makes the connection between racism and antisemitism, and also explains what's different between the two notions. Indeed, there's a reason why we use two different words, *racism* and *antisemitism*. And the Great Replacement theory, with its neofascist historical background, makes clear what the difference is.

In the US, a somewhat distorted illustration of what the Great Replacement theory is about may be found in, for instance, the Ku Klux Klan's rhetoric that argues that the civil rights movement in the '60s in this country was in fact the result of a Jewish plot to help the "brown races" to conquer the West; a most extremist and demented version of that narrative links the civil rights movement with the slave trade itself as two parts of that same plot to destroy Christian civilization and patriarchy and the Christian values.

But the theory itself was born in France. It is true that it has been popularized recently by the until then virtually unknown novelist Renaud Camus, as Ian Buruma just pointed out, and I'll come back to him in a minute; but it is worth noting that the name itself was born first just after World War II, under the pen of someone called René Binet, a former Trotskyite leftist militant turned Nazi, who enlisted in the Waffen-SS during WWII and, like several former French SS, ended up joining Jean-Marie Le Pen's then neofascist National Front as soon as that party was founded in 1972. It is Binet who first came up with the expression "Great Replacement theory" in the early '60s, and it is important to understand what he meant by that, at a time when mass immigration did not exist in France.

Eager to rewrite history from the margins of history where the defeat of Nazism had put them, midcentury former and postfascists considered that Europe was occupied since 1945 by two competing imperial forces: the capitalist United States, on the one hand, and the Soviet Union on the other. Both were forms of the one true enemy: cosmopolitanism, today we would say globalism, engineered and controlled by an international Jewry looking for revenge. Although Binet and other neofascists such as Walter Mosley in England, for instance, fiercely defended the remnants of the French and British empires, including French Algeria and apartheid South Africa, against independence; yet, as soon as the former colonies freed themselves from the colonial power, their obsession against globalization was so strong that they changed his mind, and by the mid 1960s began to side with the new nationalisms emerging in the Third World. Some went as far as supporting the Black Panthers in the US. So, how does that possibly fit with today's anti-Muslim, anti-immigration rhetoric?

Since the 2000s, the essayist Renaud Camus defines the Great Replacement theory as a fight against a mass immigration—a Muslim invasion of the West that threatens white Europeans with a new genocide. Renaud Camus, today 73 years old, was for a while the official intellectual of the National Front in France; he has founded his own party since then called the Party of Innocence, and he remains mostly known for the Great Replacement formula that is now quoted everywhere. An anonymous English-language website called greatreplacement.com, for instance, quotes Camus in an epigraph and claims that mass immigration of non-European people poses a demographic threat, and that European races are facing the possibility of extinction in the relatively near future. Brenton Tarrant, who killed forty-nine Muslims at Christchurch, New Zealand, in 2019, called the "manifesto" he left behind him "The Great Replacement." John Earnest, who killed two at the Poway synagogue in Texas that same year, quotes Tarrant's notion in his own manifesto. Before them, the slogan sung by the white supremacists in Charlottesville in 2017, "You will not replace us," is a direct reference to Camus, whose last book, directly written in English, uses the slogan as its title, and it is interesting to note that in Charlottesville the "they" in this phrase defines not the migrants but the Jews.

No less interesting is the fact, previous to his antimigrant rant, Camus wrote some antisemitic statements, something he tries hard to hide today. As it turns out, back in 2000, a time when Camus was hailed by the Left for being publicly gay and for having known Roland Barthes, I was the first to expose him, after he published a volume of his journal in which he claimed that representatives of "the Jewish race" could not fully understand nor express French culture, never mind how long their families had settled in the country. Basically, it meant that writers such as Proust, for instance, could not "really" be French. The article I wrote then started one of those big intellectual dramas that can only happen in France, to decide whether Camus was or wasn't an anti-Semite, and whether I was or wasn't a snitch and a *dénonciateur* on the French literary scene.

Then 9/11 happened, and it changed everything. After 9/11, Camus stopped being officially an anti-Semite. He became instead as ardent a Zionist as could possibly be, while beginning to rant against migrants. He was not alone in this. He was followed by Éric Zemmour and a bunch of other French polemicists who either took on Camus's Great Replacement theory or denounced globalization or both.

Since then, the success of those polemicists, coupled with the virtual disappearance of the old guard inside the National Front, has given way, among the Left, to the notion that, today, antisemitism in the extreme right has disappeared, that it has been replaced by Islamophobia, and that the Great Replacement theory is, simply put, Islamophobia in disguise. But then, what are we to do when the Great Replacement theory is being sustained as a justification for the mass murders of both Muslims in Christchurch, New Zealand, and of Jews in Poway, California, and at the Tree of Life Synagogue in Pittsburgh? Or when Germany, earlier this week, an extreme-right killer attacks a synagogue, kills two people, and, although he does not officially speak about the Great Replacement, the video he films and posts on social networks afterward shows him yelling that Jews are responsible for everything in the world, including mass immigration—as it happened last week in Germany?

Adam Shatz: Thank you. That was such a superb summary of the Great Replacement theory; I don't know what there is to add.

But the Great Replacement theory that Camus is credited with having come up with is, of course, a theory of the far right and of white nationalist extremists. But I want to suggest that, particularly but not only in France, it finds fertile terrain because it also connects with ideas that are not so uncommon in mainstream political life.

I want to quote a passage—I'm not going to identify the author at first. This statement was made in 1959, three years before Algeria achieved its independence from France. One thing that you have to keep in mind here is that Algeria, which had been colonized by the French for 130 years, was formally and administratively a part of France, although the idea that Algeria was French was an ideological fiction imposed by the French conquerors. For all intents and purposes, Algeria was a part of France and was divided up into three departments. So the events of the 1950s that led to Algeria's independence were particularly wrenching for France, leading to the fall of the Fourth Republic, the rise of the Fifth Republic, and de Gaulle's return to Paris in 1958.

The statement is, "Do you believe that the French nation can absorb 10 million Muslims, who tomorrow will be 20 million, and the day after, 40 million? If we adopt integration, if all the Arabs and Berbers of Algeria were considered Frenchmen, what would prevent them from coming to settle in mainland France, where the standard of living is so much higher? My village would no longer be Colombey-les-Deux-Églises, Colombey of the Two Churches, but Colombey-les-Deux-Mosqués, Colombey of the Two Mosques." This statement was made by Charles de Gaulle when he was explaining to his adviser Alain Peyrefitte why he did not support giving full citizenship to the Algerians, and why he was going to move France toward withdrawal.

At the time of independence, a million Europeans leave Algeria and become what are later known as the Pied-Noir. The parties of the French far right are populated, or were at one time—things have changed, but in the '70s and '80s they were dominated by people who had ancestral ties to Algeria, either as Pied-Noir or as people who had fought against the Algerian rebels during the War of Independence. Benjamin Stora, a great French historian of the Algerian war, himself of Algerian-Jewish extraction—he was born in Constantine—has described this phenomenon as *sudisme,* or southernism, that crept into the French far right. Now, the idea of the Great Replacement had not yet been coined, but certainly anti-immigration politics that powered the French far right in the '70s and '80s was driven by the same fears of a kind of countercolonization by Algerian immigrants. This was the time that Jean Raspail also published his book *The Camp of Saints,* which imagined France being overrun by poor, dark-skinned immigrants from the Third World and destroying French civilization. So, long before Renaud Camus, long before Michel Houellebecq's novel *Submission* (2015), imagining an Islamic takeover of France, the idea that immigration, but especially Muslim immigration, and especially Algerian immigration because the Algerian was the most feared figure in some way, was very much a part of French discourse on the far right.

I mentioned de Gaulle's speech because these ideas are not exclusive to the far right, and unfortunately in recent years I think a space has been created in the French mainstream for some of these ideas. We've seen this with

Racism and Antisemitism

celebrity figures like Éric Zemmour and even to some extent with figures like Alain Finkielkraut, a French intellectual who has expressed views very close to Renaud Camus's and who has been a defender of Renaud Camus, even though Camus has made very antisemitic statements, as Marc was just saying, and even though Finkielkraut himself is the son of Holocaust survivors.

Interestingly, one of the slogans of intellectuals and figures on the far right has been the need for freedom of speech. They feel that they've been muzzled by the sensitivities of political correctness and Islamophilia, and so on. And although I agree with Marc that there's a difference between racism and antisemitism, there are distinctions to be drawn. At the same time, the figure of the unassimilable Muslim is a cousin, I think, in some ways of the figure of the unassimilable Jew. In the late nineteenth century, one of the great stars of French intellectual literary life was Édouard Drumont, who published a book called *La France Juive*, and who warned that French society was being Jewified, who spoke in a sense very much as Renaud Camus does today. He also ran a newspaper called *La libre parole*—Free Speech.

Thomas Chatterton Williams: Thank you all for being here today. Replacement theory, I think, is the intersection of racism and antisemitism, and xenophobia as well. I think it really gets at everything that we have been trying to talk about and think about for the past two days. Marc did do an exhaustive kind of recap of what it is, but I'll try to add my relevant insight if I can.

I first got interested in replacement theory shortly after Donald Trump was elected, because I was watching a lot of clips of Richard Spencer. He's the coiner of the term *alt-right*. He's a kind of white nationalist. He dreams of an ethnostate. And I saw a clip of him after he got sucker-punched in Washington, DC, shortly after the inauguration. And everybody was talking about, is it okay to sucker punch Nazis? And, yes. But one thing he said when he was being interviewed was, "I'm not a Nazi. I'm not a white supremacist. I'm actually an identitarian. Like white supremacists, Nazis hate me. It's like an idea that comes from France." I live in Paris, and I was kind of like, what is that?

So I talked to an editor at the *New Yorker*, and I decided to read a bunch of books. There are a lot of other theorists who are much more sophisticated than Renaud Camus, like Alain de Benoist, but Camus came with this term that's like a branding coup. *The Great Replacement* just sounds better than *white genocide* or *reverse colonization*, which makes you sound crazy. But if you say, "Well, I don't like things being replaced—it would really bother me if the Japanese were replaced by Chinese people because then we'd lose something nice, which is Japanese culture"—that's harmless, right? He kind of really magnified this concept that's been around for a long time.

I went down on a train and a car, and I went to this fourteenth-century fortified castle in the whitest region of France with the least amount of tourists and immigrants, in Gascony, near Toulouse, and I climbed the steps up into the watchtower, where he has an office filled with books and self-portraits of his blue-eyed gaze surrounding him, magnifying himself, and he looks out over this expanse as though he's waiting for invading hordes to come and he tweets dire warnings of impending white doom and writes books. He's written 100 books, mostly like gay erotica and travelogues; but then he wrote, in 2011 I believe, *The Great Replacement*. And I'm sitting there with my mixed-race child and my wife who had to drive me because I lost my license, and myself clearly not being a white man and certainly butchering the language of Rabelais and Racine with my American pronunciations, asking him if I'm not myself an agent of replacement as a black man sitting there, a so-called black man sitting there in his study.

And he kind of began to reveal to me how none of this has to be logically coherent or make much sense because it's not really about replacement; it's just a way of hiding hatred and prejudice behind kind of like word games. He said, "Oh no, it's fine. There's nothing more French than a black American in Paris. That's fine. And individuals can always be absorbed, and you're welcome in my castle anytime you want to come here because individuals are actually great. I have lots of Muslim friends. That's great. What matters is anytime that it happens on a larger scale and that I notice a difference. And it doesn't even have to be that I notice a difference where I live—there's not a single Muslim woman for miles around me—but I know that my soil has changed."

I thought about that and I kept reading these books, and then two months later Charlottesville happened, and all of these white Americans were walking around chanting, "You will not replace us. Jews will not replace us." Most of them had no idea where the ideas even came from, never had heard of Renaud Camus. Most of them—I don't even know—most Americans who heard this were like, "What the hell are they talking about? Jews won't replace us? There's like 12 million Jews in the world, you know."

But it makes sense when you spend time with these thinkers. Jews are the original stateless, rootless people that have no soil. There's no blood in soil that they represent. They are agents of change in any society that they infiltrate. And they actually work—many of these people in different ways will say they work to dilute strong, old, rooted identities. And when Jews arrive—they don't have to arrive in numbers—the people that really are not agents, are just the hordes and the masses that enter society, come with them and follow them, and then some of them will explain how Jews actually find ways to profit off of this. So it's a really strange kind of mix of racism against outsiders, certainly Islamophobia or anti-Islam sentiment, and a kind of visceral distrust of the cosmopolitan Jew that's as old as it gets. This kind of became the final scene in my *New Yorker* piece, and I've been thinking about it ever since, because it's only been getting more potent. There was the Christchurch shooting, where the shooter mentioned the Great Replacement, and the El

Paso shooter titled his manifesto "The Great Replacement." So this idea is staying with us.

Thank you.

Nacira Guénif-Souilamas: Thank you for having us for this conversation that might seem to be kind of anecdotal coming from France, but I will try to give some account, as I notice that I'm the only female speaker on the panel. So I want just maybe to add this matter to the conversation and see what it speaks for.

So, I'm left with trying to understand where does gender stand. The fact that I represent, as far as I know, a gender, a sex who can technically reproduce the human kind, as I have—I host, I'm home to, a womb, and I declare that I used it for that purpose. Taking seriously this matter of fact, I come to realize that for some partisans of white nationalism as it unfolds in France, such as Génération Identitaire (Identitarian Generation) or the Republican Spring—sic?—this is a French organization that is rather close to the Great Replacement—or those who blame the post/de/colonial theories and accuse the importation of the intersectional theory from American campuses, and mainly, just last week in *Le Monde*, point at fellow academics, among whom I stand, and at books that unearth the "Colonial Trauma," or for that matter anyone who revives the repressed memory of the French colonial empire, are denounced as attempting to colonize the minds of students, readers, activists. Similarly in the US, as I've seen implemented at the Mexico-US border last August by a deliberate policy of starving and controlling undocumented foreign civilians by drones and CCTV, as it was purposefully reminded to me through intimidation at the JFK US Immigration and Customs just two nights ago.

All of this, I argue, makes the case that I embody the Great Replacement as its actual realization in demographic terms and potentially as a scholar and academic in epistemological, intellectual knowledge building and dissemination terms; one may add ideological and civilization terms. I and before me many women, but more significantly today, multitudes of women who are overlooked, if not invisibilized or eliminated, are carrying children across borders, bearing them while crossing one, giving birth while on their way, hoping they will give birth once they have reached one of those [hoped-for] destinations, not so much because they think that their child will replace another, eventually outnumbering the local population; but because this newborn may protect them from deportation, and, most of all, give meaning and purpose to their journey and its outcome.

Therefore, many things could be said about the fact that the main device of the so-called Great Replacement, the womb, is never mentioned or discussed. To begin with, it could be said that this outrageous stance is male-centered and very straight, held by men, endorsed by other men who share a common sense of entitlement and yet claim to feel disempowered as white Christian and/or secular—*laïc*, as we say in French, Western-European-civilized-modern—in a word, superior, superior to women, to other men, and to other civilizations. The condition for supporting such a stance, is that it presupposes the sustainability and persistence of a patriarchal point of view, including the protection of women—provided that they subscribe to the Western script of action being prescribed to them by moral and gender entrepreneurs. Most of the time, such men simultaneously express their fear of being invaded by un/desirable men, physically, psychically, maybe explicitly sometimes—thus exposing their own sexual and social anxieties—and their deep anger for face the risk to be demographically outnumbered. Therefore what matters most is who will be born and brought to life, and whether it is by people that have the same genealogy as mine. I'm of Algerian descent, my parents were born under the French colonial rule known as le Code de l'indigénat (the Indigeneity Code). What I will teach and share with students and audiences both as an intellectual and an academic has always been under control and a matter of fear and caution.

Disclaiming, disavowing my roots, my histories, my memories, my ties, my attachments was expected from me since day one, since I was born during the Algerian War, and is still today an issue: how to make me, and people similar or resembling me, agree to the terms of a more and more explicit contract to resign and relinquish anything that may look or sound like a threat to the hegemonic culture and political order inherited from a not enough mentioned norm, the canon of the colonial rule and imperial narrative of French whiteness that is not yet dismantled.

Not embodying the Great Replacement can be understood as a way to yield to all demands of whitening and whitewashing. Embodying the Great Replacement in the white gaze means to embrace any oddness that is labeled as a threat to sameness. A stark example of this lies in the status of Islam in France, when sameness is supposed to be whiteness and embodied by non-Muslim citizens. Therefore, white supremacy and white nationalism, as displayed, without almost ever being stated, are synonymous with universal color blindness and ultimately to a narrow conception of humanism.

Yet it would be inaccurate to assume from this quick depiction that such moral panic translates into some groups dominated by circumstances—declining Europe, economic crisis, migrant crisis. Rather one should see them for what they are: fighting for privileges—economic, symbolic, cultural, social, ethnic—recast as rights to live as they have always lived, and pretending that these so called rights are stripped from them by invaders. This is the depiction of the castle that was just offered to us.

So the question would be, who are the accomplices of this ideological entrenchment in today's France? I ask the question since France pioneered and empowered some killers, keeping in mind Christchurch, as [we were] reminded, but also El Paso, but also Utoya in Norway—maybe you remember this mass killing of young people in 2011? Whoever is not opposing the Great Replacement theory becomes its accomplice. So are those corrupted white intellectuals or artists that take pride in exiting the marked history of their parents or forebears to be granted the unmarked place of the universal order, that is, under Western white standards, the only acknowledgment they should aspire to. So are those writers who gain success and recognition in prestigious US publications. My question, and I will leave you with that, is how not to be the accomplice of the Great Replacement toxic expansion, not only willingly but also without really noticing it?

Thank you.

Marwan Mohammed: I would like to talk about the mainstream level of the Great Replacement. These different reminders and perspectives are necessary to grasp the entire reality and forms taken by this ideology. I think it's not a terrorist ideology. *Terrorist*, for me, is something else, ideology with a political project. But I'm afraid that a discussion that is only at the level of the ideas and pictures would take us away from what I think is absolutely essential to understand: the in-depth place of this ideology in French society.

To put it in a provocative way, it must be assumed that the ideology of the Great Replacement takes its current strength from the success of many mainstream instigators, instigators of what we can call the Small Replacement ideology. It's less a question of the nature or mechanism of thought than a question of the scope and political solutions that distinguish these two levels of denunciations of the alleged replacement or invasion by Muslim people in Europe.

Voices and thinkers of the Small Replacement don't consider themselves like that. Forget the public visibility of certain forms of activity, particularly Muslim religion, science, and markers. They consider that the republican values, the hegemonic, and the democratic culture are by Muslim visibility and some of their local mobilization. The issue of the Islamic culture by women and, increasingly, any form of Muslim religiosity, even discrete, is sinful.

The topic of invasion, of conquest, has taken on its strength in the French context through the images of Islam in which the social practice of visible Muslims have been presented as a problem contrary to accepted norms of cultured civilization. The power of the Great Replacement idea comes from the accumulation of a struggle on behalf of the rescue of the republican value of a secular model of feminist conquest. The Muslim women [wearing head scarves] became as famous as—you know this book for children, *Fancy Nancy*, "*Fancy Nancy* here, *Fancy Nancy* there"—it's the same thing. The Muslim women wearing head scarves is a new *Fancy Nancy* in the French context because she is constructed as a problem at school, at the beach, at the campgrounds, at the university, at the nursery, at the hospital, in the French version of the NBC TV show *The Voice*, in sports shops. . . . Wherever she is, she is considered a public problem, and a final solution is important; it's often to ban the veil, its exclusion.

Why exclusion? Why ban the veil? Because Muslim women and Islamic people, Muslim people want to replace the liberal lifestyle [with] a dark one. Think of media voices of the Small Replacement questioning the legitimacy of the Muslims present in public institutions and increasingly in the public space. The stigmatization of this Muslim visibility is intended to prevent it from normalizing. The solution provided is exclusion—exclusion by law, exclusion by internal regulations, exclusion by refusal to offer naturalization, exclusion by increasing tuition fees for foreigners in French public universities that mainly impact West and North African students, exclusion by the strong society of vigilance and denunciation of Muslims showing small signs of radicalization by the last government as well as the Macron one a few days ago after the last terrorist attack. And the first prime minister just told us that one of the signs, the small sign, of radicalization is, for example, when you start to grow a beard, like me; this is a small sign of radicalization in his [mind]. He also said that a small sign of radicalization could be when Muslim people increase the practice of their religion during Ramadan. But Ramadan, this is a time when you [re-create] your practice of your religion. He just said [this] at the congress.

The link between the Small and Great Replacements is summarized by Pierre Bourdieu in 1989. He said, the obvious question whether or not to accept at school the wearing of the so-called Islamic veil obscures the latent question, *should we or should we not accept immigrants with North African origins in France?*

The central thinking and the narrative, the structure of the narrative, are the same between the Small and Great Replacements, but the political response is different so far. They have the same targets, and the central issue is the legitimacy of the Muslim national territory, as well as for the antisemitism of the nineteenth and twentieth centuries, and probably today as well in some European countries.

It's also important to know that the link between the Small and Great Replacements, the main difference, is the level of radicality of the political response, you know, between those that just want to ban the Muslim visibility in some states, and those that want to ban Muslim persons in the whole country; but the structural narrative is the same.

To conclude, I can say that the link between Small and Great Replacement is also a link between intellectuals on each side. They write with each other, they frequent the same space, they talk in the same space now, and this is a sign of a kind of mainstreamization [sic] of the Great Replacement.

Thank you.

IB: Thank you very much for all those presentations. Nobody ever claimed that racial ideology was either coherent or rational, and there seem to be contradictions that have been brought out, but still, perhaps this could be explained a bit further.

One is that on the left there are many people who are extremely sensitive about and actively engaged in antiracism, but still occasionally—you see it in the British Labour Party—can be antisemitic at the same time. On the right you see that people can be antisemitic and ferociously pro-Zionist at the same time. And there are Jews who are on the right, like Stephen Miller in the United States, and Alain Finkielkraut and so on in France who [don't see themselves as right-wingers] but who espouse many of the same views on immigration and the dangers of Islam.

This reminds me of an anecdote about a British historian, Lewis Namier, before the war, who was himself of Polish-Jewish ancestry. He was in Oxford, and there was a German scholar there at Oxford in the 1930s. He was rather pro-Nazi, and he was explaining to his audience that what the Nazis wanted was *lebensraum,* and the Nazi project was really no different from the British imperial project, which, after all, was an admirable one, and surely his British listeners would agree that the Nazi project was equally admirable. Whereupon Lewis Namier said, "We Jews and other colored people beg to differ." Now, is it possible that this idea of the Jews as a colored people has disappeared so much from our consciousness that it's very easy for a left-wing antiracist to believe that antisemitism per definition can't be racist, because after all, the Jews are white; and at the same time, on the right it's possible for Jews to be on the same side as those who warn against Islam and immigration and so on because it gives them the hope that they can be more authentically white? Would anybody like to respond?

MW: I'd like to say something and rectify some of the things that have just been said by Marwan, and I'll answer your question afterward.

First of all, in principle, you can criticize as much as you want the French notion of assimilation. Perfectly audible arguments for doing so have been examined, most famously by Frantz Fanon's *Black Skin, White Masks* but also by others, in connection with the specifics of what I would call the French Balzacian dynamics, characterized by a series of codes and manners, an obsession for the centrality of power, and, above all, an inexhaustible need to belong, not just to the right class but to the right circles, the right people, and so forth. This is the need of the "parvenu," the dynamic of arrivism. And although you certainly may find it in every country today, the depth and intensity of its French version remains unparalleled. Why? Not just because the French invented it, or because its roots go deep into the Versailles court culture of the ancien régime, where misunderstanding the codes of the milieu you had the ambition to enter would condemn you for life to become a ridicule outcast, but because this arrivism is denied as such in contemporary France, by the circles whose very existence depends on it—to put it simply, the French dream of being part of an aristocracy that they claim to despise when they do not deny its very existence. The perversions of such dynamics are endless, and sometimes murderous—like, for instance, in 1940, when most French Jewish institutions went along with Pétain and the Vichy regime to blame the Polish migrant Jews for the rise of antisemitism and, in effect, helped in their discrimination if not later in their arrest. It is true, too, that after migrants from the former colonies began to set foot in France, and, above all, after their children started to claim they belonged to the country as much as anybody else, this already complicated dynamic became even more complex—in part because of the bitterness of a former empire and the resulting social discrimination of unheard magnitude against these migrants, but in part, also, because in a good number of cases, the migrant fathers were too proud to acknowledge that their children were French. It is a complicated and very French story with very specific conflicts. But to call the perversions of the French assimilation system and its flaws to deal with migrants and their offspring a "Small Replacement" of which the Great Replacement would only be an extension is both historically wrong and politically dangerous. Historically wrong because, in doing so, you reject the good side of assimilation; it exists too, you know—the emancipation of the Jews during the French Revolution, for one, whose example allowed the rise of a secular Jewish culture across Europe, or the abolition of slavery in 1848, and even the notion of the Republic. Politically dangerous because by giving up any sense of nuances you stop seeing who the real enemy is. The real enemy is the extreme right and the Great Replacement theory. By the same token, when you quote the prime minister on the minor signs of radicalization, you forget the context. You take this statement as evidence that the French elite have "built" a fantasized notion of the Muslims. But this statement was made a few days after a radical Muslim who had converted to Islam ten years before killed four of his colleagues out of radicalization. This, in a country that has been going through a terror wave of unprecedented magnitude, a wave that claimed more than 200 dead between 2015 and 2016 and left thousands of people damaged for life. It is not incidental. In such a context, the prime minister was not speaking about "the Muslims." He was speaking exactly of what he was speaking of: the "minor signs" that Islamic extremists can display.

But there is more. By equating the Great Replacement theory, which exists, with a Small Replacement that you're making up you somewhat change the subject, in that you go from criticizing a postfascist notion to praising identity. Are Muslims discriminated against in France because of one form or another of racism, or because they reach out to their own identity religiously or culturally? What you're implying with your idea of "small replacement" is that one goes with the other. You take for granted that it is the "authenticity" of the true Muslim that sets up racism, and that the more Muslims try in good faith to practice their religion, the more they are marginalized or discriminated against for it. In other words, racism *is* Islamophobia. But is it?

I'd like to come back a minute to the difference between racism and antisemitism. In modern history, Jews were not persecuted, when they were, because they reached out to their religious traditions or their identity, but the other way around, because they ceased to do so. Take Spain in the fourteenth and fifteenth centuries, when the Inquisition rose after Jews converted en masse to Catholicism. Take Vienna and the Austro-Hungarian Empire of the nineteenth century, when Jews, under French influence, turned massively urban and secular, to the point where you could not distinguish them any longer from the rest of the population—and that's when antisemitism reached a peak, slowly paving the way for Nazism. Or take France: in each and every case, it is the assimilation that is the problem; it's not the difference.

All the theoreticians of the Great Replacement theory are defenders of identity and cultural difference, just like you are. Take Alain de Benoist, one of the founders of the New Right. Benoist defends identity; he even claims that identity—including the Muslim one—should replace nationalism. In fact, he *defends diversity*. "The true wealth of the world," he wrote, "is first and foremost the diversity of its cultures and peoples." Accordingly, Benoist, over the years, has proved himself a supporter of political Islam in Iran and in Algeria. He's also an extreme-right essayist and thinker, a defender of the Great Replacement theory.

As I tried to say earlier, the Great Replacement theory has to do with the refusal of miscegenation, of mixing cultures. The shooter at the Christchurch mosque in New Zealand left in his manifesto a very clear statement that I could quote here, saying that he has nothing against Muslims; he has something against *migrations*. He has something against miscegenation, multiculturalism, the way people can interact and mix with each other. He has something against *assimilation*. And it seems to me that this is precisely what you're up against as well.

IB: Marwan, would you like to respond?

MM: Yes, of course, of course. I will try to respond. I will try to find my words.

First, I'm talking about how Muslims, they are constructed as a problem—the political construction of Muslims by elites. This construction of Muslims as problems started before the terrorist attacks, before the [?] attacks of, for example, Saint Michel in 1985. That started in the current period of time in the early '80s. That is the first stage. It's important to know that. It's not only about identity, how Muslims feel, etc. It's how some part of the elite, they constructed the Muslim "prisons," the Muslim visibility as a problem, and how they target the legitimacy, the normalization, of the Muslim prisons in some of the public spaces. . . .

The second thing is that when I talk about radicalization, I don't talk about terrorist attacks and the necessity to find solutions to be safe in this country. I'm talking about the consequences, the huge, the *massive* consequences on [the] public population after attacks, after each attack. It's not about what a little number of dangerous groups are claiming, but I'm talking about the mass system of surveillance, the mass system of *comment dire signalement*—signaling of little signs of radicalization that lead the country and the institutions to a mass discrimination system. We have lots of cases like that. After the terrorist attack in 2015, there were more than 6,000 of—I don't know, searches targeting Muslim people. [Fewer] than ten led to some discovering something wrong, you know. I'm talking about everything in the French context, and the link between them is not to say everyone is from [the] far right, everyone shares the same ideology; but . . . I agree with [the statement] that thirty years of construction of Muslim problems led the country, led the opinions, to accept more easily this kind of ideology, to be more receptive to this kind of ideology, and led to this ideology, as Adam said, to become mainstream, to become accepted. This is a huge difference. . . .

IB: Nacira, do you want to add something?

NGS: First of all, I want to say that it's all about trying to target the main enemy, the principal enemy, and that in such case in France it would be only the far right, or the extreme right. I think there has been a lot of damage done to any kind of possibility to live together and to accept France as it is today, which is partly nonwhite, . . . multiracial, multireligious, and so on and so forth, by the leftists in France. They have built some sort of a specific kind of Islamophobia of their own that has to do with the way they relate to secularism, to feminism, whatever. I mean, there has been this kind of blend also that cannot be overlooked when you want to understand how the Great Replacement is maybe not endorsed by the leftists, but they have their own part in the fact that it has become something that can be discussed and not strongly opposed. And to some extent it has—the fact that we're not able to understand the leftists in France, especially when they were in the government, which is up until today, although Macron is not really on the left. So they not only disempowered themselves as being able to build some new narrative about what France could become but they also failed in the fact that they were not expressing any kind of solidarity for groups that were oppressed because of their minority, because they were minoritized, because they were racialized, because they were criminalized. The lesson completely failed when it came to this, and this speaks to some sort of a liberal society that we all want to build but have failed to achieve so far.

MW: I'm not suggesting that there's no discrimination in France, of course, I guess this should be clear. I'm saying that by minimizing the context in your first remarks, you mislead people. You imply a kind of religious apartheid that is preposterous. Between the early '90s and today in France, the number of mosques has reached 1,600 to 3,000. Most of these mosques have been built with the help of public funding. You can find these numbers at the Ministry of Interior or more fastidiously you can list them on the internet, even though a good part of them are not registered as mosques but as cultural centers so they can receive public subsidiaries, since French law forbids the government to fund religious establishments. Let me finish. What I'm saying—I don't want to enter a discussion on Islam in France—it's not the subject. The subject is that by focusing exclusively on the religious aspect of things you miss the point, you miss the main enemy, because the main enemy is the killing one. Who kills? It's either, in France, the Islamists who share a lot of ideas with the right-wing identitarians; or, in the US and in New Zealand, the extreme-right adherents of the Great Replacement theory. Those are the killers, and those are the people we should understand in order to defeat them. But you're not interested in that. You're interested in defending your identity, which, frankly, is both narcissistic and meaningless.

IB: Adam?

AS: I take the point that the question of murders might take priority, but I think it's entirely reasonable for people of Muslim origin in France to be concerned about housing and job discrimination, about the conditions of life. And for that, the French political mainstream has a lot of responsibility.

I wanted to piggyback, though, briefly on some of the comments that have just been made, because it seems to me that anti-Muslim prejudice in France, or discrimination in France, has been provoked not just by a failure to assimilate, as I think Marc is suggesting, or by the expanded construction of mosques for that matter; but it's much more about success of assimilation, because there's been a double and paradoxical movement in French society, which is that on the one hand, yes, there is this ghettoization—you have the Cité, you have a disproportionate poverty and police violence, and so on, in Muslim communities in France; and at the same time, you have growing upward mobility. I mean, you have people who are making inroads into French society, who are doctors and professionals and scholars and so on, and they're facing the kind of resistance that Nacira was describing. So I think it's actually partly the success, to some degree, of assimilation that is responsible for some of this racist pushback.

In a way, I think Marc was—I don't know, intentionally or not—underscoring this when [he] talked about the question of assimilation, because France is distinguished by a very intense culture of Jacobinism. There's so much pressure on people to be one thing. There's a general skepticism about the possibility of a hyphenated identity, which is of course [present] here. What makes you more of an American, or has until the arrival of the unnamable, has been that you have a hyphen, not that you don't have a hyphen.

IB: You mean God—the Unnamable.

AS: Well, He thinks He is. I think there are a lot of French people who want to be simultaneously—who are simultaneously—French citizens and Muslims, practicing or not. Actually, the level of religious practice—mosque attendance is actually fairly low in France, even if there are these new mosques, and I think that Jacobinism and that powerful expression of French universalism which suggests that you have to 100 percent assimilate in order to be French—I think that also accounts for some of the problems.

IB: We have two more minutes, Thomas, for you to add your voice.

TCW: I just want to make an observation and bring in some things from earlier this morning.

One thing that's very important about this, which you touched on, which I was trying to allude to was Richard Spencer saying he's an identitarian and not a white supremacist, is the cooptation of terms. One reason why I think it's not enough to be an antiracist but you actually have to *be* antirace, is because the language is so easy to coopt and racists can use antiracist rhetoric and logic very easily. So diversity is good, strong identities are good, people should be proud of their identities; but diversity without mixing—it's absolutely not true. The endpoint of racism is to have a raceless, postracial society where divisions are invisible. Racists want Moroccans in Morocco, French people in France, Jews in Israel. That's why you have racists who can be Zionists. It's not enough to be antiracist. You have to oppose these artificial categories that we box ourselves into and find a transcendent humanism, and you have to have mutually shared values.

IB: Nacira, two words.

NGS: To achieve what you just suggested, which I completely agree with, that would be, to start with, something that you know very well about in the US. If we speak about murders, we should start to think about how police brutality kills precisely those that are targeted by the Great Replacement in France and beyond. Hence the young black and Arab men who are killed at the hands of the police in France should be considered as a way to prevent the Great Replacement at the local level and at the police level, man by man, death after death.

IB: On that very happy note, we will conclude the entertainment for this morning. Thank you.

The New Racism?

Etienne Balibar

The title with which my talk was announced, chosen some time ago in order to keep several possibilities open, alludes to a debate in which we were participating in the 1990s about the alleged transition from a "biological racism" to a "cultural racism," also called a racism of "cultural differences." A few weeks ago, I had the dubious honor of being attacked in the German newspaper *Junge Freiheit*, which is an organ of the neo-Nazi party Alternative für Deutschland (AfD) and the promotor of the idea of "*Rassismus ohne Rassen*" (a racism without races), which, according to them, would make it possible to blame patriotic citizens who "resist" their country being "invaded" by migrants. The truth is that, in a context when, in Europe at least, controversies about the demographic effects of migrations from the global South toward the global North were increasingly affecting the political discourse, I was trying (with many others) to describe what Stuart Hall has characterized (in his Du Bois lectures from 1994 on "The Fateful Triangle: Race, Ethnicity, Nation") as the *sliding* of the "signifier" (or the *name*) "Race," moving along a chain of equivalences with others that, in different contexts, can perform the same function, such as *ethnicity, culture, difference, otherness*, etc.

Today, I do not believe that such discussions are obsolete—far from it—but I believe that they need to be relocated and reformulated, by taking into account the new political and ideological structures that are revealed in the current situation, where the tensions between the *demographic* and the *democratic* aspects of our political institutions have reached a very dangerous level of acute conflict.

This question, of course, calls for a much longer discussion than what I can offer now. So, I should probably go directly to what forms the main idea that I want to submit for critical examination and, if necessary, refutation: namely, the idea that *antisemitism* and *Islamophobia* are twin narratives of hatred, with a global, transnational influence and a myriad of local manifestations. They are integral parts of "racism" in a broad sense. But they also differ from it—symmetrically, albeit not exactly in the same modality—because they belong to singular histories of the articulation of the *racial narrative* within the *theological register* of meaning. But before I come to this with a few more details, I need some preliminaries, which I will try to make as elliptically as possible. I have two such preliminaries.

Preliminary 1: there is no single—therefore also no simple—form of racism, because racism is essentially diversified: it traces back to different histories, it is linked to many different structures of power and discrimination, and it is always combined with other political passions. However, periodically, attempts are made at producing a "definition," or at *unifying* the various definitions of racism. And, of course, this is both problematic and helpful, at least to suggest strategic questions. The most important such attempt remains the one that *gave its name* to what we call "racism," therefore remaining implicit in all our debates, even when we depart from its content. This is the definition that was coined by UNESCO in its two successive "Statements on the Race Question" from 1950 and 1951.[1] I leave aside (although with regret) the history of the writing of the Statements, why there are two (not only one, which would make its "implementation" easier), and which differences they bear (they are quite significant). My essential point relates to the fact that they base their critique of the so-called "myth" of the biological races on the consideration of three intersecting historical "cases" with profoundly different genealogies: the case of *color discrimination* in postslavery societies (implicitly the United States, but also Latin America, etc.); the case of subjugation and inferiorization (or even dehumanization) of indigenous populations in *colonial empires*; and the case of persecutions against Jews in Europe (and, by extension, in other continents), leading to their extermination during the Nazi rule. So, in a sense, what "racism" meant was that these three cases could be subsumed under a single concept with the help in particular of pseudobiological theories of evolution and degeneracy.

Preliminary 2: returning to Stuart Hall's idea that the *name Race* is essentially a "sliding signifier" that enters into "chains of equivalence" with other names, which appear either as *correlates* or as *substitutes*, we may notice that the importance of this signifier comes from the fact that it makes it possible to ground institutions of discrimination and elimination in a "theory" that is also a "grand narrative." Essentially, as it was invented with the initial steps of European colonization, this was a theory of *origins* and *descent* (following what we can call a "genealogical scheme" applied not only to individuals, but to entire populations), articulated with a theory of heritage and degeneracy (especially through "*metissage*" or "hybridization"). We know that this discourse was transformed several times, with the signifier "race" sliding toward new definitions and applications. *Biological heredity*, relying on the "scientific ideology" of social Darwinism, was already sliding away from the starting point. *Cultural racism*, or the racialization of cultural differences, was another shift, closely linked to decolonization and the advent of neocolonialism. It is not really "without races," in fact, but rather grounded on *a denial of the permanence of the name race* under the pseudonyms "culture" and "civilization," which had always been associated with racial typologies. None of these discursive formations have disappeared, in fact, because it is an essential characteristic of the genealogical scheme to be conservative. In addition to social practices, even institutions, this might explain why the trace of slavery and the color bar are still with us, why the trace of colony and the "indigenous" non-European stigma of being *"issu de"* (coming from), as Nacira Guénif calls it, is still with us in France and elsewhere. *But,* and this is the crucial question that I want to ask now, isn't it the case that a *new sliding* is taking place, or a new metonymy of the name "race" is developing, which is linked to the new Nomos of the Earth, or the new demographic and territorial pattern of settlements, migrations, refugees?

I believe this is the case, and I intentionally borrow for this a category, the "Nomos of the Earth," the title of his 1950 magnum opus, from Carl Schmitt, an ultraconservative, ultranationalist author, because he insists on the articulation of every *nomos* (which in ancient Greek means both "law" and "distribution") with the identification of an *interior enemy*. The typical interior enemy today (I am tempted to say) is the interior enemy *who comes from outside*, especially the arch-"outside," which is the South, the former colony, but in fact is already present and "at home" *inside*, in great numbers. It is the "Southern" migrant or immigrant. This explains, of course, why we need to take very seriously the ideology of the "great replacement," invented about ten years ago by a French essayist (Renaud Camus) and now widely adopted worldwide by neo-Nazi and ultranationalist, or *white nationalist*, (as our colleague Eric Ward called them in his presentation yesterday) groups.[2]

I am now, at last, perhaps in a position to return to the point that I had announced in the beginning: antisemitism and Islamophobia as internal "exceptions" to the general pattern of "racist" discourse. Perhaps I should speak of *Western racism:* not because there would be no racism, and also no antisemitism and Islamophobia outside the West (just think of the situation in India or China today), but because this is where we are meeting today, and try to perceive things from.

My point is twofold. First, I believe that we ought not to exclude Antisemitism and Islamophobia from our broader definition of racism, both because they are typical cases of persecution and elimination based on what I called the "genealogical scheme," and because we observe today that antisemitism, Islamophobia and all sorts of other racisms are intensely combined in the ideology of the most active, militant, and politically organized groups. However, as we know, these groups also develop other hatreds, especially homophobia and antifeminism and misogyny. An important component of their ideology is the defense of "family values" and "Christian values"—which takes us back to the issue of religion.

I want to push this issue one step further by suggesting that the important element which we must analyze regarding the singularity of antisemitism and Islamophobia, within the broad spectrum of racism, has to do with a *theological* (rather than simply "religious") determination, which is present in both the case of antisemitism and Islamophobia: a history of "elect" peoples and communities, a privileged relationship to the "revealed truth," and an absolute notion of the "law." Of course, this has roots in the history of conflicts internal to the developments and diversifications of monotheism. It is therefore a *symbolic* element, on a par with the name "race," which is also symbolic. This element is *not erased* by the so-called process of "secularization" (which goes along with commodification of social relations) in our capitalist societies. The philosopher Jacques Derrida once suggested (at a conference on "Race, deconstruction and critical theory" held at UC Irvine in 2003) that a theological "power" of subjection is at work in the combination of ideas of *election* and *selection*, one that is intrinsic to the dilemma of Western racism and nationalism. Along the same line, I tend to believe that, when antisemitism was combined with colonialism and color prejudice in the "biological racism" that UNESCO attempted to deconstruct in 1950 and after in the wake of the fight against Nazism and the shocking discovery of the Holocaust, the Jews were selected as the degenerate and malevolent Other of the Christians (even "secularized Christians") featured the counterpart of the *other Other*: the so-called "inferior" or "subject races" (in the colony), thus testifying for a latent theological determination in the sacralized hierarchy of the human "races." However, at the time, the Arabs and Muslims remained indistinct within the ensemble of colonial "subject races" (the category officially used in the British Empire). At least, *apparently*.

This appearance, in fact, is increasingly fragile. Already in the nineteenth century, Arabs and Jews are associated in the racial-philological construction of the "Semites," the eternal rival of "Aryans," a metonymic name for Europeans as the "master race" or the race of "natural rulers." This, in a sense, was the ideal type to which, with several others, I was trying to return when, in the early 2000s, I suggested including Islamophobia in an *enlarged* or *generalized antisemitism,* which would combine Judeophobia and Islamophobia.[3] Of course, there were political intentions behind this suggestion—and I know that they are problematic. One of them was the intention — not to deny that there is virulent antisemitism in the Arab and the Muslim world (there is, just as there is virulent Islamophobia among Jews and Judeophiles (not to mention the institutional anti-Arab racism in Israel))—but to counter the idea that the "new Judeophobia," or the new wave of antisemitism in Europe (or especially in France), is essentially a product of anti-Zionism among Arabs and Muslims, something that we clearly know is a mistake, with the rise of neo-Nazi groups in particular.

But I no longer exactly believe in this symmetry or in a construction of a "countermyth" of the Semites. More precisely, I believe that the elements of *dissymmetry* are just as important as the elements of symmetry. Of course, they have to do with the very different histories of Christian/Islamic rivalry and Christian/Jewish persecutions, and with the very different places of Jews and Muslims in today's Nomos of the Earth—including their different relationship to the process of global migrations. The Jews, especially Eastern European Jews, were once the prototype of the *wandering* and *stateless* people, essentially because they were confined within or expelled from national territories. But they are no longer. Conversely, Muslims form an important part of today's errancy of *migrants* and *refugees,* which is compounded by their traditional image as *nomads*, and their more recent assimilation with transnational *terrorism*. Their "negative privilege," however, does not only come from there: it comes from the representation of Islam as the *absolute theological Other*, since it can be presented paradoxically *both* as the inveterate enemy of Christianity or "Christian civilization," *and* as the arch religious group that is resisting every form of *secularism* (since, in a sense, it is always already "secular" in its own rigid, legalistic manner). To this we should add another crucial element of dissymmetry: namely, the fact that, at least in the West, antisemitism has been increasingly *deracialized*, that is, *extricated* from the "racial" paradigm with the regression of the "biological" model; whereas Islamophobia remains, or perhaps becomes ever more intensely, *racialized*, especially in places like France (more generally, Europe), through the complex catachresis of the names *Arab* and *Muslim*, and the permanent relationship between colonialism and imperial policies of "governing Islam" that are transferred from the colony to the postcolony.

So, as you see, the pattern, in my eyes, remains very complex. What I would like to insist on, nevertheless, to conclude these remarks and open a debate, are the following ideas: *First*, there is an absolute necessity to *add Islamophobia* to any label or discussion program such as "Racism and Antisemitism" (a fortiori an educational or civic campaign against group hatred); because, in fact, there is a third term that is important, one with the same overlappings and singularities, posing its own problems. *Second*, any politics that aims at reversing discriminations and combat hatreds today must be just as intransigent against antisemitism and against Islamophobia, with no hierarchy or primacy of objects—not *despite* the dramatic conflicts between Jews and Muslims (or rather part of them), but *because* of these conflicts and their murderous capacity to foster racism. And *third*, more abstractly: however this investigation proves to be, it reminds us of the importance of the theological element, and of the fact that there has always been, and there is now more than ever, a theological dimension in the development of racism, which has symbolic sources but very material and practical effects.

---

1. See *Four Statements on the Race Question* (Paris: UNESCO, 1969).
2. I am referring to Eric K. Ward's presentation on day 1 of the conference: "How Antisemitism Animates White Nationalism."
3. Etienne Balibar, "Un nouvel antisémitisme?," in *Antisémitisme: L'intolérable chantage—Israël-Palestine, une affaire française?* (Paris : Editions La Découverte, 2003), 89–96.

Are "They" Us? The Intellectuals' Role in Creating Division

Peter Baehr

Intellectuals of varied occupations—journalists, artists, teachers, and academics—repeatedly lament the corrosion of Western democracy. Trumpism, racism, and populism are the chief culprits, we're told, of a growing intolerance and irrationality. But could it be that intellectuals share responsibility for the problems they deplore? That the divisions in society and the resentments pulsing through it are in part the intellectuals' creation? That *they*, the ill informed and dismissive, are *us*, the learned? Intellectuals are harming democracy not through ill will but through a way of speaking and writing—I'll call it the unmasking style—inherited from the revolutionary tradition. Instead of elevating public discourse, this style coarsens it. It does so by reckless exaggeration, by cruel parody, by stretching concepts like race beyond their proper compass, and by treating large groups of people as idiots or pariahs.

We meet this afternoon under the auspices of the Hannah Arendt Center. I pay tribute to its director, Roger Berkowitz, to its staff and donors. For several years, Roger and his colleagues have hosted conferences on controversial issues, which means issues that actually matter. No stranger to controversy herself, Hannah Arendt would surely approve of the Bard initiative. And for the purposes of my talk today, there is still another reason to invoke Hannah Arendt's legacy. I'm referring to the distinction that she makes, in several books and essays, between disclosing and unmasking.

In disclosing, Arendt says, we reveal ourselves to others and ourselves to ourselves through their responses. In unmasking, it is others who reveal us, and they do so from a hostile, outsider's standpoint. If disclosing highlights a unique and idiosyncratic individual, unmasking exposes a category of person—an imposter, an enemy, a conspirator—that attracts suspicion and disdain.

During the French Revolution, unmasking was the term of choice among Jacobins to expose "enemies of the people," supposed renegades bent on undermining the new republic. Thousands fell victim to a frenzy of exposure when their words were wrenched out of context or when false motives were ascribed to their actions. Later, the Bolsheviks adapted the unmasking idiom to root out "objective enemies," people deemed guilty of a crime not by virtue of any act that they had committed but because of their class or status position—landlord, kulak, teacher, priest; in a word, nonproletarian. This was an early version of what today we call identity politics. Within three decades of the Russian Revolution, unmasking encompassed intellectuals and "cosmopolitans" (Jews). In the show trials of the 1930s, and in a series of purges, people who considered themselves to be good Communists were forced to confess to impossible, imaginary crimes. Stalin's aim was to create total compliance, unremitting loyalty, a unified society in which no space existed for discord.

It would be comforting to think that the unmasking of motives and identities is restricted to revolutionary situations. Alas, over the past century or more, unmasking has become increasingly normal in both the academy and the broader public culture. Typically, but not always—ask Allison Stanger and Charles Murray—this unmasking avoids physical violence. Academics have developed an extensive language of unmasking: ideology, false consciousness, symbolic violence, implicit bias, microaggression, the hermeneutics of suspicion, and so forth. Meanwhile, Twitter and other social media outlets are engines of doxing and trolling. An indiscretion committed years ago is disinterred, a word pounced on, a gesture reframed to throw the worst possible light on the target. Self-abasement is demanded, an apology is given, and the apology is never enough.

It might appear bizarre, or at least unfair, to associate the academy with internet fanaticism. But whether sophisticated or vicious, unmasking has similar effects. It truncates our sympathies. It abridges our understanding. And it degrades our tolerance of disagreement. In fact, unmasking, by its dogmatic assertion of one indivisible truth, makes disagreement redundant. After all, if you know the truth already, what's the point of debating it?

Unmasking Techniques

How do people unmask? What techniques do they use? I'm going to give just three, though I could mention several more. The most violent technique is *weaponization*, a kind of intemperate language in which persons, groups, and ideas are condemned out of hand as evil or inhuman. The Nazis unmasked Jews as vermin, and Islamists do the same. The Protocols of the Elders of Zion, a fraudulent document that purports to reveal a Jewish conspiracy to dominate the world, is taught as authentic across the Middle East and in several of the Muslim lands of Southeast Asia.

Now you might think that university intellectuals would steer clear of such hyperbolic accusation; but not at all. They gain kudos from using it. Look no further than Rutgers University women's studies professor Jasbir Puar, a prizewinning writer and a star of the Boycott, Divestment, and Sanctions movement against Israel. The title of her book *The Right to Maim* abbreviates her inflammatory assertion that it is Israeli policy to shoot Palestinians to disfigure rather than kill them; that Israel has embarked on a policy of harvesting the organs of Palestinians; and that Israel deprives living Palestinians of nutrients so that their children will grow up stunted. Even to contest Puar's claims with facts is to be complicit in Zionist evil.

It is of course true that intemperate speech is a fixture of politics more generally today. Donald Trump has described the press as enemies of the people, and Democratic politicians as traitors and lowlifes. During the last general election campaign, when Trump was competing against Hillary Clinton, "Lock her up!" was one of the uglier chants in pro-Trump rallies.

But Donald Trump's opponents are no better. In fact, they are worse because they claim to be better. Since his inauguration, Trump's critics in the liberal media, Hollywood, and Congress have refused to accept his electoral legitimacy, have dubbed his regime fascist, have depicted his supporters as morons, and have fantasized in public about hitting, decapitating, or in other ways murdering the president.

And why not? Maxine Waters, a congresswoman, has called Trump a demon. Duke University professor Allen Frances adds for good measure that because of his indifference to climate change, President Trump is as destructive a person in this century as Stalin, Hitler, and Mao were in the last. Denunciation spans the gamut from the murderous to the foolish. It hits below the intellect, as Oscar Wilde once remarked.

Inversion, a second unmasking technique, is no more edifying. Inversion is the practice of taking a person's words as evidence of interests diametrically opposed to those professed in that person's utterances. In Germany in the 1930s, it was common for Communists to call their socialist rivals "fascists," an inversion of the truth that catastrophically helped the Nazis win power. Unmasking inversion is even more familiar today. You say that there are sound reasons to be concerned about the impact of rapid mass immigration on resident communities. I say that you are a xenophobe. You say that you are indifferent to a person's color. I say that such indifference is itself a covert form of racism. We end in deadlock because no persuasive denial of these accusations is possible. In fact, to deny an unmasking accusation is to look as if one is *in denial*.

Such unmasking techniques gloss over the most striking features of human relationships; namely, their ambiguity and their complexity. As we steer through life, it is rarely clear where we and others are going, how a particular problem should be solved, and whether we are the best person to solve it. Time and again, pundits make predictions with the greatest of certitude. Time and again, events prove them wrong. The limits of our knowledge and control, even of the smallest matters of life (as any parent will attest!), should astonish and chasten us. All this suggests that we should doubt the certainty, the formulaic reduction, that unmasking writers bring to their topics; and we should doubt our own certainty when we too succumb to dogmatism.

Few areas of understanding are as complex as race. But you would never know that from much that gets said about it. To illustrate this point, I'm going to introduce the third and final unmasking technique for my purposes today. I'll call it *elongation*, and it refers to the stretching of a concept potentially to infinity. The concept in question loses its boundaries and its limits. Such elongation is evident in the rhetoric of racialization: the notion that racism and white supremacism, or white privilege, are ubiquitous in American society.

Racialization

It is a commonplace today on the American Left, as much a premise of critical race studies as it is of the *New York Times*'s 1619 Project, that the Republic's foundational ideas of liberty and equality are fraudulent. In *Democracy in America,* Alexis de Tocqueville could marvel at the Republic's practices of freedom and equality, while simultaneously condemning as evils the existence of slavery and the dispossession of native Indians. That kind of distinction is unfashionable today. Instead we are told that every aspect of American history and society, both in the past and now, is tainted by the experience of slavery. While Tocqueville offered nuance, observing that the good and the bad coexist but are also irreducible to each other, we demand a single key to history. And for many intellectuals, as distinct from ordinary folk, that key is race.

But is it race? And is it racism? Few people will doubt that a system as wicked as slavery has had manifold consequences for America, and some of these consequences are evident still today. But to describe every aspect of American society as affected by the legacy of slavery is like saying that every aspect of American society is affected by the legacy of religion, or by Westward expansion, or by the greenback, or by the fact that the geography of the United States constrains it to be both a Pacific and an Atlantic power. A concept that embraces everything fails to explain anything in particular.

Racialization, by which I mean the ever-expanding list of conducts and attitudes to which the accusation of racism is applied, culminates inevitably in the charge of pervasive white privilege or supremacism. This kind of allegation has chilling analogs. The most notorious is the Nazi idea of the Judaism of thought, so-called Jewish intellectualization. As David Nirenberg points out in his book *Anti-Judaism,* the Nazis boasted many intellectuals among their supporters. Even Joseph Goebbels, the Reich's propaganda minister, held a doctorate in German literature. But Nazi doctrine wasn't interested in real Jews, in actual Jews, what particular Jews did, how particular Jews lived. Jewishness, or Judaism, was a kind of demonic ether, or spirit, that emanated from Judaism and saturated an entire society with its poison. Judaism stretched to art, the history of ideas, linguistics, physics, and, of course, biology.

I submit that the accusation of generic white supremacism or generic white privilege is the same kind of claim. It attaches white supremacism not simply to neo-Nazi gangs who openly brag of supremacist ambitions but to white people in general, regardless of what specific white people do, what they believe, what they say, and how they live. Much like Judaism in the abstract, there is something about whiteness that appears metaphysically depraved.

It should be obvious that what I've been calling racialization, this stretching of the concept of racism, has an obvious polemical advantage for the people who espouse it. To insist that America is integrally racist, rather than contingently or intermittently racist, is to suggest that any counterargument advanced by a white person is tainted with racism. Now admittedly this dance runs into some embarrassment when the critic is black; but then, following the logic of racialization, a black person who refutes racialization may be deemed spiritually white.

Racialization has a severe weakness, however. The more blanketly that racism is alleged, the less it appears credible, particularly to ordinary folk. In consequence, racism, a real wrong deserving serious attention, becomes trivialized by racialization, as an avalanche of petty complaints overwhelms urgent ones in need of redress. Besides, ask yourself what the accusation of pervasive white privilege or supremacy is supposed to achieve among white people. Is it going to persuade them? You're joking. No one is going to be persuaded by being insulted. Will it encourage conciliation? Indignation is the more likely response. What about solidarity? That's unlikely too, because solidarity, unlike pity, is a two-way street. It cannot exist where one party sits above the other in patronizing or censorious judgment.

I conjecture that, for most white people, the notion that whiteness is a matter to be "problematized" (to use the jargon of critical race studies), or that whiteness is a privilege in itself, is nothing more than a racist slur, since it attaches privilege and a problem to a color and not to a real person or to an actual activity or condition of life. Indeed, the very language of privilege betrays not just arrogance toward those it depicts, who for the most part have difficulty just getting by in life, but also a tin ear to common decency. That defect was grotesquely on show just a few weeks ago when a journalist of the *Guardian* newspaper remarked that, while the former prime minister of the UK, David Cameron, doubtless suffered at witnessing the death of his disabled six-year-old boy Ivan, it was nonetheless "privileged pain."

When concepts become all encompassing, and when presumption drowns out dispute, intellectual life shrivels. People stop asking hard questions. And they avoid telling hard truths. For that reason, it is inspirational to recall models of intellectual honesty. Hannah Arendt is one such model. Albert Memmi— still living, and whose 100th birthday we celebrate in 2020—is another. His work is especially germane to the topic of Bard's conference.

No intellectual has a more impressive record of opposing racism and of supporting national independence than Memmi, a Tunisian Jew of Berber heritage. In textbooks, he's often bracketed with Frantz Fanon and Aimé Césaire. Yet, surveying a host of decolonized African and Middle Eastern countries fifty years after independence, Memmi poses a series of disquieting questions about them. Why are these lands today, he asks, overwhelmingly dictatorships? Why do their most militant groups focus on the plight of the Palestinians, while downplaying systemic theft, autocracy, violence, and religious intolerance in their own countries? Why has the position of women and religious minorities not improved overall, and in some cases deteriorated, since independence? Why are Muslims slaughtering Muslims by the thousands? Why, if Islam is a moderate religion, is apostasy from Islam a capital crime in many Muslim states? Why are citizens of a decolonized country desperate to immigrate to Western lands? Why are the rulers of decolonized countries willing to accept subsidies from their former colonial masters? And why are the latter's troops invited to come in and sort out domestic problems?

You know the standard answer for these ills. They are the vestiges of Western colonialism. They are products of neocolonialism.

No, says Memmi. These ills are now, after fifty years of independence, thoroughly indigenous. Memmi reserves his choicest words for Western intellectuals. By prioritizing solidarity over truthfulness, these intellectuals contribute to evils they should be attacking. Solidarity based on evasion is not support at all for citizens of former colonies who need support most. Instead, it displays a mandarin condescension toward those people by obscuring the wrongs that truthful intellectuals would expose.

I've been summarizing some remarks from Memmi's book *Decolonization and the Decolonized*. When it was published in 2004 in France, Memmi says, it received an enthusiastic response from readers in decolonized countries. It was the postcolonial intellectuals of Paris who hated the book. Radio Libertaire canceled an interview. "Your comments are inappropriate for our listeners," an editor sniffed. An interview for *Libération* failed to appear in print.

Facing Facts in Hong Kong

I said that unmasking is a mode of speech and writing that differs from disagreement. Whereas a disagreement supposes that there is something worthwhile to disagree about, unmasking denies that contention. Its practitioners already know what the truth is: the truth about whiteness, about race, about gender, about identity, about colonialism, and so forth. And, tediously, that truth always boils down to domination. Unmasking virtuosi are also convinced that people who have not come to truth are defective in some way. They're phobic or they're irrational or they're delusive. The unmasking attitude expects unanimity. To ensure it, speech is censored by speech codes, by public humiliation, by collective letters of denunciation. To its shame, the academy is Ground Zero of this stultifying, authoritarian ethos.

At this point I want to return briefly to Hannah Arendt, or rather to a phenomenon that I think she would have considered remarkable: the contrast between the hypersensitized emoting on American campuses and a drama unfolding in a city 8,000 miles from here in which students are taking the leading role, my own students among them. In this city, something like a miracle has occurred in Hannah Arendt's understanding of that term: a totally unexpected event with potentially momentous consequences. This city, renowned for its order, its commitment to hard work, its cleanliness, its ease of doing business, is now in open revolt against a totalitarian power. The city is, of course, Hong Kong, engaged in an agonizing effort to shake free from its Communist overlord.

Hong Kong's history and its current plight raise a striking anomaly for those who like their history simple. I refer to the fact that Hong Kong was freer and more secure under a colonial British government than it is under the present Chinese administration. Let me be bolder: the greatest blessing for Hong Kong people following the establishment of the People's Republic in 1949 was living in a British colony, for without that status, and the protection it conferred, Hong Kong would have fallen victim to the mass famine known as the Great Leap Forward and the murderous turmoil of the Cultural Revolution. The great expansion of Hong Kong in the 1950s was wrought by Chinese refugees fleeing Communist terror. They sought asylum and they found it in Hong Kong; and together, not alone, the British and the Chinese, the Chinese and the British, built this extraordinary city.

To be sure, British arrogance and entitlement were real, and they infuriated locals. Hong Kong under British rule was never a complete democracy, but nor was it a tyranny. Riots and protests occurred; when they did, the colonial government responded sometimes with violence, but mostly with pragmatism, gradually expanding representation both at the municipal level and in the Legislative Council, the city's equivalent to a lower chamber. Hong Kong Democrats who felt stymied by the colonial governor appealed over his head to the British Parliament. Democrats in Hong Kong today no longer have that option. And the common law and the rule of law, both British legacies, are ever more embattled.

A lesson I draw from Hong Kong is one that Albert Memmi anticipated. It is worthless to judge states abstractly and programmatically on the basis of, say, their colonial, ex-colonial, or noncolonial status. It is far more sensible to compare states as they actually exist. Using that measure, a Hong Kong colonial state was a far better regime than the Hong Kong noncolonial state under the thumb of Communist China. That is obvious to anyone but a hardened ideologue.

I began by saying that intellectuals contribute to social division when they adopt the unmasking style. The style's weaponized rhetoric is intemperate; its inversion of argument renders disagreement void; and its elongation of concepts such as racism imposes a simple formula on a complex set of experiences. Together, these unmasking reflexes encourage an intolerant and dismissive attitude toward those who think differently.

No society can cohere for long in a state of mutual loathing, nor can solidarity grow out of cynicism and contempt for those who do not think and vote as we do. If we are serious—if we are really serious—about nurturing a plural society, we will have to stop unmasking our fellow citizens and start to address them as equal members of a common world.

Reflections on Hannah Arendt's "Reflections on Little Rock"

Roger Berkowitz

Hannah Arendt wrote "Reflections on Little Rock" in the fall of 1957, occasioned by a picture in The *New York Times*. There were actually two pictures in the *Times* on 4 September 1957. It is widely assumed that Arendt refers to the photo of Elizabeth Eckford, a 15-year-old black girl being taunted by a white mob of adults after she was refused entrance to Central High School in Little Rock, Arkansas. But it is as likely that she describes the other photo, which shows Dorothy Counts, another 15-year-old black girl also being harassed by a mob of white students as she and a family friend walk toward Harding High School in Charlotte, North Carolina. Arendt speaks of only one photograph: "I think no one will find it easy to forget the photograph reproduced in newspapers and magazines throughout the country, showing a Negro girl, accompanied by a white friend of her father, walking away from a school, persecuted and followed into bodily proximity by a jeering and grimacing mob of youngsters."[1] Arendt seemingly combined the two photographs in her mind's eye, describing the scene in North Carolina while attributing it to Little Rock.

Arendt makes several factual errors in her account of the photograph. She mistakenly refers to the man accompanying Dorothy Counts, Dr. Edwin Thompkins, as a white friend of her family; but Dr. Thompkins is black.[2] She writes that Dorothy Counts's father was absent, when in fact he had driven her to school. And Arendt criticizes the NAACP and other adults who she says were wrong to foist that struggle on their young children. But Dorothy Counts had prepared for this struggle. She had spent weeks in a white summer camp to prepare for racism at Harding High. And Counts willingly and courageously took on her role as a civil rights warrior, one she continued to embrace throughout her life.

Arendt's critics contend that her "several errors of judgment, coupled with factual errors" discredit her essay and show Arendt to be biased and even racist in her judgments.[3] For Kathryn T. Gines, Arendt has already made up her mind that the black parents and the NAACP are "neglectful and opportunistic."[4] Anne Norton agrees, writing that Arendt deprecates the intellectual reasons for integrating the schools. For Norton, black families "are moved by need, and so, according to Arendt's strict dichotomies, they operate in the realm of necessity, not in the realm of freedom and will."[5] Patricia Owens believes that "Arendt's anti-black racism is rooted in her consistent refusal to analyze the colonial and imperial origins of racial conflict in the United States."[6] And Michael D. Burroughs writes, "Arendt is yet another racist

Western philosopher, one inexcusably indifferent to the political strivings and oppression of blacks and African Americans."[7]

A more nuanced critique was offered by the novelist Ralph Ellison. In an interview with Robert Penn Warren in 1965, Ellison said that Arendt "has absolutely no conception of what goes on in the minds of Negro parents when they send their kids through those lines of hostile people." Arendt had written that black parents should fight their political battles and not send their children to do so. Ellison explained that parenting black children requires initiating them into the racist world; he argued that "the child is expected to face the terror and contain his fear and anger *precisely* because he is a Negro American."[8]

Arendt found Ellison's response persuasive. She wrote him a brief letter admitting that her original criticism of the NAACP for using black children to fight adult political causes misunderstood the "ideal of sacrifice" so important in the black community.[9] "You are entirely right; it is precisely this 'ideal of sacrifice' which I didn't understand; and since my starting point was a consideration of the situation of Negro kids in forcibly integrated schools, the failure to understand caused me indeed to go into an entirely wrong direction."[10]

Most Arendt scholars argue that Arendt's letter to Ellison is an admission that she has abandoned her essay. Seyla Benhabib argues that in the wake of Ellison's critique, Arendt had the "grace to reverse her position."[11] Elisabeth Young-Bruehl also apologizes for Arendt's well-meaning but mistaken attempts to carry over her analysis of antisemitism to American racism.[12] And Jill Locke struggles with what she calls Arendt's lack of perspective regarding racial realities; she challenges Arendt scholars to conceptualize exactly "*why* Arendt is so wrong and *what* she fails to understand."[13] There is a desire amongst Arendt's supporters to see her "Little Rock" essay as a mistake and to suggest that Arendt herself abandoned her arguments.

But while Arendt admits she was wrong in her characterization of black parents, she never retreats from her principled criticism of forced integration. Arendt fully opposed legal segregation and Jim Crow. It is necessary to abolish the Jim Crow laws enforcing segregation; but it is another thing entirely to force desegregation on Southern whites who were vehemently opposed to integration. The effort to forcefully integrate schools against the wishes of white Southerners would rob them of their personal rights to decide how to raise their own children; it would also take away their social rights to free association. These are rights that Arendt argues belong to all people in a free society.[14] For Arendt, discrimination in the social sphere may be the result of unjust prejudices, but it is also a basic right.

Arendt's argument begins with her distinctions amongst legal, social, and private segregation. Legal segregation is wrong because it attacks the fundamental equality of the political realm. Arendt's political thinking insists that equality is an achievement of politics rather than a natural characteristic of human beings. We are made equal by politics, and political equality means that in spite of our real differences, we are all equal as public citizens. This means we can vote, serve in public office, and appear in public with dignity as who we are. This public equality is the most fundamental human right; it is the right to belong to a political community, to speak and act in public in ways that matter—it is the right to have rights.[15] Insofar as segregation laws prevent black Americans from fully appearing in public as voters, officeholders, and public citizens, they deprive them of fundamental human rights to be full members of a political community.

As strong as Arendt's commitment to public equality is, she is adamant that the principle of equality is dangerous and out of place in social and private life. In our social lives, the lifeblood of society is "like attracts like." Chess players hang out in the park with other chess players; Muslims gather in the mosque, Jews in the synagogue, and gentiles at restricted country clubs. We choose who we want to hang out with, which means we discriminate. Arendt: "What equality is to the body politic—its innermost principle—discrimination is to society."[16] In society, we are not abstract human beings who are equal; instead, "people group together, and therefore discriminate against each other, along lines of profession, income, and ethnic origin."[17] To oppose discrimination is to oppose a basic human drive, which is why "discrimination is as indispensable a social right as equality is a political right."[18]

Given the need and also the justification for social discrimination, the question Arendt poses is "not how to abolish discrimination, but how to keep it confined within the social sphere, where it is legitimate, and prevent its trespassing on the political and the personal sphere, where it is destructive."[19] When discrimination oversteps the boundaries of society and enters politics, it denies people their political rights to full citizenship. But when equality traverses its political realm and imposes itself on society, it threatens to impose conformity on a pluralist state that can encompass many nations, religions, and groups.

As she does so often, Arendt supports her argument by way of an example: just as it is wrong and unconstitutional to enforce segregation in schools, it is also wrong to enforce segregation in marriage. Arendt was married to a non-Jew and saw the right to marry whomever one wants as "an elementary human right."[20] To say, however, that we all have a right to marry who we want is very different from enforcing interracial marriages for all people.[21] For Arendt, to force people to go to school with who we think they should go to school with is like forcing them to marry who we think they should marry. "The crucial point to remember," she writes, "is that it is not the social custom of segregation that is unconstitutional, but its legal enforcement."[22]

Arendt's essay reminds us that demands for social equality can lead to a dangerous denial of freedom. This is especially true in a country like the United States that is incredibly heterogeneous; in such a country, the demand for equality in society can lead to conformism that seeks to enforce the sameness of political and moral opinions. To forget the distinction between social and legal or political rules risks allowing law to follow social prejudice. When that happens, "society has become tyrannical."[23] Concerning the practice of social discrimination and its possible reasons, Arendt insists that the task is not to do away with discrimination, but how to limit such discrimination to where it is legitimate.

Arendt's claim that education is a social activity in which segregation and discrimination is necessarily permitted is deeply unpopular. In the eyes of her critics, Arendt ignores the political relevance of naturalized racial hierarchies. In arguing that segregation and thus inequality can be permissible in education, Arendt risks assigning black Americans to a second-class status. Thus Norton argues that Arendt's refusal of forced integration naturalizes black Americans and justifies their exclusion from politics: "according to Arendt, they are not present in the polity at all. They remain in the realm of nature, outside politics."[24] For Arendt's critics, the relegation of education to the social realm ignores the political importance of education and naturalizes racial hierarchies. She is said to miss how the desire for desegregating schools is a form of reparation for the way in which African American people had been institutionally discriminated against.

What critics of Arendt's defense of social discrimination overlook is that she adds a second and more important argument against enforced segregation. Just as the principle of politics is equality and the principle of society is discrimination, the principle of the private sphere is uniqueness and exclusiveness. In the private realm, "we choose those with whom we wish to spend our lives, personal friends and those we love." If we choose to marry someone of the same sex, there is no objective standard or rule that guides us. No person and no government should tell us who we can marry, with whom we can live our lives, or how we should raise our children. And yet our private choices, particularities, and eccentricities generally constitute "a challenge to society" insofar as social discrimination will force us to bear the burden of our personal choices at odds with social customs.[25]

Our private lives are important because it is in the refuge of private life that every young person can grow into an independent and self-thinking adult. Privacy matters for Arendt because it secures depth, through which young people become independent and self-thinking persons: "A life spent entirely in public in the presence of others becomes, as we would say, shallow."[26] It is in private that we develop our independent and plural selves. The reason to defend the private sphere from equality is to protect plurality and uniqueness. Privacy protects freedom that is compromised when social discrimination is legalized.

In "Reflections on Little Rock," Arendt argues that we are increasingly losing privacy. There are few more private acts than raising one's children.

"Children are first of all part of family and home, and this means that they are, or should be, brought up in that atmosphere of idiosyncratic exclusiveness, which alone makes a home a home, strong and secure enough to shield its young against the demands of the social and the responsibilities of the political realm."[27] The home is a wall against society and politics, and only in a strong home free from enforced conformism can individual persons grow up into independent citizens in a pluralist society. That is why "the right of parents to bring up their children as they see fit is a right of privacy, belonging to home and family."[28] If privacy is to be preserved, we must protect the right of parents to raise their children as they wish.

There is, however, a danger in protecting privacy. Privacy protects the dark side of the inscrutability of human motivations. In private we humans do shameful and at times antisocial things, hold unorthodox opinions, and challenge the social and political consensus. Above all, it is in private—especially in childhood—that we learn prejudices. "Man cannot live without prejudices,"[29] Arendt writes. Prejudices "crop up in our own thinking, we cannot ignore them, since they refer to undeniable realities."[30] "The danger of prejudice lies in the very fact that it is always anchored in the past" and blocks judgment.[31] Prejudices "are not judgments" and thus cannot be silenced with rational arguments.[32] Rather, prejudices crumble when they are revealed as ideologies and pseudotheories.[33]

For Arendt, the way to attack prejudices is to interrogate them honestly and manifest their outdated partiality. She argues that "whole battalions of enlightened orators and entire libraries of brochures will achieve nothing" in the fight to end prejudice. Instead, we must take prejudices seriously and "discover the past judgments contained within them," so as to "reveal whatever truth lies within them."[34] Revealing what is true in prejudices shows also the untruth in every prejudice, as it exposes the historical and partial nature of prejudice. Eradicating prejudice requires a political effort over time to reveal the truth and the falsity that lie within the prejudice.

To simply claim that prejudices are wrong and to integrate schools *as if* the prejudices underlying segregation could be wished away is to deny the power of prejudice in human life. It is not an accident that sixty-five years after the beginning of school desegregation, American schools are nearly as segregated as they were before.[35] While it may be true that segregation favors the privacy of whites over the privacy of blacks, to forcefully desegregate the school leaves prejudices intact and breeds resentment.

Arendt's assumption that how one raises one's children inclusive of where one sends them to school is a private matter is controversial and possibly wrong. She concedes that children are future citizens and that the government has a claim on them and their education.[36] The state can make education compulsory, prescribe minimum requirements necessary for citizenship, and promote desirable professions. It may be the case that in a multiethnic and multiracial democracy, public education serves an integrating function that is essential. Public schools in the United States serve multiple functions, one of which is to equalize differences.

And yet, even as she recognizes that schools serve an essential public and socializing function, Arendt argues that any principled judgment about school desegregation must distinguish between the need for political equality, the social discrimination, and private uniqueness. School is that institution that mediates between the private world of home and the public world of the citizen. In school, the young person is gradually, over time, introduced into the common world. If we are to guard and preserve plurality, we must also find ways to protect the right of parents to educate their children as they wish.

In the United States, it is essential to address the inequalities grounded in racism and enforced segregation. But Arendt asks us to recognize that to "force parents to send their children to an integrated school against their will" deprives "them of rights which clearly belong to them in all free societies—the private right over their children and the social right to free association."[37] Integrated schools are essential for American democracy; but forced integration, Arendt argues, is a violation of the fundamental private right of parents to choose how to raise their children and the social right to free association. It is also, as history shows, rarely successful.

I thank Anne Burnett for research assistance and for reading earlier versions of this essay. I also thank Thomas Wild, who read and commented on a draft. The opinions are mine, not theirs.

1. Hannah Arendt, "Reflections on Little Rock," in *Responsibility and Judgment,* ed. Jerome Kohn (New York: Schocken Books, 2003), 203.
2. Kathryn T. Gines, *Hannah Arendt and the Negro Question* (Bloomington: Indiana University Press, 2014), 17.
3. Ibid., 15.
4. Ibid., 18.
5. Anne Norton, "Heart of Darkness: Africa and African Americans in the Writings of Hannah Arendt," in *Feminist Interpretations of Hannah Arendt,* ed. Bonnie Honig (University Park: Pennsylvania State University Press, 1995), 247–61 (251).
6. Patricia Owens, "Racism in the Theory Canon: Hannah Arendt and 'the One Great Crime in Which America Was Never Involved,'" *Millenium* 45, no. 3 (2017): 403.
7. Michael D. Burroughs, "Hannah Arendt, 'Reflections on Little Rock,' and White Ignorance," *Critical Philosophy of Race* 3, no. 1 (2015): 52–78.
8. Ralph Waldo Ellison, "Leadership from the Periphery," in Robert Penn Warren, *Who Speaks for the Negro?* (Toronto: Random House, 1965), 344.
9. See Arendt to Ellison, 29 July 1965, Library of Congress, no. 005820, General 1938–1976, n.d.—'E' miscellaneous. http://memory.loc.gov/cgi-bin/ampage?collId=mharendt_pub&fileName=02/020340/020340page.db&recNum=6&itemLink=/ammem/arendthtml/mharendtFolderP02.html&linkText=7.
10. Ibid.
11. Seyla Benhabib, "Feminist Theory and Hannah Arendt's Concept of Public Space," *History of the Human Sciences* 6 (1993): 104.

12. Elisabeth Young-Bruehl, *For Love of the World* (New Haven: Yale University Press, 2004), 311–12.

13. Jill Locke, "Little Rock's Social Question: Reading Arendt on School Desegregation and Social Climbing," *Political Theory* 41, no. 4 (August 2013): 540.

14. Arendt, "Reflections on Little Rock," 212.

15. Hannah Arendt, *The Origins of Totalitarianism* (New York: Harcourt, 1976), 296–96.

16. Arendt, "Reflections on Little Rock," 205.

17. Ibid.

18. Ibid., 206.

19. Ibid.

20. Ibid., 203.

21. Ibid.

22. Ibid., 202.

23. Ibid., 208.

24. Norton, "Heart of Darkness," 257.

25. Arendt, "Reflections on Little Rock," 208.

26. Hannah Arendt, *The Human Condition* (Chicago: University of Chicago Press, 1958), 71.

27. Arendt, "Reflections on Little Rock," 211.

28. Ibid.

29. Ibid., 99.

30. Hannah Arendt, *The Promise of Politics* (New York: Schocken Books, 2005), 96.

31. Ibid., 101.

32. Ibid.

33. Ibid., 103.

34. Arendt, *The Promise of Politics,* 101.

35. Alexander Nazaryan, "School Segregation in America Is as Bad as It Was in the 1960s," *Newsweek*, 28 March 2019. https://www.newsweek.com/2018/03/30/school-segregation-america-today-bad-1960-855256.html.

36. Arendt, "Reflections on Little Rock," 211.

37. Ibid., 212.

Dialogue

A Republic of Discussion: Habermas at 90

Raymond Geuss
Originally published in the digital edition of the Point, *18 June 2019.*
Used with permission.

Is "discussion" really so wonderful? Does "communication" actually exist? What if I were to deny that it does?

The public discussion of exit from the European Union has already caused incalculable, probably irreversible and completely superfluous damage to Britain. Obviously, the "conditions of discussion" before the vote were not in any way "ideal." There is no need to belabour that, but one should also recall that ten years ago *no one*, except a handful of fanatics, had any real interest in discussing relations with the EU; they were not on the table, and nothing was any the worse for that. It is only the discussion of the last four years, stoked by a few newspapers owners (many of them not domiciled in the UK at all), a small group of wealthy leftover Thatcherites, and some opportunistic political chancers, that generated any interest in the subject at all. Dyed-in-the-wool Europhobes didn't constitute more than 10 percent of the population. It was only the process of public discussion that permitted that hard core to create conditions in which another 10 percent of the population articulated what was antecedently a merely latent mild discontent of the kind any population will be likely to have with *any* political regime, and express it as scepticism toward the Union. A number of further, highly contingent historical factors caused another 17 percent of the population to join the vote for Brexit. The most important of these factors was the ability of the Brexiteers to convince people (falsely) that harms they had in fact suffered at the hands of politicians in Westminster were *actually* the direct result of action by bureaucrats in Brussels. Structural features of the archaic and rather ridiculous "first-past-the-post" electoral system transformed the vote of 37 percent of the electorate into a politically effective, and constantly cited, 52 percent of votes cast (in one single election), and that has now been treated as the Irresistible Voice of the People for three years. The irony of the Conservative Party, which had spent two hundred years vociferously opposing this Rousseauist conception, now experiencing a sudden conversion to it, is clearly lost on Tory Brexiteers like Jacob Rees-Moog. A strange sequence of accidents, including the inflexibility and monumental incompetence of the Prime Minister, has now created a situation in which 30 percent or 40 percent of the electorate really is anti-European, and no discussion, no matter how ideal the conditions under which it is conducted, can now in the short run change that. A person who has been brought, for whatever reason and by whatever means, to take a public position, is, for obvious psychological reasons, not eager to admit to having made a mistake. Discussion is not neutral, but changes the situation. Once the government, whatever the rights and wrongs of the original decision, fails to act on it, that changes the situation again, and can generate additional resentment and turn the issue into an existential one. To use the current jargon, for many of those who voted for Brexit, it has become a matter of "identity." When I talk with Brexiteers, I certainly do not assume that what Habermas calls the "power of the better argument," will be irresistible. And I am certainly very far from assuming that an indefinite discussion with them, conducted under ideal circumstances, would eventually free them from the cognitive and moral distortions from which they suffer, and in the end lead to a consensus between them and me. What makes situations like this difficult is that arguments are relatively ineffectual against appeals to "identity." Sören Kierkegaard in the nineteenth century was very familiar with this phenomenon, and much of his philosophizing is devoted to trying to make sense of and come to terms with it. "We do not under any circumstances wish to be confused with Europeans because we have nothing but contempt for them." What is one to say to that? Only real long-term sociopolitical transformations, impinging external events, and well-focused, sustained political intervention has any chance of having an effect. In the long run, however, as Keynes so clearly put it, we are all dead.

When, at the beginning of his *Minima moralia*, Adorno expressed grave reservations about the "liberal fiction which holds that any and every thought must be universally communicable to anyone whatever" (*MM*§50), he was criticizing both political liberalism, and also the use of "communication" as a fundamental organizing principle in philosophy. This hostility toward both liberalism and the fetish of universal communication was not maintained by the members of the so-called Frankfurt School and was abandoned even before the next generation had fully come on the scene. Even as early as the beginning of the 1970s, the unofficial successor of Adorno as head of the school, Jürgen Habermas, who turns 90 this week, began his project of rehabilitating a neo-Kantian version of liberalism. He proposed to do this by having recourse to a normatively highly charged concept of "discourse." What exactly "discourse" meant was to be explained in what he called a "theory of communicative action." His program is "neo-Kantian" in three senses: First of all, it is dominated by the idea that the central philosophical issue is one of "legitimacy" (just as for Kant, the central philosophical question was "*quid juris?*" not "*quid facti?*").

Second, Habermas is fixated, as Kant was, by the idea that there are historically invariant structures that are capable of generating normativity endogenously. In Kant's case these are structures of "reason"; in Habermas's, structures of communication. Finally, Kant was obsessed with clear, strong dichotomies, and deeply anxious about possible violations of the boundaries between what he took to be radically different domains (such as morality and prudence or the a priori and the a posteriori). This Kantian preoccupation is mirrored in the sharp opposition between the central concepts of "discourse" and of "instrumental action" one finds in Habermas's position. Adorno took the "liberal fiction of universal communicability" to be a clear pathology. Habermas, on the contrary, makes no attempt to distance himself from this "fiction"; he actively embraces it, takes it seriously, and even promotes it to being a criterion for legitimacy: "Legitimacy" is to be defined by a certain kind of universal communicability. His liberalism is supposed to have foundations, and to find them in a transcendental theory of communication.

"Communication" is not for Habermas a simple empirical phenomenon. Rather, it has, in his view, the dual structure which is characteristic of the major ideological constructs of Western history, for instance the theories of "freedom," "democracy," and "rights." On the one hand, the term "communication" has an empirical and entirely unproblematic use in everyday life. This fact itself has potential ideological implications because it makes it seem as if "communication" were beyond question, a self-evidently fundamental feature of all human life. On the other hand, the mere existence of communicative structures is taken by Habermas to imply that the agents communicating stand in what he calls a "*Verständigungsverhältnis*," a term which seems inherently confused (and a breeder of further confusion) when looked at through the prism of English, because it seems to put together two things that in English seem patently to be completely different: linguistic comprehension and moral agreement. To use a single word for these two things seems to be an invitation to replace argument with linguistic sleight of hand. If he ever reflected on this at all, which I assume he has not, Habermas presumably would say that here everyday German usage expresses in a pretheoretical way a fundamental truth about the inherent connection between understanding and normativity. To admit that this general point is (in some highly unspecific way) right is not, of course, necessarily to endorse Habermas's particular version of the connection. He holds that to speak is to be committed to coming to (ideal) moral agreement with the person to whom one is speaking. Only a form of speech which is guided by this orientation toward ideal moral agreement can be called "communication" in the full sense, that is, "communicative action." The space that exists between the merely empirical and the emphatic, full-blown, normative sense of "communication" is the potential playground for ideological distortions. To express it paradoxically, for Habermas most communication in our society is not an instance of "communicative action"; it is "distorted" to the extent to which it does not conform to the normative rules that are implicit in communication itself. So it is crucial to distinguish between (distorted) pseudocommunication, which takes place under conditions of social coercion, and genuine "discourse," a form of speech-action that is free of all forms of social domination. To respect this distinction, police the boundaries between pseudospeech and true speech, and never confuse the two, is as important for Habermas as it was for Kant never to permit the corresponding confusions between "duty "and "inclination" or "empirical motivation" and the demands of the categorical imperative.

The natural affinity between this kind of theory and certain motifs of traditional liberalism are too obvious to require discussion. After all, the high value placed on the ideal of "free discussion" is part of the stock in trade of the classical liberal.

To be sure, by proceeding in the way he does, Habermas also finds himself confronted with some of the same problems that traditionally plagued liberals.

One frequently noted problem is that liberals seem to presuppose—although they don't usually admit it, and certainly do not draw attention to it—that discussion is always possible, and always a good thing, assuming, of course—a huge, idealizing assumption, but one liberals are in general willing to make—that the situation is not an emergency with imminent danger to life and limb in which action must be taken immediately. One way of taking the opposition between a liberal and a certain kind of religious fanatic is that the religious fanatic, like the early Christians, believed that *all* the situations of human life were emergencies because the End of Time was nigh and judgment would be pitiless and its consequences eternal. There is a further tacit assumption among most liberals that free and uncontrolled discussion will always contribute to clarifying and resolving problematic situations, and that it is, at least "in principle," always possible to attain consensus. J. S. Mill notoriously thought that liberalism was not for "undeveloped" populations—meaning, presumably, Indians living under the benevolent rule of the British Empire—but even he would probably have found it difficult to come out publically against the ideal of free discussion itself.

In any case, it is important to recognize that these assumptions are actually empirically false. Discussions, even discussions that take place under reasonably favorable conditions, are not necessarily enlightening, clarifying, or conducive to fostering consensus. In fact, they just as often foster polemics, and generate further bitterness, rancor, and division. Just think of Brexit. I get along with most people better the less I know about what they really think and feel. Anyone who has had any experience of discussions in the real world knows that they can get nowhere and peter out, that they can cause people to become even more confused than they were at the outset, and that they can lead to the hardening of opinion and the formation increasingly rigid and impenetrable fronts between different parties. The longer and more intense the discussion, the worse it can get. This is precisely what motivated Habermas in the theory of communicative action to appeal to the topos of an "*ideal* speech situation" as a means for removing these difficulties. However, it is not at all obvious that anyone who performs a speech act, necessarily thereby "presupposes" that his current situation is to be evaluated vis-à-vis what would be decided in an "ideal speech situation," nor that in such an ideal situation a consensus would necessarily be reached.

In the first part of the twentieth century, half a century before Habermas began to write, the American philosopher John Dewey also developed a "theory of communication." To be sure, he, in contrast to Habermas, was clear to emphasize that he conceived communication as a "naturalistic process" (*Experience and Nature*, 1925), and that in problematic situations it is, in the first instance, only human *action* that could bring about clarification and resolution. Any "clarification" is a response to a given situation and set of problems and it remains, unless specifically modified, relative to that configuration. Only a set of further actions, in particular specific acts of abstraction, can transform it into something with more general application. In some, but by no means all, situations the action in question can take the form of discussion, but there is no form of discussion which is given a priori as ideal. If discussion does not help, as it often does not, one must intervene to change the situation, and the "change" required may not be the sort of thing those of delicate sensibility automatically welcome. It may be necessary even to use one's hands rather than some purportedly more ethereal organ. Many people may find this a hard saying, or even a sacrilege against the very principles of liberalism. Not, of course, that self-confessed liberals have ever really hesitated to act harshly when they deemed it necessary (especially to protect their interests—think of J. S. Mill and the East India Company), but they have not usually been rather willing to admit this.

The pendant in analytic philosophy to Rimbaud's "*Je est un autre*" is Quine's assertion that "radical translation begins at home" [*Ontological Relativity and Other Essays*]. Even, Quine claims, in the inner dialogue my soul conducts with itself, I encounter a speaker who uses a language that is utterly alien and completely untransparent to me. This language, too, must be "translated," and the only basis on which the translation can be done is the *actions* of the speaker (to the extent to which they are visible or otherwise accessible to me), that is, in this case, the actions of the person with whom I speak when I am speaking with myself. If, then, I do not even stand in a fully transparent relation of normative understanding with myself (again we are back to a German word "*Einverständnis*," with the same root as "*Verständigungsverhältnisse*" above), and if it is true, according to Quine, that the very idea of such a state is incoherent, what are we to make of Habermas's ecstasies about normative understanding and genuine consensus in politics?

No amount of human exertion will suffice to permit us to establish within the domain of the natural phenomenon "communication" a safe zone which is actually completely protected on all sides from the possible use of force, nor can we even realistically "anticipate" in some utopian sense a form of communication where relations of domination were completely suspended or canceled out. Even if, as Habermas suggests, there is something in the "inherent logic" of speech that "implies" freedom from domination, any *particular* theory which tries to claim that it is insulated against history and the real existing forms of communication will eventually turn out to do nothing more than absolutize some contingent features of our present situation. The historical precedents for this are Kant's arguments in favor of eighteenth-century conceptions about capital punishment and against a right to suicide as purportedly following from demands of the very structure of human reason itself.

There is good reason to be sceptical about the main thesis Habermas proposes in this context: that the main contemporary problem is a deficit of legitimacy for social institutions, and that this can be remedied by developing a theory of communication. First of all, as has been mentioned above, it is a Kantian prejudice that "legitimation" is the basic problem of philosophy or even the basic problem of philosophy in the modern era. It is even less plausible to think that it is the basic *social* problem of the modern world. Then, Habermas's conception of "discourse without domination" makes no sense: "communication" has no stable, invariant structure, certainly not one that would allow us to infer from it criteria for a universally valid set of norms, and for the identification and criticism of all forms of "domination." In other words, there is no "communication," at any rate, [not] in the following sense: there is no rule-governed form of linguistic behavior that is necessarily oriented to universal norms that are implicit in it, can be anticipated, and are always presupposed by those who participate in that form of behaviour.

The theological foundations of early liberalism (Spinoza, Locke) began to crumble in the late eighteenth century, and there followed a period of about two hundred years (from Constant and Humboldt, through Mill, to Hobhouse) during which liberals tried to forge ahead without making appeal to the concept of God and the theoretical apparatus that had developed in dependence on that concept. This freestanding, non-theology-based liberalism seems in retrospect to have been a lengthy experiment, the temporary success of which was actually dependent on the fact that it was protected by the strong hand of one or another of the great colonial powers, the British Empire in the first instance, but then also its successors and imitators. If the empire was large, powerful, and self-confident enough, it could allow itself, within certain limits of course, to defend tolerance, freedom of speech, a diversity of opinion, and even to protect certain civil rights. The end of the old imperial orders with the great moral collapse of the First World War and the catastrophe of the Second, meant that all that remained was the sheltered internal space of the American Empire, which provided a continent-size open-air zoo for the various subspecies of *homo liberalis*. Since the events of 11 September 2001 and the economic crisis of September 2008, even this sphere is slowly but surely collapsing in on itself under our very eyes. One can see President Donald Trump as acting on the Nietzschean maxim: "Give what is falling already a further good kick."

The soft nostalgic breeze of late liberalism that wafts through the writings of Habermas carries along with it the voice of a particular historical epoch; nothing unusual about that. After 1945, the pressing question was how Central Europe would be politically, economically, and socially reconstructed. The alternative was, crudely speaking, integration into the West or into the East. There was no room for more radical suggestions, nor were they attempted. The integration of the German Federal Republic into the West had long been a fait accompli by the early 1970s, when Habermas's works began to appear, but it was the framework within which one should place his project, a project which culminated in the publication, in 1981, of his book *Theory of Communicative Action*. Hegel noted that philosophy always comes after the fact, and such was the case here, too: a quasi- transcendental philosophy which consecrated "discourse" as the central medium of public reason, and gave ideological cover to further "*Westintegration*" by combining the tradition of liberalism what was particularly strong in Britain, the Netherlands, the US, and France, with motifs from Kant that had strong appeal in Germany.

There was little prospect for the "experimentalism" of Dewey—who called his position, almost interchangeably, "pragmatism," "instrumentalism" and "experimentalism"—to gain any kind of foothold during the formative period of the Federal Republic. Too many people were terrified of any kind of political or social "experiment." There were perfectly comprehensible reasons for this, given the fear of a recurrence of the "experiment" of fascism, and anxiety in the face of the "great cultural experiment in the East" (as Freud put it *Die Zukunft einer Illusion*). "No experiments!" was a highly effective slogan used by the German political party CDU [roughly the equivalent of the US "Democratic Party"] in the late 1950s. However, the inherent attraction of some aspects of socialism, despite the negative example provided by Eastern Europe, was not negligible, and it increased in the 1960s and 1970s. So it was advisable to try to proceed against possible "experiments," not only in an overtly political way but also, indirectly, by excluding them from the realm of discussion altogether, and ensuring that they couldn't be discussed at all. So, there was a vogue for Karl Popper, who claimed that experiments that were too "large-scale" were a violation of the "logic of scientific investigation"; Dewey, in contrast, had claimed that there was no such thing as an invariant "scientific method" or "logic of investigation," because one of the most important aspects of science was that as it progressed, its *methods themselves changed*. Habermas, too, should be seen in this context, paradoxically, as an ally of Popper, especially when he claimed that there were a priori limits to rational communication and that these excluded the very possibility of certain "instrumental" political interventions which were to be considered "undiscussable." So his transcendentalism is not just the shiny ornament of a philosopher who had enjoyed a decent education, but it was an indispensable instrument for ramming firmly into the ground the border posts that were to enclose the area within which discussion could take place, and keep out unwelcome topics. That this policy of limitation of discussion was not merely a local phenomenon in Germany is indicated by the fact that Rawls, at about the same time in the US, saw himself forced to borrow some similar bits of kit from Kant's great philosophical drugstore, in his attempt to protect the American way of life from alternatives that were considered too radical.

The foolish claim that "we live in the best of all possible worlds" is not the best defense of the status quo. It is much more effective to hide one's affirmation of the given social and economic structures, while trumpeting the opportunities one's philosophy provides for criticizing a wide variety of *individual* flaws, defects, and inadequacies. An ideology of "discursive criticism" also has much better chances of establishing itself because of certain psychological advantages it gives to those who adopt it. It is well suited to absorb, deflect, and channel destructive energies that might otherwise get out of hand, by, thanks be to Kant, imposing discipline on existing discontent and dissipating it in small packets of reformist criticism of individual imperfections and blemishes of the social system.

Philosophers have no special competence as prophets. On the other hand, humans can hardly avoid thinking about the future, one way or the other, and speculating about its course. So one can wonder whether the next generation of young people will be as focused on and obsessed with "discussion" as their predecessors were between 1950 and 2000. If it should turn out to be the case that they are not only different from those who went before but also have different values and desires, and a different orientation, what grounds could one have for objecting to that? Disloyalty to some ideal of free discussion? Even if they were "disloyal," who could blame them?

This is a translation by the author of an essay that appeared in the German-language journal Soziopolis *on 18 June 2019 (Habermas's 90th birthday). The author wishes to thank Martin Bauer of* Soziopolis *for commissioning this piece, suggesting the specific topic, and for numerous helpful discussions of these issues over the years.*

Jürgen Habermas's 90th Birthday

Seyla Benhabib
Originally published on Medium by the Hannah Arendt Center, 2 July 2019.

Raymond Geuss saw fit to celebrate Jürgen Habermas's 90th birthday with a poisoned polemic called "A Republic of Discussion: Habermas at 90." Originally commissioned by the German journal *Soziopolis*, with essays by other contributors reflecting on Habermas's work and significance, the article appeared on the website of the *Point* magazine.

Amor Mundi then featured Geuss's essay on 23 June 2019, with no discussion or alternative commentary. A thinker of Habermas's stature deserved a more measured exchange of opinions about his work on such an occasion. The introductory note in the *Point* magazine to Geuss's essay also credited him with having brought critical theory into mainstream Anglophone philosophy with his 1981 *The Idea of a Critical Theory*. But Geuss's early book is just as polemical and dismissive of Habermas's work as his current article and it did not give rise to any significant exchange between the two traditions. Instead, the work of Thomas A. McCarthy, *The Critical Theory of Jürgen Habermas* (1978), and Richard J. Bernstein's *Restructuring Social and Political Theory* (1976) have initiated the serious conversation between Habermas's work and Anglo-American philosophy.

This may not be important for Geuss, who denies that "communication" is even possible and who asserts that discussions lead only to further discord and disagreement. Why, then, should one respond to Geuss at all? And why, indeed, does Geuss himself write at all, if communication is impossible?

Obviously, his paradoxical claims intend to provoke: while denying the possibility of communication, we will continue to communicate, and seek some understanding. Karl Otto-Apel, Jurgen Habermas's senior colleague at the University of Frankfurt and the greatest interpreter of the ideas of Charles Sanders Peirce, called this predicament a "performative contradiction": a situation in which my speech and action can take place only under certain conditions which I continue to contradict through explicit statements such as, "Believe me, reaching an agreement through discussion is impossible, and Habermas is wrong."

Apel and Habermas have argued that in speech acts, such as the one above, we implicitly raise a number of validity claims. Such validity claims include assumptions about *what exists or what is the case* (i.e., if I did not assume that Habermas had made such a claim, my statement would make so sense). In saying "Believe me. . . , " I further assume it is *appropriate* for you to trust me and that I am prepared to convince you on the basis of evidence and reasons, and not through threats of force or violence. Furthermore, we take it for granted that you and I are speaking a language that is more or less *comprehensible* to both (intelligibility claims); and that we are in some sense *sincere* in trying to convince each other of the validity of the proposition that "Believe me . . . Habermas is wrong." These four validity claims—to truth (*Wahrheit*); to appropriateness according to some norm (*Richtigkeit*); to intelligibility (*Verständlichkeit*); and to truthfulness (*Wahrhaftigkeit*)—are presupposed in every communicative action, which itself is situated in a concrete lifeworld. Habermas has called his analysis of the validity claims presupposed in speech acts and their embeddedness in communicative acts of our lifeworld "quasi-transcendental." Serious questions have been raised about whether such transcendental analysis, quasi- or not, can convince. Unlike Kant, Habermas acknowledges that a presuppositional analysis alone will establish neither necessity nor inevitability, and therefore he has appealed to sociolinguistics, pragmatic theories of meaning, and even socialization theory to further shore up his claims. Like Wittgenstein, for Habermas, too, language becomes the medium in and through which we articulate and try to solve the puzzles which the philosophical bequeathed to us in the vocabulary of mind and consciousness.

Geuss reduces this idea of "communicative action" to a formulation which he names a "Verständigungsverhältnis," through which he accuses Habermas of conflating "comprehension and moral agreement." But the confusion is Geuss's own. Habermas claims that in ordinary transactions, we act within the shared assumptions of our lifeworld and we transmit cultural knowledge about our tradition and we coordinate our actions and express our desires, wishes, etc. It is only when communication breaks down and we can no longer understand or trust one another or bring our actions into sync that it becomes necessary to engage in special argumentation practices called "discourses." It is then that we must seek "Verständigung," both in morals and politics; that is, we must seek to come to some kind of agreement about the conflictual and contentious situation at hand—if it is even only to agree to disagree. There is no guarantee that we will achieve this. Habermas's point is that if the certainties that guide our lifeworld are disrupted and torn apart, and can no longer be restored through communication, we will experience crisis-like phenomena in our societies and in our selves. Intergenerational cultural transmission will cease to convince and enhance our lives; we will become less and less able to achieve social coordination in politics, economics, and administration, and we may fall into anomie, isolation, and loneliness. In other words, the failure to reach some such understanding can produce crises in the lifeworld.

Geuss reduces the complex architectonic of Habermas's theory of communicative action, which blends language analyses with social theory and a critique of contemporary capitalist societies, into a series of insultingly simpleminded propositions. He has very little to say about Habermas's theory of the legitimation crises of modern societies, which tried to show how the dsyfunctionalities of the private appropriation of capital could or could not be compensated for by the democratic welfare state; not a word is spent on Habermas's theory of modernity in terms of the distortions caused by the intrusion of systems of instrumental action from the economy and administration into the family, into neighborhoods, into parliaments and other associations. Geuss makes no attempt to link Habermas's views of discussion and argument with his theory of the public sphere and its place in a democracy—admittedly, one of the crown jewels of Habermas's political theory. Geuss, who invokes John Dewey contra Habermas in the final pages of his essay, also misses the influence of Dewey's *The Public and its Problems* (1927) on Habermas's work,

That Geuss is not interested in Habermas's complex and subtle defense of democratic constitutionalism, as discussed in *Between Facts and Norms* (*Faktizität und Geltung*), is nowhere more evident than in his claim that discussions are "not necessarily enlightening, clarifying, or conducive to fostering consensus." That is undoubtedly sometimes the case, but if we desist from engaging in discussion altogether, if we cease to try to persuade each other with the best arguments possible as we believe them to be, if we do not seek to understand each other's reasons and reasoning, then there can be no democracy, no parliamentarism. Period. The tired gesture of the misanthrope ("I get along with most people better the less I know about what they really think and feel") or the nimble touch of the psychoanalytically enlightened critic ("In the dialogue my soul conducts with itself, I encounter a speaker who uses a language that is utterly alien and completely opaque to me") leads Geuss to sigh over what he calls Habermas's "soft nostalgic breeze of late liberalism."

Geuss's dyspeptic article appeared just a few days before Russian President Putin announced in the *Financial Times* that liberalism was dead and its credibility spent. Hiding the millions of dollars that the Russian government secretly and not-so-secretly spent to stir up the Brexit campaign (look at what the extraordinary website *Open Democracy* has done to unearth the "dark money" behind Brexit); or to finance Marine Le Pen in France or the populist fascist Matteo Salvini in Italy, Putin attacked Angela Merkel for admitting under a million of refugees into Germany, where he said, with little evidence, that they were raping, stealing, and attacking—and all because liberalism had given them "human rights." Putin and Steve Bannon share talking points apparently!

Let us listen carefully to what Putin is saying, because the battle lines are drawn: a new authoritarianism that is sweeping across the globe from Brazil to Turkey, from Hungary to India, is upon us. It intends to destroy democratic constitutionalism, the liberal culture of tolerance and diversity, and yes—*pace* Geuss—government based on the idea of reaching agreement among citizens and residents of a polity who show one another equal respect. In this current climate, whether we criticize liberalism à la Rawls or à la Habermas, it is incumbent upon us to state more clearly where we draw the lines between an *internal critique* of liberal democratic constitutionalism and autocratic authoritarianisms—lest we end up with strange bedfellows!

Professor Benhabib and Jürgen Habermas

Raymond Geuss

Originally published on Medium by the Hannah Arendt Center, 6 July 2019.

When I have been invited, I have published things on the internet, but I don't myself regularly read anything published there. However, yesterday two friends pointed
out Seyla Benhabib's reply to my piece on Habermas, and I thought those who have been following the discussion might find the following clarifications helpful.

Professor Benhabib is the author of what seems to me to be the best philosophical study of the thought of Jürgen Habermas, *Critique, Norm, and Utopia*, and she is an internationally recognized expert on his writing. She is entirely correct, in her recent response to an article I published in the *Point*, to note that I was not the first to introduce Habermas (or, for that matter, "The Critical Theory"—she tends to use these as if they were interchangeable expressions, although for me they are distinct) to English-speaking thought. This claim is made in the preface added to my essay by the editors of the *Point*; I was not shown this text or consulted about it in advance. I would not consider myself at all to be a scholar of the works of Habermas. In fact, in 1976 or 1977 when I was writing the manuscript which I eventually published as *The Idea of a Critical Theory*, it was the publisher's idea to add the subtitle *Habermas and the Frankfurt School*. I had conceived the work without reference to any particular figure, and had three aims. First, I was interested in rehabilitating the concept of "ideology," which at that time was widely criticized. I thought that these criticisms were unwarranted, and motivated by a confusion of different senses in which the term "ideology" was used. Second, I was interested in the idea of people having and pursuing or failing to pursue their own 'real interests'. Third, I was keen to try to suggest that there could be forms of "enlightenment" that were not in any sense analogous to scientific theories but were nonetheless important. I merely mentioned this third point at the very end of the book, without developing it. Despite the book's external success, I thought that on my own terms it was a huge failure, if only because I discovered that several careful philosophers (including Dick Rorty) thought I was trying to do the reverse of what was my intention; namely, that I was trying to discredit the use of the term "ideology." In addition, others thought I was asserting dogmatically that there were real interests that existed independently of their construction by agents. Finally, no one seemed to pick up the point about enlightenment and science/knowledge at the very end, which seemed to me to be key.

So the book is not about Habermas, and the criticisms I leveled at him in the book were not even original. In about 1971, the colleague with whom I shared an office as an *Assistent* in the *Philosophisches Seminar* in Heidelberg, Konrad Cramer (later professor at Göttingen), said something to me that stuck in my memory. One could, he said, go through the work of Habermas and simply strike out all occurrences of the word "transcendental" (including in the expression "quasi-transcendental"), and if one did that, not only would the resulting text lose nothing, but palpable falsehood would often be transformed into truths. The only problem was that the result would be philosophically trivial. This is basically what I had to say specifically about Habermas in the book. I did him what I took to be the philosophical courtesy of treating his use of the word "transcendental" as if it were serious and considered, and modeled on Kantian usage. To say that there were "transcendental conditions of communication" did *not* mean merely (1) that there were *important* conditions, nor (2) that there were universal conditions—because these could be *merely empirically* universal, nor indeed (3) that there were necessary and universal conditions, but (4) that there were necessary, invariant, universal conditions *that could be the grounds of further cognitions a priori*. What was crucial then was that the purported necessary and universal conditions of communication told us a priori about commitments we (purportedly) had to have, commitments about how we had to evaluate things, and how we had to act.

Perhaps I ought to have resisted the addition of the subtitle to the book, but at the time I was an emollient young fellow and I thought the publisher knew better. (I should also mention that in the original German version of the text published in translation in the *Point*, I started the piece with Adorno and *Minima moralia*, relegating the material about Brexit to later, as merely an instance of the many ways in which discussion may go wrong. The editors suggested this transposition, and I acquiesced. I suppose they thought that more people in Chicago, where the *Point* is published, were interested in Brexit than in Habermas. [Now, in retrospect, I think that this transposition was a mistake, because it distorts the structure of my argument.]

I stopped reading what Habermas wrote in about 1980, when I discovered that he continued to be committed to pursuing a general line which seemed to me a dead end. I did, in fact, read a further one of his books, *Diskurs der Moderne*, when I was asked to review it (for *Zeitschrift für philosophische Forschung* in 1987), but I thought it was a tissue of misunderstandings, and so that was my last attempt to keep up with his writing.

So if I am not an expert, and think Habermas's project is terminally flawed, why don't I keep my mouth shut about it? I have tried to do this for the past thirty years or so, but in March of this year I happened to find myself in Vancouver, Canada, with nothing much to do, and on the computer in my hotel lobby I found a message from my old friend Martin Bauer of *Mittelweg 36* and *Soziopolis*, inviting me to write something on the topic of Habermas and communication. Martin had a knack of suggesting topics I myself would never have picked and thought myself unqualified to treat (for instance, Cervantes's *Don Quixote*). Martin was keen to avoid conventional pieties—who can blame him for that? What is the point of publishing mere panegyrics? It is, I assume, commonly accepted that public philosophers should not be immune from public criticism, or even expressions of public dissent; also, anyone may speak. Adoration, on the other hand, is an inappropriate attitude in philosophy; it went out with the Pythagoreans, who had a religious cult of their founder, and we have no good reason to revive it. So finding myself at a loose end for four or five days in Vancouver, I wrote a short essay in German about what I remembered about Habermas (and also T. W. Adorno and John Dewey) on communication. I praised Dewey for his open-ended idea of communication as an empirical process with potentially *changing* rules, and also Adorno for his criticism of liberal claims about the universality of the communication of truth. In doing so, I contrasted their views with those of Habermas, who held that communication had invariant, universal rules which imposed forms of behavior on all speakers. In the sense in which Habermas used the term "communication," I thought, did not exist. My main target, just to repeat, is transcendentalism (or, in Habermas's formula, "quasi-transcendentalism," which seems to me in fact to amount to the same thing). Professor Benhabib's response to this is to restate the structural rules which Habermas thinks govern communication and the implications which these rules have. It would be unfair to expect her to outline in full and convincing detail Habermas's complex theory and to defend it in the compass of a single paragraph, and of course I did not expect her to do that, but the reader will also understand that if reading Habermas's work in extenso in the 1970s did not convince me, reading her bald summary did not either.

I note that the position I outlined was not that what we usually call "communication" is never possible or never a good thing, only that Habermasian "transcendental theory of communicative action" was an illusion. Now perhaps I am wrong about this, although I see no reason in Professor Benhabib's text to think so. There is, however, something in her piece that bothers me, and that is the suggestion that if we wish not to endorse the views of Vladimir Putin, the *only* way to proceed is by accepting Habermas's construction, or that the only way to avoid playing into Putin's hands is to avoid any criticism of any position that can reasonably be construed as "liberal" (as Habermas's position, in my view, clearly is). Following Karl Kraus (and my old teacher Sidney Morgenbesser), I would say that if I have to choose between Putin and Habermas, I choose neither. Just as when Tony Blair told us that if we opposed the invasion of Iraq, we were supporting Saddam Hussein, there too I permitted myself to choose neither of the proposed alternatives. If you tell me I "*must*" choose, I would wish to know what the force of that "must" is (apart from "I would very much like you to choose between exactly these two").

The most interesting passage, for me, in Professor Benhabib's note is the characterization of my view that I often get along better with people the less I know about their deepest inner opinions, feelings, and motivations. Professor Benhabib thinks that this is a form of misanthropy. This seems to me naive, and it is also potentially dangerous to make public order depend too strongly on a deep understanding of shared impulses and opinions. I merely point out that there is another—dare I say, a related?—strand of recent liberal thought (Rawls) which emphasizes precisely the necessity for a good society to create institutions in which different people and groups can get along *despite* differences in their final conceptions of the good.

Professor Benhabib dismisses my remarks about Rimbaud and Quine, which were intended to suggest that Habermas's ideas about communication were unsophisticated, for reasons that are not completely clear to me. In fact, I think that the nineteenth century saw four "revolutions" in our way of seeing and thinking about society and politics: first, the great upsurge of socialist, anarchist, communist thought (Marx); second, the new aesthetic sensibility associated especially with figures like Rimbaud (*"dérèglement de tous les sens"*); third, Nietzsche's transformation of epistemology in his "perspecticism"; and fourth, Freudian psychoanalysis. Moving from reading Adorno, who whatever else one might think of him, made some attempt to assimilate and deal with *all* of these, to reading Habermas, who makes a serious attempt at thinking about the first, a desultory stab at dealing with the fourth, completely misses the point of the third, and does not even seem aware of the second, always strikes me as regressing from the contemporary world to some point at the start of the nineteenth century.

To return to the issue of adoration, the phenomena of philosophical affiliation and loyalty deserve more study than they have received (which is, as far as I can tell, none). Since antiquity, philosophers have formed "schools" and conducted polemics. It is perfectly understandable that philosophers take especially seriously, and think twice about criticizing, the views of their main teachers. It is also understandable that someone who specializes in mastering a set of highly convoluted, difficult systematic views will not wish to have that investment of time, patience, and energy devalued. Defending one's favorite position or philosopher tenaciously is a perfectly laudable impulse and some philosophers seem especially to inspire this in their admirers (for instance, Wittgenstein), but this is different, I think, from cases in which the identification with a particular philosopher is so strong that criticism of him or her is taken as a personal affront. This seems to be the case with Professor Benhabib and Habermas. There is something mysterious about the way in which some philosophers become iconic for some people; whatever the reason for this, it cannot be that these philosophers, and no others, are always right.

If I have misunderstood Habermas, I regret that, but I have yet to see any evidence that that is the case. Being 90 is no intellectual get-out-of-jail-free card for a public philosopher (or, in my view, for anyone else who is still compos mentis). I am 72 years old and not a public figure, but I expect to be criticized when I speak or write, not blandly and indiscriminately praised, not even on my birthday.

Contra Geuss: A Second Rejoinder

Seyla Benhabib
Originally published on Medium by the Hannah Arendt Center, 6 July 2019.

As Raymond Geuss admits in his reply, having published his initial critique of Habermas in 1981,[1] he no longer followed the work except for a review of *The Philosophical Discourse of Modernity* (German, 1985; English, 1990), which he considered equally to be a "tissue of misunderstandings." I did not harbor any illusions that I would be able to change Raymond Geuss's mind about Habermas's work through my reply, but I just wanted to set some of the record straight, particularly for new generations of students and scholars, out of whose milieu the *Point*, which first published Geuss's article, seems to have emerged. (Martin E. Jay has now written an in-depth rejoinder to Geuss on this website: https://thepointmag.com/2019/criticism/the-liberal-idea-has-become-obsolete-putin-geuss-and-habermas.)

Geuss's principal critique of Habermas is that the program of searching for "transcendental conditions of communication" is a philosophical failure. This is a perfectly legitimate philosophical disagreement but Geuss simply does not state the problem precisely. Habermas is NOT searching for transcendental or quasi-transcendental conditions of communication überhaupt; rather, in the tradition of speech-act theory, he is analyzing the conceptual presuppositions which we as speaking agents make in order for our utterances to be intelligible to each other. The distinction here is between "knowing what" and "knowing that," or between implicit and explicit knowledge. Speech acts are embedded in communicative actions in the lifeworld.

As is well known, J. L. Austin's theory of speech acts presupposes an institutional analysis of the background conditions against which our utterances become intelligible performances for our interlocutors. We can do "things with words" (as when the couple gets married by saying "I do" in front of the justice of the peace or other relevant official) because these statements are uttered in certain lifeworld contexts. In such contexts, we take certain assumptions about what is the case, what is proper to do or say, the language in which we communicate, and why we communicate, always, already for granted. Habermas digs deeper than Austin in analyzing just those assumptions that make speech acts possible and uncovers the four validity claims. It is these four conditions (and their world references, which I will not go into) that Habermas names "transcendental." Geuss does not sort out speech-act theory from communicative action.

For Habermas, the distinction between illocutionary and perlocutionary speech effects is one that we must presuppose for communicative action to be possible. It is, of course, obvious that in many cases this distinction may be blurred. "Illocutionary" are those effects which one speaker communicates forthrightly to the other in order to coordinate their actions, whereas "perlocutionary" are those speech acts through which one speaker wants the other to behave in a certain way without communicating overt intentions and sharing mutual understanding. The key to Habermas's work, in my opinion, is the relationship between this speech act analysis, the social-theoretic conception of communicative action, which is both action and communication, and the logic of modernity as rationalization. Having misconstrued one part of this complex program as a transcendental argument about communication as such, Geuss dispenses with the whole structure.

Geuss is not alone in rejecting transcendental arguments or in denying that philosophy ought to be concerned with policing boundaries among different kinds of speech acts. The fundamental dispute between Derrida and Habermas rested on this issue, and Derrida denied the necessity as well as viability of the illocutionary/perlocutionary distinction. For Foucault and Foucaultians as well, who see speech acts as interlaced with and imbricated in relations of power, this distinction makes no sense. All speech is perlocutionary in their view.

These are crucial questions in philosophy which go as far back as the dialogue between Thrasymachus and Socrates in Plato's *Republic* about power, persuasion, and justice. Reasonable and smart people can disagree about them, even while trying to convince each other with the best arguments they can marshal against each other—as Geuss and I are (hopefully) trying to in this exchange. Therefore, I find the insinuation that my arguments are motivated more by "adoration" and by "philosophical loyalty to a school" rather than by rational conviction offensive.

Raymond Geuss may or may not be a misanthrope and we may all be better off if we do not know about each other's "deepest opinions, feelings, and motivations." As one of my mentors at Harvard, Judith Shklar, argued convincingly, society is dependent for its functioning upon a certain hypocrisy, and many of us do not even know our "deepest opinions, feelings, and motivations." But democracies cannot simply be republics of hypocrites. Sometimes, somewhere, we must speak truth to power and to each other if we are to succeed in living together with respect and dignity.

Hence my final paragraph on Vladimir Putin. It was intended to provoke Geuss to state more clearly, and not by his dismissals of Habermas's position alone, how he would distinguish his critique of liberal ideals of government by deliberation and argument, tolerance, and respect for individual dignity, from Putin's critique. Sometimes, "*les extremes se touchent*," the extremes touch, and there can be a convergence between right-wing and left-wing critiques of these ideals. I don't know much about Geuss's politics, but I sense a certain ultraleft critique of labor and social democratic politics in his statements. It would have never occurred to me to pose this as a choice between Putin and Habermas. Indeed, the whole idea is so preposterous, that I will rest my case contra Geuss here: Putin OR Habermas? Really, Raymond Geuss?

---

1. Geuss's disclaimer that the book is not about Habermas is disingenuous. I took out my tattered copy of *The Idea of a Critical Theory* (1981) from the shelf. The series editors' introduction, by Alan Montefiore and Hide Ishiguro, refer to Geuss's arguments with reference to Habermas throughout (vii–ix); the list of abbreviations in the front of the book are all to works by Habermas. And Geuss himself writes in the introduction, " I have decided to focus my discussion on the views of Habermas because his work is the most sustained attempt by a member of the Frankfurt School to get clear about the underlying epistemological assumptions of the critical theory, and so raises the issues that interest me in a particularly striking way" (3). The discerning reader may want to check out pages 55–88 for Geuss's further critique. But there is one oddity in a book in which Habermas is discussed on nearly every page: the index makes no reference to him at all!

"The Liberal Idea Has Become Obsolete": Putin, Geuss, and Habermas

Martin E. Jay
Originally published in the digital edition of the Point, *5 July 2019.*
Used with permission.

From the Editors of the *Point*: This essay is a response to a widely discussed piece we published last month by Raymond Geuss. In "A Republic of Discussion," Geuss offered a critical reassessment of Jürgen Habermas's theory of communicative action.

I was first alerted to Raymond Geuss's sour anticommemoration of Jürgen Habermas's 90th birthday, "A Republic of Discussion," coincidentally on the same day that Vladimir Putin declared the obsolescence of liberalism in a meeting with Donald Trump. Trump, with the exquisite cluelessness that has made him so easy to mock, took the remark to refer to American political liberals, such as those in the Democratic Party. But Putin's target was something much larger: the tradition of liberal democratic norms and institutions he and his fellow authoritarian populists are determined to undermine. It is the tradition that Geuss finds so lamely defended by Habermas's theory of communicative action, which believes in discursive deliberation as a fundamental principle of a liberal democratic polity.

Since guilt by association may not be a fair tactic—although in this case, it is hard to resist—let's look at Geuss's argument on its own terms. The first point to make is that it is, in fact, an argument, made publicly, drawing on reasons and evidence, employing Geuss's characteristic rhetorical flair and keen intellect, and not a mindless rant. It is hard not to see it as an attempt to communicate, intending to sway its audience, and thus betraying some residual faith in the power of persuasion through the better argument. As such, it immediately invites the reproach, which Habermas and his followers often level, of committing a performative contradiction. That is, if Geuss denies that communication and discussion are laudable endeavors, how can he still engage with such brio in precisely what he is so eager to trash? It is not as if there are no examples of performatively consistent denials of communication—see, for instance, the way Derrida dismissively thwarted Gadamer's attempt at hermeneutic dialogue in the stillborn "encounter" between them in 1981—but Geuss is too deeply steeped in Oxbridge civility to act out his disdain. If such an option is not then possible, why not just withdraw into silence, retreating, as Orwell would have put it, inside the whale?

There is, in other words, a certain amount of bad faith in Geuss's arguing against argumentation, giving reasons against the power of reasoning. But the performative contradiction reproach, let it be admitted, only goes so far in rebutting Geuss's disillusioned take on the role of communicative rationality in the public sphere. It smacks too much of a clever schoolboy trick to stifle a discussion before it can begin. Geuss's case should be addressed on its own merits, taking his points, both empirical and theoretical, at their strongest. Otherwise, the defender of communicative rationality will be open to the charge of performative contradiction in turn.

Let me begin by conceding that the current political discourse in liberal democracies—Geuss's main case is the cacophonous Brexit debate, but it would be easy to give other examples on both sides of the Atlantic—provides ample evidence that we are a long way in practice from Habermas's ideal speech situation. Of course, he always posited it as a counterfactual, which could only be approached asymptotically with no guarantee that we are going in the right direction. Like the democracy that is always "to come," as Derrideans are wont to say, or "the perfect union" that is always a task, not an accomplished state of affairs, it is an aspirational goal. By making the obvious point that we have not yet achieved it, does it follow that its function as such a goal is negated? Geuss is thus setting up a straw man in asserting that "no amount of exertion will suffice to permit us to establish within the domain of the natural phenomenon 'communication' a safe zone which is actually completely protected on all sides from the possible use of force." Would the same disconnect between imperfect achievement and enduring aspiration also render otiose other such laudable goals as, say, equality, dignity, autonomy, or abundance for all?

Although it would be challenging to determine conclusively, the real issue is how much progress, however uneven, has been made moving in the right direction. Ironically, Habermas's own study of *The Structural Transformation of the Public Sphere* ruefully concluded that the institutional breakthrough that was the bourgeois public sphere was losing ground in the late twentieth century, when media manipulation was overwhelming the power of the better argument. Rather than being a starry-eyed utopian, he showed himself to be realistic about the obstacles to communicative rationality, even if the ideal, once articulated, was hard to suppress entirely. Although he later postulated a latent telos of communicative rationality in discursive interactions, it was always a regulative ideal and never a constitutive one. Only weakly transcendental, it has always been understood as dependent on specific circumstances for its potential actualization. Although it is easy to cite examples of its imperfect realization, to deny its aspirational function—to join with Putin in deriding it as "obsolete"—is something else entirely. Would Geuss abandon all ideals if they have not yet been universally achieved?

Geuss's skepticism toward Habermas's position is buttressed by his appeal to an earlier Frankfurt School figure, Theodor W. Adorno, whose scorn in *Minima moralia* for the "liberal fiction which holds that any and every thought must be universally communicable to anyone whatever" he cites approvingly. Written during his exile, when Adorno was exasperated by the demand that his esoteric writing be made accessible to a middlebrow audience, this critique of the fetish of communicability was an understandable defense against a reductive view of language as conversational and transparent. It was the plea of an aesthetic modernist and philosophical outlier for the necessity of difficulty and indirection in expressing complex ideas. It was based on an appreciation, one later shared by deconstruction, of the distinction between verbal conversation and written discourse. As we know from his later musings on the alleged virtues of clarity in philosophy—see, for example, his defense of *skoteinos* (darkness) in Hegel—Adorno never accepted the imperative to simplify his prose in the service of painless comprehension. While attacking Heidegger and other exponents of the "jargon of authenticity" for deliberate linguistic obfuscation, he remained ambivalent about the role of discursive argumentation in his own work.

But it is no less the case that Adorno never claimed that esoteric obscurity was inherently superior in all circumstances. Nor did he consider the fiction of universal communicability, as Geuss asserts, "a clear pathology," as if the state of mutual incomprehension were somehow a "healthy" normality. Although it is hard to imagine Teddie giving a TEDtalk, his pedagogy, as shown by the wonderfully lucid lectures that have been posthumously published, was based on a strong desire to make difficult ideas accessible to his students. And as demonstrated by the series of radio broadcasts he delivered after returning to Germany from his American exile, he appreciated the responsibility of intellectuals to intervene in the public sphere in such a way that large numbers of people could be influenced by the power of an argument. To do something as important as "working through" the Nazi trauma, it was absolutely necessary to have a public discussion in which the occluded past was brought to light and frankly confronted. Geuss acknowledges as much when he claims that Habermas's turn to communicative rationality also reflected the postwar era of reconstruction (which he then bizarrely dismisses as merely "ideological cover" for the Western integration of Europe). For the very same imperative can be discerned in Adorno's own communicative practice at the same time.

But whether or not Adorno can be as easily enlisted in Geuss's anti-Habermasian campaign as Geuss assumes, there are larger points he raises that transcend any quarrel over the putative blessing of an authority. One is the issue of legitimation, another that of the relationship between identity and discourse. Geuss disdainfully charges that for Habermas, and Kant before him, the question of legitimation is both a fundamental philosophical issue and "the basic *social* problem of the modern world." That it may also be a burning political question, however, he neglects to mention. Once again, it is hard to ignore resonance in current headlines, as only the day before this is being written, a former American president, Jimmy Carter, explicitly denied the "legitimacy" of the current president because of the irregularities of his election. Legitimate authority as opposed to naked power has, of course, been a theme of political theory and a concern of political practice ever since the Romans struggled over the meanings of "*auctoritas*" and "*potestas*." In *A World without Why* (2014), Geuss has an essay on "Authority: Some Fables," in which he considers various candidates for authority, weakly concluding that none is really convincing.[1] In a secular world, one in which questions of sovereignty, human rights, and constitutional constraints are constantly negotiated, to dismiss the quest for a plausible notion of legitimacy through discursive will formation as merely a hypocritical liberal experiment within the protected space of the American empire is appallingly cynical. First of all, it ignores the issues of popular sovereignty and the exercise of democratic agency, and makes it only a question for bloodless liberalism with its jejune faith in reason over will. The political instantiation of communicative rationality is less narrowly a liberal polity, with all of the restrictions that implies, than a robust deliberative democracy, based on a powerful egalitarian imperative. It is not one that seeks legitimation in discourse alone, but also in the institutions and practices that enable moving from argument to decision to implementing action.

In his recent collection, tellingly titled *A World without Why*, Geuss confesses that, immersed as he is in an academic environment where justifications are always demanded, "I suffer from recurrent bouts of nausea in the face of this densely woven tissue of 'arguments,' most of which are nothing but blinds for something else altogether, generally something unsavoury; and I feel an urgent need to exit from it altogether."[2] It is thus not surprising to see him dismissively denigrate communicative rationality without offering any alternative way of establishing legitimate authority, oddly siding with that latter-day Nietzsche, Donald Trump, who knows when to push over a tottering idol when it is poised to fall. For a disillusioned realist nauseated by the annoying demand to give reasons and justify values, is there any way to make right besides naked might? Maybe the resemblance to Putin is not so far-fetched, after all.

Geuss's second major point, and perhaps his most arresting, concerns the relationship between identify and discourse. It is, of course, often argued that prior identities are so strong that it is impossible, or at least very difficult, to dislodge them by counterarguments alone. When ultimate value systems are involved, religious faith being the favored exemplar, it is hard to dissuade a true believer who says with Luther, "Here I stand. I can do no other." The same intransigence often seems to accompany secular worldviews held with conviction. Geuss is fond of citing his former Cambridge colleague, the eminent philosopher Bernard Williams, who "took an extremely dim view of the powers of reason to persuade. He once told me he had only one time in his life seen a case of a person convinced to give up a deeply held belief by the force of rational argumentation."[3] Such conversion experiences that do happen can be explained, if at all, by unconscious processes that operate in less transparent and reflective ways.

One might, of course, note that identities and belief systems are now often considered in far greater flux than ever before, and the bald alternative between rational reflection and emotional involvement may be too rigid a way to capture how they are negotiated. It is also the case, moreover, that many significant decisions made in the public sphere are not based on hardwired worldviews or impermeable identities. Despite the ticket mentality that does so often prevail, there are sufficient numbers of "undecideds" in any large population to make outcomes uncertain. And although Williams was certainly right to note that, say, few analytic philosophers have been persuaded by reasons to become raving Heideggerians (who themselves scorned the very need to give them), it is quite possible to say that Quine's refutation of the analytic/synthetic distinction gave a good number of Kantians second thoughts. That is, communicative rationality may have a weak ability to work its magic on the most fundamental identity levels and belief systems, but it is often effective within more local communities of discourse. It is wrong to measure its power only against the most recalcitrant existential identities or entrenched belief systems.

Geuss, however, makes a larger claim than that prior identities or worldviews resist the blandishments of rational communication. He argues that discussion itself is often the cause of their emergence in the first place, as it can lead to the hardening of inchoate opposing positions rather than their convergence. Instead of enabling consensus, he asserts, discussions "just as often foster polemics, and generate further bitterness, rancor, and division. Just think of Brexit. I get along with most people better the less I know about what they really think and feel." No performative contradiction here: instead of a reasoned argument, Geuss gives us an extreme example—the current mess in the UK—and his own personal experience. Other examples and other experiences might easily be adduced for the opposite effect, but what is striking about Geuss's claim is that it suggests that identities and worldviews are not necessarily formed prior to discussion, like, say, a preference for chocolate over vanilla ice cream, but are rather their product. For what this implies, against his intentions, is that they are far more vulnerable to discursive modification and perhaps even dissolution than if they were a priori givens before the discussion began.

The homely example I would offer from my own experience concerns my service on jury duty, when we deadlocked six to six at the first ballot. Without spelling out the details, I was in favor of a guilty verdict, but by the end of the third day of our sober and careful discussion, I and the five others on my side were convinced by the arguments of one of the other jurors that we couldn't convict beyond a reasonable doubt. What made the experience particularly moving was that the persuasive reasoning came from a postal worker, who had succeeded in convincing a professor at a prestigious university and five other professionals through the sheer power of his arguments. I suppose no one had come in with a strong investment in a prior outcome, but still, what made the experience so powerful an instance of communicative rationality working to reach a meaningful consensus became clear after we announced our verdict. We had exit interviews with the attorneys for both sides, and the prosecutor admitted that he had a weak case and thus tacitly confirmed our judgment. Jury deliberations are, of course, imperfect models of public discourse in general—our interests weren't involved and we had strict rules of admissible evidence—but they draw on the same aspirational imperative as deliberative democracy: giving justifications and listening to the justifications of others before decisions are made.

Geuss, embracing his dyspeptic allergy to this kind of process, concludes that the Habermasian age of communicative reason, whose heyday he places between 1950 and 2000, may well be drawing to a close. Rather than lamenting what is lost, he wonders if the generations to come "have different values and desires, and a different orientation, what grounds could one have for objecting to that? Disloyalty to some ideal of free discussion? Even if they were 'disloyal,' who could blame them?" These are phony questions. For having already abandoned the very idea of grounds or reasons or justifications, Geuss has preempted the possibility of objecting to anything at all that might happen in his postdiscussion future world. If there is any blame to assign for such an outcome, it is to those who turn their own bitter world-weariness into a recipe for resigned indifference. A meaningless world without "why?" easily turns into a brutal world in which atrocities can be committed without ever asking "why not?"

---

1. See Raymond Geuss, "Authority: Some Fables," in *A World without Why* (Princeton: Princeton University Press, 2014), 112–34.
2. Geuss, "A World without Why," in *A World without Why*, 231–36 (232).
3. Geuss, "Did Williams Do Ethics?," in *A World without Why*, 175–94 (189).

Presuppositions: A Reply to Benhabib and Jay

Raymond Geuss
Originally published on Medium by the Hannah Arendt Center, 11 July 2019.

I am grateful to the Editors of Medium for sending me a copy of Professor Benhabib's response to my comments on her defense of Habermas, and I wonder if I might reply to her and also to some comments by Professor Martin Jay which appeared recently in the *Point*.

Of course, in everyday life we all—but who exactly is "we"?—make innumerable presuppositions and assumptions about the world, have commitments to and expectations about others, and would dearly love to be able to live up to various ideals we have in various ways acquired and invented. What is perhaps more important, we would dearly love to hold others to (unrealized) ideals we have, and would like (in some cases) to impose commitment to these ideals on them. If I speak French to a waiter in Lille, it is because I assume he will understand that language, and I presuppose all sorts of other things in our encounter. I also project onto him various ideas about how I think he ought to behave toward me.

None of this is at issue; it is taken for granted and trivial. If that is all Habermas has to say—here are a set of presuppositions *we* make, they are connected with many of our other institutions and we think they are bloody important—he is, as my friend Konrad Cramer thought, philosophically irrelevant. He hasn't said anything interesting yet. Things move on only when we go on to ask three further questions:

1. How fixed and invariable are the assumptions and presuppositions "we" make, or that "we" could make?
2. What reasons or grounds do I have for presupposing what I presuppose?
3. What expectations and commitments can I properly *impose on you*?

I contrast two sets of responses to these questions, the transcendentalist (say, "Kant") and the nontranscendentalist (say, "Dewey"). The transcendentalist thinks (question 1) that at least some of our basic "presuppositions" are very fixed indeed, perhaps even couldn't be changed; (question 2) that I have some very special grounds for making at least some of the basic presuppositions I (always) make; (question 3) that I have some noncontextual reason for imposing (some of) my commitments on you. Kant and Habermas disagree about the answer to question 2: Kant appeals to "special grounds" purportedly rooted in some structures of universal reason, whereas Habermas mobilizes his version of speech act theory, but that, in the larger scheme of things, is a trivial distinction. In contrast to the transcendentalist, "Dewey" would say (question 1) that what "we could" come to assume or presuppose is inherently undefined. The basic fact is that the future is genuinely open and our knowledge is changing, and we can't predict apodictically how it will develop. We have to act in the present, but we should do so tentatively on the basis of our best *present* assessment, not taking that to have any absolute standing. "Our best assessment" is what we think at the moment, given our best lights, nothing more (but nothing less). These lights have to be enough, because they are *all that we have* (although in the future we may have, certainly, other and, perhaps, better). The motivation of the transcendentalist is the inability to tolerate this thought, namely that what is in fact cognitively available to us changes and is limited, and that nothing more than it is actually given: no God, "pure reason," no ideal speech situation. "Dewey's" response to questions 2 and 3 is precisely that there are no special, noncontextual reasons or grounds for dealing with these questions.

For these reasons, then, I do not see that Habermas's appeal to "speech act theory" (rather than "pure Reason") makes any difference. Professor Benhabib writes: "Habermas is NOT searching for transcendental or quasi-transcendental conditions überhaupt, but . . . he is analyzing the conceptual presuppositions which we as speaking agents make." This does not address the point. If Professor Benhabib means: "We make these presuppositions now in the sense in which we agree on the rules of chess in order to play a game, *but we could just as easily change the rules of chess or decide to play go or bridge*, and, what's more, *you could unilaterally* act in a way that did not conform to the rules, and I would then have to decide what to do," this, I submit, confirms Konrad Cramer's suspicions about the vacuousness of Habermas's position. If I start a game of chess and then begin to ignore the rules, you may say, "That's not chess," and you would be right, but *so what*? I may perfectly legitimately have more pressing concerns than conforming to the rules of chess.

In chapter 1 of my book *Changing the Subject* I try to discuss this. Do rules about lying, sincerity, etc. have *this* status, like the rules of chess? To defuse Cramer's suspicion would require saying, for instance, why we *can't* change these "presuppositions." Repeating that they are the ones we make is not an answer to this. If I say: "I *don't* presuppose that if I were to discuss this matter with Professor Benhabib for an indefinite period of time under ideal conditions, we would reach agreement"; she says: "Oh, yes, you do; you just don't know that you do." Why is that? No answer apart from further repetition.

Professor Jay takes a surprisingly flat-footed approach to my paper "A Republic of Discussion." I begin by asking: "What is so wonderful about discussion?" He then canvasses the possibility that I think that no discussion can ever be valuable in any respect at all. I go on to ask: "Does 'communication' even exist? What if I were to deny that it does?" Does this, he wonders, mean that I deny that communication ever takes place? So why do I bother writing? I would have thought that for a careful reader the quotation marks around "communication" would be some kind of tip-off that I was speaking of someone's conception of "communication." I go on to talk about different conceptions of "communication," and make it clear that my objection is to Habermas's conception of "communication" as presupposing a transcendental framework, which imposes on all speakers certain ineluctable obligations.

Habermas's theory of the ideal speech situation is, precisely, ideal (that is, unrealized at least as yet), and Professor Jay assumes that my objection to it is that it has not yet been realized. He asks whether I would like to "abandon all ideals if they have not been universally achieved." I don't understand what I can have said to give Professor Jay this idea. What is supposed to be so wonderful about his ideals, according to Habermas, is that they are "*transcendentally grounded*," so we are right always to impose them on others. This is what I am at pains to deny.

I return to Vladimir Putin, because both Professor Benhabib and Professor Jay bring him up. If Professor Jay insists that I should refrain from even well-founded criticism of liberalism because at the moment Vladimir Putin is also attacking it, this demand represents an odd version of liberalism. Many critical theorists were deeply suspicious of the tribal instinct expressed in call to rally round "our" institutions. Adorno thought that the Enlightenment to remain true to its own deepest impulse must enlighten itself about itself. One of the most disappointing things about Habermas's work is his complete failure to try to pursue this thought.

It is true that I simply do not believe, as Professor Jay does, that "legitimation" is the "burning" political (and philosophical) issue of the modern world. I think that a lot of other things are at least as "burning" as the question "what is legitimacy?" and that turning the focus of attention from genuinely pressing practical issues to discussion of "legitimacy" often serves as a mask for the protection of entrenched existing interests. I submit that anyone who looks at ecological questions, questions about the politics of gender, and the issues raised in a pamphlet like the anonymous *L'insurrection qui vient* will be hard pressed to deny their importance, and equally hard pressed to force them into the Procrustean framework of a "legitimation theory." Since I find that I must be hyperexplicit in this discussion, I merely mention that this does not mean that I think that "legitimation" is in no sense an issue at all.

Professor Jay suggests that I misread Adorno when I attribute to him the view that the liberal fiction of universal communication was a "pathology." I took the word "pathology" from Ästhetische Theorie (115) where Adorno speaks of "*Unwesen*."

Perhaps my German is not good enough here and "*Unwesen*" means something more anodyne. I also refer the reader to *Minima moralia §§* 5, 130 (in addition to §50).

I also continue to hold that identities are much more resistant to transformation by discussion than philosophers have traditionally thought (and than Professor Jay seems to think), and that in most cases changes in identity do not come about through the magic force of "the stronger argument" alone, but through long experience, the pressure of external events, and complex processes of re-education, including changes of circumstance and participation in new and different forms of experience, which will certainly not have the form of mere discussion.

Finally, Professor Jay states that I have "abandoned the very idea of grounds, reasons, or justification." No, I reject Plato's dichotomy: *either* one must be committed to Ideas (in a strong metaphysical sense) *or* one must accept chaos and unintelligibility, and also Habermas's analogue: *either* notions of reason are transcendentally grounded in an ideal speech situation *or* there are no reasons at all. I decline this choice. I also decline to accept that unless I can give a full alternative account of what a "reason" is, I am not at liberty to reject Habermas's view.

Since, as I said, I don't believe that unlimited discussion *must necessarily* result in consensus (which, to repeat again, does not mean that discussion is never under any circumstances useful), this is the last comment I am going to write on this issue.

Geuss, Habermas, and the Rose of Unreason

Martin E. Jay
Originally published on Medium by the Hannah Arendt Center on 13 July 2019.

Interaction, let me concede, can ultimately be exhausting. High-minded exercises in inferential logic and evidentiary demonstration descend into ad hominem polemics and clever put-downs. Accusations of misrepresented arguments on both sides grow more heated as civility morphs into a pissing contest. Getting the last word may reward stamina or at least persistence but doesn't necessarily turn into a conclusive victory, as telling points made along the way continue to reverberate. It is therefore no wonder that Raymond Geuss concludes his response to Seyla Benhabib's second critique of his original essay on Habermas (and my one entry into the fray) with a vow of future silence: "Since, as I said, I don't believe that unlimited discussion *must necessarily* result in consensus (which, to repeat again, does not mean that discussion is never under any circumstances useful), this is the last comment I am going to write on this issue."[1]

Because it may seem unfair to counterpunch an adversary who has taken off his gloves, any attempt to continue the argument risks appearing churlish. But not if one takes seriously the concession made in the parenthesis. For the discussion that we have entered had been going on for a long time before Geuss's initial effort and our responses, and will doubtless continue for a very long time after. It transcends, we might say, the proper names affixed to our little essays, by raising perennial questions that have never been fully resolved. Happily, Geuss's final entry helps clarify what is at stake, and does so without the tone of misanthropic *ressentiment* that made his initial essay so inappropriate a way to commemorate a 90th birthday. So it is in the spirit of trying to move the discussion forward rather than to score debating points that the following remarks are intended.

But before I take the high road, I have to take one detour to highlight what has so troubled Benhabib and myself in Geuss's characterization of Habermas's position. Having admitted that he stopped reading Habermas's work around 1980, he cannot avoid presenting a cartoon version of the latter's nuanced and evolving position. One of the exemplary characteristics of Habermas's extraordinary career has been his ability to listen to and learn from his critics. The issue of transcendental norms has been one repeatedly raised in his encounters with them, resulting in an ongoing attempt to clarify a complicated argument.[2] Some of his interlocutors, such as Karl-Otto Apel, have, in fact, chided him for abandoning transcendentalism entirely, but most applaud his attempts to find a way beyond it. In my own attempt to present his position in *Reason after Its Eclipse: On Late Critical Theory* (2016), I characterized it as "the detranscendentalization of reason," and argued that Habermas clearly sought to distance himself from Kant's belief in a universal "consciousness philosophy." By short-circuiting the process of actually grappling with Habermas's dauntingly large oeuvre (which is about to be extended by a massive new book dealing with secularization), Geuss is able to create an easily vulnerable target, whose "irrelevance" he takes on faith from his friend Konrad Cramer.

Perhaps Geuss's casual essentialization of Habermas's position reflects his belief that identities are enduring and solid formations that cannot be shaken by argumentation. But if so, how are we to deal with such familiar distinctions in the history of philosophy as those dividing the precritical and critical Kant, early and late Marx, Heidegger before and after his "turn," early and late Wittgenstein, Sartre the existentialist and Sartre the Marxist, and so on? Habermas may not be subject to such a radical periodization, but it behooves any serious critic to pay attention to the development of his work before dismissing its crudest formulation. For those inclined to see where Habermas now stands on some of these issues, one good place to begin is the interview published last year in the *Oxford Handbook on Deliberative Democracy*.[3]

Geuss's haste in interpreting the positions of others is, alas, also on display in his reply to my piece—sorry for playing the misrepresentation card, but I will only provide this one example—when he writes that "it is true that I simply do not believe, as Professor Jay does, that 'legitimation' is the 'burning' political (and philosophical) issue of the modern world. I think that a lot of other things are at least as 'burning' as the question 'what is legitimacy?,' and that turning the focus of attention from genuinely pressing practical issues to discussion of 'legitimacy' often serves as a mask for the protection of entrenched existing interests." In my essay, I had in fact not called the question of political legitimacy "*the*" burning question of our world, but rather "*a*" burning question, which makes his objection meaningless. No one denies there are lots of other pressing issues, but at a time when the president of the United States is doing all he can to subvert constitutional safeguards against arbitrary rule and the presumptive British prime minister is threatening to prorogue Parliament to get his way on Brexit, to dismiss the issue of legitimacy as merely an ideological mask seems remarkably tone deaf to reality. And, of course, doing so raises the question of whether or not there is a pattern in Geuss's work of attributing extreme versions of a targeted position and then subjecting them to easy ridicule.

Okay, enough petty parrying. Let me turn to the main substantive issue raised in this little contretemps: the vicissitudes of normative transcendentalism. In the title essay of *The World without Why*, Geuss invokes the infamous episode in Primo Levi's wrenching account of his time in Auschwitz in which a camp guard cruelly snatches an icicle from his thirsty lips and responds to Levi's astonishment with "*Hier gibt es kein 'Warum'*" ("Here there is no 'why'"). It was with this episode in mind that I concluded my piece by saying that "a meaningless world without why easily turns into a brutal world in which atrocities can be committed without ever asking 'why not?'" Geuss anticipates this reproach by arguing that there is a less diabolical reading of the question exemplified by the famous lines of the seventeenth-century German Catholic mystic Angelus Silesius: "The rose is without why; she blossoms because she blossoms." Insofar as the cover of his book depicts a rose, it is clear which he prefers.

The opposition, however, is clouded by the fact that the lines from Silesius became familiar to those of us unschooled in early modern German religious poetry—and I would imagine Geuss is one of our company—when they were cited approvingly by the philosopher whose sympathies for the regime that put Levi in Auschwitz have come increasingly into focus: Martin Heidegger in *Der Satz vom Grund* (The Principle of Reason).[4] Significantly, they were mobilized in a polemic against Leibniz's principle of sufficient reason, which Heidegger understood as the *principium reddendae rationis* (the principle of rendering reasons). In addition to whatever philosophical objections he raised, there was also a personal motivation. Annoyed by those who were offended by his Nazi engagement and pressed him for an explanation, Heidegger complained that "lately we have had the demand to render reasons all too oppressively in our ears."[5]

Now, it may seem that by recalling Heidegger's tacit embrace of both versions of "here there is no 'why,'" I am insinuating that Geuss is somehow a closet Nazi, whose visceral disgust at being asked to give reasons hides some sort of crime for which he is culpable. But remember, I have committed to taking the high road in this response, and so want to make clear that I am making no such accusation. Not only would it be entirely unwarranted but it would also inevitably end any chance of moving the discussion forward. Here, what has come to be called "Godwin's Law of Nazi Analogies"—"as an online discussion grows longer, the probability of a comparison involving Nazis or Hitler approaches 1"—would kick in, and we would all go home disgruntled.

Instead, by dragging Heidegger into the conversation I want to make a very different point. In many respects, he has been positioned as the anti-Habermas and strongly identified with the battle against transcendentalism, wherever it might be found. Inspired by the pre-Socratics, he rejected the Platonic quest for abstract truths disclosed by inferential reasoning. Despite his debts to the phenomenology developed by his former teacher Edmund Husserl, he never endorsed the latter's "transcendental idealism," and in his famous debate with Ernst Cassirer at Davos, he lambasted the Kantian tradition. Not surprisingly, his fingerprints are all over later antitranscendental philosophies such as Gadamer's hermeneutics and Derrida's deconstruction. When American pragmatists like Richard Rorty sought a continental partner for John Dewey, it was Heidegger who seemed most appealing. So if Habermas can serve for Geuss as the exemplary transcendentalist, Heidegger can justly function as the poster boy for what can be called radical immanentism, hostile to both traditional metaphysics and the subjective idealism of Kantian epistemology. Not surprisingly, in this role he has been a useful resource for critics of the alleged Eurocentrism of Habermas's position.[6] Each distinct *Lebenswelt*, he can be taken to argue, contains its own immanent self-justification, which cannot be judged from without on the basis of allegedly universal norms. Like roses that bloom without a reason, they don't ask why, they just are.

Or so it seems. For a case can be made—and in fact has been very powerfully presented by the philosopher Daniel Dahlstrom, in a 2005 essay called "Heidegger's Transcendentalism"[7]—that for all of his fulminating against the evils of normative thinking, the constitutive function of the epistemological subject, and the imperative to give reasons, palpable traces of what Heidegger tried to abject can nonetheless be discerned in his own thought. This is obviously not the place to attempt a summary of Dahlstrom's claims or argue their merits. But acknowledging their possible plausibility leads to an important insight: the suspicion that behind traditional transcendental claims—or even ones, such as Habermas's, that seek universal normative grounding in different ways—there lurks a rationale for the privilege of specific interests must be mirrored by a comparable suspicion of the latent transcendental norms in their immanentist opposites. That is, if it can be shown that abstract, universalizing claims are generated by concrete, particular contexts of origin, it then becomes necessary to examine closely those putative contexts to see if there are impulses that transcend their putative boundaries, perhaps even cryptonormative imperatives that have universalizing implications. Should these be found, and I would venture they quickly would be, the conclusion follows that there is no self-sufficient discursive community, be it linguistic, ethnic, religious, cultural, national, gendered, or even "civilizational," that is so homogeneous that it lacks tensions, even outright contradictions, which push beyond its limits. Similarly, there is no historical *Zeit* ruled by a uniform and coherent *Geist* without residues of earlier periods or intimations of later possibilities. When Geuss himself asks "who exactly is 'we'?," he shows that he understands the perils of locating a coherent, watertight collective subject or discursive community with no remainder. It is always possible, to give a familiar example, that a young girl from an orthodox Muslim background in certain sections of Africa or the Middle East will reject her culture's mandate and appeal to transcendental values of woman's rights in the hope of avoiding genital mutilation.

To recognize the mutually limiting power of both the transcendentalist and immanentist positions, the ways in which contexts of genesis both inflect the validity of the norms they generate and are in turn left behind by them, is perhaps what Adorno meant by a negative dialectic (and which is illustrated in one of his earliest essays on "The Idea of Natural History").[8] Habermas has always been sensitive to this dynamic, which informs, for example, the ways in which he pits the insights of Kant against those of Hegel.[9] Ironically, despite his one-dimensional cartoon of Habermas's position, Geuss seems to arrive at a somewhat similar conclusion when he proclaims, "I reject Plato's dichotomy: either one must be committed to Ideas (in a strong metaphysical sense) or one must accept chaos and unintelligibility, and also Habermas's analogue: either notions of reason are transcendentally grounded in an ideal speech situation or there are no reasons at all. I decline this choice." Because of his self-imposed ban on keeping the argument going, we will never know for sure. But in the discussion that is certain to continue well after both of us have left the room, it is an insight that may move a future "us"—understood as inclusively as possible—just a little bit closer to that elusive deliberative consensus that provides a compelling telos for interminable discussion itself. And which distinguishes humans who need reasons in order to flourish from flowers that can blossom without them.

---

1. Raymond Geuss, "Presuppositions: Reply to Benhabib and Jay," *Medium*, 11 July 2019. https://medium.com/@arendt_center/presuppositions-reply-to-benhabib-and-jay-835c4898d848.

2. The concept of "transcendentalism" is, of course, itself highly contested. In addition to referring to the American movement associated with Margaret Fuller, Ralph Waldo Emerson and Henry David Thoreau, it has been identified with everything from Kant's epistemology, which distinguishes between "transcendental" and "transcendent," to the Maharishi Mahesh Yogi's meditation techniques. For the purposes of this exercise, we can define it as a belief in norms or grounds that transcend their parochial contexts of origin, providing a point d'appui for critique.

3. Jürgen Habermas, "Interview with André Bächtiger," in *The Oxford Handbook of Deliberative Democracy*, ed. André Bächtiger, John S. Dryzek, Jane Mansbridge, and Mark Warren (Oxford: Oxford University Press, 2018).

4. Martin Heidegger, *The Principle of Reason*, trans. Reginald Lilly (Bloomington: Indiana University Press, 1996), 35.

5. Ibid., 28.

6. Dipesh Chakrabarty, *Provincializing Europe: Postcolonial Thought and Historical Difference* (Princeton: Princeton University Press, 2008).

7. Daniel Dahlstrom, "Heidegger's Transcendentalism," *Research in Phenomenology* 35 (2005).

8. Theodor W. Adorno, "The Idea of Natural History," *Telos* 60 (1984). Here, the mutually imbricated opposition is between history and nature rather than immanence and transcendence, but many of the same issues are raised.

9. See, for example, Jürgen Habermas, "From Kant to Hegel and Back Again: The Move toward Detranscendentalization," in *Truth and Justification*, ed. and trans. Barbara Fultner (Cambridge: MIT Press, 2005).

Essays

Introduction to the Arendt-Gaus Interview[1]

Natan Sznaider

The date is 16 September 1964. A man and a woman enter a studio to record an interview for the German television program *Zur Person*. As you will see, the man looks rather tense. She is a famous philosopher. He, twenty-three years her junior, is one of Germany's most prominent journalists.

The interview is supposed to air one time only. Moreover, the first thing the woman says is that she is no philosopher—a statement quite confusing to the journalist, who keeps insisting that in his eyes she is. However, this is of course about more than just the journalist's viewpoint. Right at the beginning she makes a point about what it means to be a thinking person in the world. Politics is about acting in the world; philosophy is about thinking about the world. The tension between the two is crucial for her and clearly defines not only her thinking.

Finally, at 9:30 pm on 26 October 1964, six weeks after its recording, the interview is broadcast on the newly established Second German TV channel—the ZDF. There was no reference to it in the newspapers, even though the interview would receive an important prize later on.

That could have been it. *Zur Person* was only broadcast between April 1963 and April 1966 in its first version. Hannah Arendt was the seventeenth guest on the program, the first female after sixteen men in a series of interviews conducted by Günther Gaus. Both he and Arendt are smoking, so you know it is an old program. As you will see, they talk about philosophy, writing, the role of women, Arendt's childhood, emigration, the Holocaust, and her Eichmann book, which had just been translated into German. You will never experience Arendt as personally as you will in this interview. She is crystal clear, her German sharper than ever. She is visibly nervous, but her nervousness just makes her more focused in her language and in her answers.

What you will see is not only a period piece but also a dialogue between generations. Gaus, 35 years old at the time, typifies the new Germany after the Nazi period. He was a left liberal journalist, very much a member of the new West German elite, very much seeing himself as apart from the generation of his parents and grandparents, thinking he can be at ease talking as a German to a Jew.

Moreover, you will see a dialogue between a man and a woman—as already mentioned, the first woman to appear on the program. Arendt is very much aware of that and talks about the role of women. She has not done this very often; it may even be the first time she does it in public. However, there is another layer, which is more difficult to make out: it is also a dialogue between a German man and a Jewish woman. The language may deceive you; both speakers are brilliant, and they express themselves in meticulous German. Arendt was educated in Germany, and you can tell. For her, the language is still very much inside her. On first viewing, you may take her for a German woman.

Listening to the interview, those of you who know German will hear at once that Gaus comes from Hamburg and Arendt from Königsberg. The language gives them away, but this is not a dialogue between two Germans; rather, it is a dialogue between a German and a Jew—even, as I would argue, an American Jew at the time of the interview: Arendt had been living in New York for more than 20 years at the time of the interview.

Language is important here. Arendt never stopped feeling at home in the language. The language did not go mad, as she pointed out. However, being at home in the language does not mean that Arendt felt at home in Germany. She is no German-speaking Athena. She speaks like a Jew and as a Jew. Gaus knows that. After talking briefly about politics and philosophy, about what it means to write, he asks her about having to leave Germany in 1933 due to her Jewishness.

This is a crucial point. Exile became a state of mind for her, very much so, as it did for many others who had to escape the country yet remained in the language. One only needs to read her essay "We Refugees," published in 1943 in the United States, to understand the urgency of language and loss of place.[2] Language discloses something, something higher than one's place of origin. Unlike Adorno, Horkheimer, and many others, she never considered going back to Germany. Arendt was very critical of the German way of dealing with the past. She wrote many essays about how she did not feel any empathy by the Germans for the fate of the Jews—ironically, the same charge made against Arendt by many Jews after having read her Eichmann book.

Look at a short essay she published in 1950 in the American Jewish magazine *Commentary* called the "The Aftermath of Nazi Rule."[3] Arendt wrote that essay after her first visit to Germany after the war, when she worked for the US organization Jewish Cultural Reconstruction (JCR) to secure heirless Jewish cultural property in the American Zone of Occupation. It is a very melancholic essay, and she reflects there on the devastation of Europe she witnessed in the late 1940s:

> But nowhere is this nightmare of destruction and horror less felt and less talked about than in Germany itself. A lack of response is evident everywhere, and it is difficult to say whether this signifies a half-conscious refusal to yield to grief or a genuine inability to feel. (349)

That seemed to be her attitude toward Germany, which did not really change much afterward. I argue that we should look at Arendt foremost as a Jewish thinker not only because she was intimately involved in the political debate and activity that defined Jewish life in the years before and after the Holocaust. Arendt defined her Jewishness primarily as a political stance. She participated in Zionist mobilization when she was still living in Germany and in the founding of the World Jewish Congress during her time in Paris. She retrieved Jewish books, manuscripts, and other artifacts from Europe in her work for the JCR. When she talked to Gaus, she talked as a Jew to a German, in German.

A decade after her work with Jewish Cultural Reconstruction, Arendt became notorious for her book on the Eichmann trial. *Eichmann in Jerusalem: A Report on the Banality of Evil* (1963) became one of the most controversial books of its time and probably the one she is best known for today in the Jewish world. The book, as you will see, was hovering over the interview with Gaus. She was in Germany at the time to promote the book's German translation. What made *Eichmann in Jerusalem* so famous was not only the phrase "banality of evil," which nurtured an interpretative literature of its own about perpetrators of mass crimes. Arendt's interpretation gave rise to interpretations of the Holocaust as bureaucratic and mechanical, even though this was apparently not her intention at all. What made the book electrifyingly famous was the enormously heated debate that it set off, among both Jews and non-Jews, about how the Holocaust should be understood and how it should be talked and written about.

The book and its German translation had enormous appeal for German intellectuals at the time. Many saw in it an attempt to deemphasize the particularity of victims and perpetrators. It changed the categories into impersonal ones. It implied retrospectively that the Holocaust could have happened to anyone and made the Nazi crimes simply one instance of a larger class of mass murders, rather than a uniquely evil event perpetrated by uniquely evil people. German intellectuals at the time drafted Arendt as one of the founders of this "functional" approach to the study of the Holocaust, which deemphasizes agency (and therefore guilt), concentrates on bureaucracy, and above all universalizes the Holocaust. This was made painfully clear by the rather lengthy introduction to the German translation of the book by Hans Mommsen, who in my opinion distorted Arendt's views.

A later icon of the New German Left, Hans Magnus Enzensberger, published around the same time of the interview a book called *Politik und Verbreche* (Politics and Crime). The German magazine *Der Merkur* wanted Arendt to review the book. Her rejection of the offer resulted in a fascinating exchange of letters between her and Enzensberger from 1965.[4] She disliked his book deeply, to say the least, and recognized that equating the Holocaust with other mass murders marked a major intellectual milestone and a mistake at the same time. (The debate about whether the Holocaust should be considered unique or as simply one instance of genocide is still being fought today.) What is intriguing about these letters, written roughly eighteen months after Arendt's exchange with Scholem, where he accused her of not having any sentiments for the Jewish people (she talks painfully about this in the interview) is that she seemed to attack Enzensberger for some of the same things she had been attacked for; namely, for describing everything in abstract, functionalist terms, which washed away the guilt. Even more striking, she told Enzensberger that he was especially wrong to make such an argument as a German, and again, she does it in German.

This is, of course, a strange argument, but I think you may understand better after watching the Gaus interview. One cannot sacrifice the particular for the universal, Arendt argued, adding, "and when a German writes that, it is even more questionable." Her point was, referring to Enzensberger, that the statement "not our fathers but all men were perpetrators" was simply untrue; and she ended the paragraph by exclaiming, "O Felix Culpa!"—an attitude of "blessed guilt" that she accused Enzensberger of harboring. Where everybody is guilty, nobody is, she claimed. Arendt defended the American tradition as well: "The non-understanding of the Germans, but not only the Germans of Anglo-Saxon traditions and American reality is an old story." Europe's relation to America and the meaning of a unified Europe was one of Arendt's preoccupations during the 1950s. She saw America as the locus of liberty through the birth of a new body politic, something that had turned into a dream and a nightmare for Europeans. What she feared most was a new pan-European nationalism that took America as its countermodel. She wrote about anti-American Europeanism, which she saw as the foundation of a unified Europe, reminding her readers that it was Hitler who wanted to destroy Europe's nation-state system and build a united Europe. Thus, in her reply to Enzensberger, which I consider a continuation of the interview with Gaus, we hear not only Jewish but also American fears about Germany's as well as Europe's possible return to totalitarianism. She clearly resented Enzensberger and his generation's anti-Americanism.

Why did Arendt deny that a German could understand the Holocaust without any reference to its particularity? Within Arendt's theory, morality is based on particularity and on identity. It is based on being able to look at ourselves in the mirror and say that we have fulfilled the moral obligations that make us who we are; this means above all the special responsibilities we have to particular others who are linked to us through the accidents of history and birth. To ignore the roots of responsibilities in identity is to misunderstand the basis of morality, and to sweep it all aside is an attempt to forget who you are and to flee personal responsibility. There is a communitarian argument at work here as well. This is a point not only about personal identity but also about who you are as a member of a community. Arendt at this point, in the mid 1960s, talked and wrote as a Jew and an American, a communitarian and a pluralist. Thus, for her, a value-free description of the Holocaust is wrong in itself because the *ought* is immanent in the *is*.

For Arendt, there is no such thing as value-free description; there is only flight from one's identity. This is the key to understanding *Eichmann in Jerusalem*. And it is, in my opinion, key in listening to her in the interview. In Arendt's view, you can only deduce the *ought* from the *is*. Everything that happens in the world has moral significance. The notion that the basis of morality lies in identity, and that the basis of personal identity is collective identity—or in overlapping collective identities—was Arendt's answer to the question of how to maintain a tension between the universal and the particular. She was not saying that all morality is based on identity but that some of it is, and that it is an essential part, because it is the part that makes us who we are. This is the part that gives us moral motivation, because it is the basis of our passions and our self. This is how you have to read her remark in the interview "that if you are attacked as a Jew, you have to defend yourself as a Jew. Not as German, not as a world-citizen, not as an upholder of the Rights of Men." She certainly was no universalist. She is very clear in the interview: "I never felt as a German," she says.

Arendt had already made a similar statement a few years prior to the interview, when she received the Lessing Prize in Hamburg. The year was 1959, and the City of Hamburg bestowed on her a prize dedicated to the Enlightenment.[5] Arendt mentions the speech in the interview as well. She didn't play along with the rules of the Enlightenment, and addressed her audience as a Jew. She talked about Nathan the Wise, and his and her own Jewishness. "In this connection I cannot gloss over the fact that for many years I considered the only adequate reply to the question, who are you? to be: A Jew. That answer alone took into account the reality of persecution. As for the statement with which Nathan the Wise (in effect, though not in actual wording) countered the command 'Step closer, Jew'—the statement: I am a man—I would have considered as nothing but a grotesque and dangerous evasion of reality" (17–18).

Arendt saw no problem in speaking with different voices, depending on the circumstances and the audience. This position should not be confused with inconsistency or hypocrisy. She spoke as a Jew when she addressed Enzensberger, Jaspers, and Gaus and her audience in Hamburg, and she spoke as an American when she corresponded with her fellow Jews like Scholem. The audience determined her vantage point. This is a point at times not really understood about Arendt. Just look at the film *Hannah Arendt* (2012) by the German director Margarethe von Trotta, who tried very much to Germanize her.[6]

But more is at stake here: the problem for Arendt was how ethnic identities could be anchored in political institutions, and fostered, and protected, and at the same time avoiding the close-mindedness and intellectual rigidity that seem inherent in nationalism. For a more current formulation of the issue, moving from a Jewish perspective to a more generalized minority perspective, an Arendtian analysis may shed light on how to translate our particular identities within a plural setting. She was indeed—as you will see—a free-floating intellectual, and the task of these kinds of intellectuals is to think of society as whole and to overcome particular standpoints by indeed floating freely over them, having wings and roots at the same time.

Thus, too much is continually made out of her apparent "non-Love" for the Jewish people, something which she wrote to Gershom Scholem after the publication of *Eichmann in Jerusalem*, and which also becomes a topic in the interview. "If you are attacked as a Jew, you have to defend yourself as a Jew," as she put it to Gaus. Giving up her Jewish identity would be a betrayal of self and of millions, but she never was an essentialist when it came to her being Jewish. "One does not escape Jewishness," as she ends her study on Rahel Varnhagen.[7]

What you will see in the interview is Arendt performing her political stance as a Jewish woman in front of a German audience. Since 2013, more than a million people have watched this interview on YouTube, a broadcast outlet that didn't exist in either Arendt's or Gaus's lifetime. What you are about to see is performance in the best sense of the word.

---

1. This essay is based on a conference presentation in Vilnius, Lithuania, in September 2019. The conference was about "Hannah Arendt and the Crisis of Education." The presentation was intended to introduce the interview Arendt gave to Günter Gaus, which aired on German TV in 1964; available at youtube.com/watch?v=dsoImQfVsO4.
2. The essay was published in the Jewish magazine *The Menorah Journal* and constitutes her interventions in American Jewish publications in the 1940s about Jewish and Zionist issues. Like many of the magazines she published during those days, they were—like Arendt—concerned with the formation of a Jewish secular culture and politics.
3. Hannah Arendt, "The Aftermath of Nazi Rule: Report from Germany," *Commentary*, no. 10 (October 1950): 342–53.
4. The English version of the exchange was recently published in English as "Politics and Crime: An Exchange of Letters," in Hannah Arendt, *Thinking without Banisters: Essays in Understanding, 1953–1975*, ed. Jerome Kohn (New York: Schocken Books, 2018), 308–15.
5. Her Lessing Prize acceptance speech was published in English as "On Humanity in Dark Times," in Hannah Arendt, *Men in Dark Times* (San Diego: Harcourt, Brace & Company, 1995), 3–33.
6. For my criticism of this movie see hac.bard.edu/amor-mundi/ the-re-germanization-of-hannah-arendt-2013-05-01.
7. Hannah Arendt, *Rahel Varnhagen: The Life of a Jewish Woman*, trans. Richard and Clara Winston (New York: Harcourt Brace Jovanovich, 1974), 216–28.

Arendt, Hölderlin, and Their Perception of Schicksal: Hölderlinian Elements in Arendt's Thinking and the Messianic Notion of Revolution

Jana Marlene Madar

> If we feel at home in this world, we can see our lives as the development of the "product of nature," as the unfolding and the realisation of what we already were.
> —Hannah Arendt, *Rahel Varnhagen: The Life of a Jewess*

Today, Hannah Arendt is above all known as a political thinker; what we hear less about is her great interest in and connection to poetry. After her first postwar visit to Berlin in 1950, Arendt writes in a letter to her husband Heinrich Blücher: "But: what still remains are the inhabitants of Berlin. Unchanged, wonderful, humane, full of humor, clever, very clever even. This was for the first time like coming home."[1] In an interview with Günter Gaus in September 1964, Arendt elaborates on this visit, stressing the difference between her German language and that of others. In the same interview, she replies to the question of continuity after she fled Nazi Germany, first to France, then in 1941 to the United States: "*Was ist geblieben? Geblieben ist die Muttersprache*" (What was it that continued? My mother tongue continued). She adds: "I felt a distance towards French and English. In German I know a great number of poems by heart. They are constantly there—*in the back of my mind*[2]—the same can never be achieved for another language." Language in general (and poetic language in particular) plays a significant role in Arendt's oeuvre: the importance of German as her mother tongue and its difference to English as her second language, the tensions between these two spheres, linguistically and also psychologically (the limited familiarity with the nuances of a language and the awareness thereof), and its overcoming through self-translating her own works into her first language as a process of *working it through*—"working through the words, the concepts and metaphors, the arguments, examples and explanations" (Weigel 2012, 72) —and last but not least her claim "to keep my distance" (Arendt 1964). Writing bilingually, "the language of poetry . . . forms the counterpart, thus providing her with the ability to remain at a distance—at a distance from the nation state and from conformism" (Weigel 2012, 64). In her *Denktagebuch*,[3] Arendt discusses the correspondence between thinking and poetry explicitly:

What connects thinking and poetry (*Dichtung*) is metaphor. In philosophy one calls concept what in poetry (*Dichtkunst*) is called metaphor. Thinking creates its "concepts" out of the visible, in order to designate the invisible.[4]

Her whole life, Arendt has expressed her great desire *to understand the world as it is*; this desire was linked to her interest in poetry—poems that she read in books or that she knew by heart. For her, poetic language is the bond, the connection, between the inner and the outer world: "The scenario of Arendt's work, which was shaped by the counterparts of philosophy and politics, was superimposed twice: first by the tension between German and American intellectual culture, and second by the antagonism between poetry and conventional language full of idioms" (Weigel 2012, 65). The German language gave Arendt the language of reflection, while the unique tone in her (theoretical) writings can be equated with the approach to political concepts through experience—the connection between *inside* and *outside*.

From 1924 to 1928, Arendt studied not just philosophy and theology but also Ancient Greek and Greek poetry in Marburg, Freiburg, and Heidelberg. In 1928, she received her doctorate, writing her dissertation on Saint Augustine with a focus on notions of love from Greek poetry to Latin confessions (see Arendt 1929). "I have always loved Greek poetry" she states, while—because of the language—feeling a special connection to German poetry: Goethe, Heine, Rilke (quoted in (Starobinski 1971, 288).

Arendt's first book (not counting her doctoral dissertation) is a biography of the late–eighteenth-century hostess and letter writer Rahel Varnhagen, whose salon in Berlin was one of the hatcheries of German romanticism. Even though mostly neglected in Arendt's canon, the Rahel biography is, according to Julia Kristeva, "a veritable laboratory of Arendt's political thought" (Kristeva 2003, 50). Arendt attests to her deep fondness for Varnhagen, calling her "my very closest woman friend, unfortunately dead a hundred years now" (Arendt 1997 [1957], 5). A special connection to the time period certainly exists as well—a connection typical for Arendt, since

> it is unclear whether Arendt appreciated her literature professor's work on Romanticism or whether his research on Varnhagen ever directly influenced hers. Nonetheless, the explored conjunctions suggest that the young Arendt's writings and thought belonged to a much wider framework of cross-disciplinary debates than has been recognised. She was never only a follower of Heidegger or Jaspers, neither an exclusively philosophical author, but possessed a remarkable ability to combine a variety of perspectives and disciplinary languages. (Keedus 2014, 319)

Arendt never embraced just *one* idea or school or field of study or intellectual framework, and the same is true of her stance on the Romantics. She
took a serious interest in German Romanticism,[5] studying under Friedrich
Gundolf, the literature professor mentioned in the quote above who was one
of the most celebrated literary theorists of the time (Grunenberg 2006, 123),
famous for his vehement criticism describing the era as "reactionary" and
"purely destructive movement and thus devoid of any creativity" (Keedus
2014, 316). At the same time, Arendt admired poets like Hölderlin.[6]

Her praise for the German romantic Friedrich Hölderlin is documented in
notes in her *Denktagebuch*—in fact, her first entry in 1950 is based on a quote
of Hölderlin: "The wrong that one has done is the burden on the shoulders,
what one bears, because one has laden it upon himself."[7] The phrase "burden
on the shoulders" refers to Hölderlin's "Reif Sind," a fragmentary poem, probably written around 1803. Arendt and Martin Heidegger had discussed it
months earlier during her first trip to Germany since fleeing the Nazis. Upon
her return to the United States, she sent a letter to Heidegger, asking for the
proper citation. She received a reply, and only weeks later, started her first
entry, on Hölderlin, of what would become a series of twenty-eight journals.
But Arendt and Heidegger had had exchanges about Hölderlin before.[8] On
23 August 1925, Heidegger compared their love affair to Hölderlin's poetry,
for instance.[9] Yet not only in letters to Heidegger but also in her writings (e.g.,
the essay "Kultur und Politik") and notes to friends we can find references to
the poet. When Arendt's husband Heinrich Blücher passed away, she wrote
to her close friend Mary McCarthy the exact same phrase that marked the
beginning of her *Denktagebuch*.[10] Moreover, in the 1950s, Arendt intended to
translate Hölderlin's poems into English, or to have them translated. Her letters indicate that she sent a first rough draft to the poet, literary critic, novelist, and translator Randall Jarell[11] asking him for his comments. However, the
project was never realized, as Arendt came to the conclusion that Hölderlin's
poetry was untranslatable (Bertheau 2016, 54).

At the end of her life, Arendt bought a copy of the special edition of
Hölderlin's works, issued on his 200th birthday by the Deutsches Literaturarchiv
Marbach (The German Literature Archive of Marbach), with the intention of
sharing Hölderlin's poetry in a letter to Heidegger on his 80th birthday. She
never sent the letter. Her personal library includes a copy of Carl Viëtor's
Hölderlin: Die Briefe der Diotima,[12] in which she wrote her name.

But Arendt was not only an admirer of poetry; she also wrote poetry herself until the 1960s (a collection was published by Piper in 2015). Seventy-one
poems have been preserved, twenty-one of them written from 1923 to 1926,
during her university years in Marburg; and fifty more between 1942 and
1961. Her lyrical production broke down when she took part in the Eichmann
trial. It is not known whether she thought of publishing her pieces, but she
typed them and collected them in folders. For Arendt, poetry was "the most

human and unworldly of the arts" and she wanted to be a part of it, even though she did not see herself as a poet. "We only expect truth from the poets, not from the philosophers from whom we expect thought,"[13] she wrote in her *Denktagebuch* in the mid '50s.

In her first entry into this series of journals—the quote by Hölderlin that is about former wrongdoings and sufferings that we bear on our shoulders while at the same time, he demands that we let go of the past and "grasp the fruit now while it is ripe" (Berkowitz 2017, 10)—Arendt calls the embrace of the present over the past "reconciliation"[14] (*Versöhnung*): "[It] has its origin in a self-coming to terms with what has been given to one."[15] This idea, the idea of "what has been given to one and what we do with that," will be at the center of this essay. I will discuss the notion of *Schicksal* (destiny, fate) found within Hölderlin's work as well as Arendt's. I shall present Hölderlin's understanding of it, beginning with his poem entitled "*Schicksal*," and then elaborate on the duality of his definition, which is—generally speaking—not just typical for Hölderlin but for many Romantic poets as well. Through his binary concept of destiny, I'll explore the realm of complementary opposites, including "individual vs. universal" which will lead last but not least to the poetic I. On that basis, I will address the following questions: How was revolution possible for Hölderlin? What did revolution mean for Arendt, and which Hölderlian elements can be found within Arendt's thinking?

Destiny, generally speaking, can be seen as an event or circumstance that a person experiences and whose effect they cannot influence. Hence, destiny can be understood as an uncontrollable power, yet a more precise description can only be made if the term is put into context of a certain worldview whereby its meaning automatically changes: destiny becomes either religious, ethical, or aesthetic. Friedrich Hölderlin's concept of destiny is a specific one, and one that was subject to change throughout his life: During his childhood and early school years, Hölderlin was someone looking for truth and in search of his calling. Then, during his Frankfurt years, he became the enlightened one who has gained knowledge; he now knows that he is meant to be a prophet (according to him, the poet). After this highly productive phase, he was diagnosed with mental illness in 1805. Hölderlin spent the second half of his life, until his death, in isolation in a tower room, where he still continued to write.

Hölderlin and *Schicksal*

Hölderlin grew up in the Christian tradition. At the request of his mother, he became a pastor. In 1787, he writes that he believes in a god "who directs our destiny by all means."[16] His relationship to this leader of destiny is naive and religious. One should believe, love, and obey. At this time, Hölderlin believes in the divine as freedom, while his religiosity is acquired through his education and not based on religious experience. He promises his mother "that the thought will never come to me again to step out of my profession—I now see! One can be so useful to the world as a village priest, one can be even happier than if one did who-knows-what?"[17] Nevertheless, it was his mother's wish that he fulfilled and not his own, which becomes clear when he writes: "Everywhere, I am so empty—am I the only one alone like this? The eternal, eternal catcher of crickets!"[18]

Hölderlin starts to doubt and begins to question happiness as the pure result of right action. In 1787, he writes: "Suddenly my favourite foolishness, the destiny of my future came to my mind—I remembered that I wanted to become a hermit after completing my university years—and the thought pleased me so well, a whole hour, I think, I was a hermit in my fantasy."[19] At the end of this first phase of his life, Hölderlin writes the poem "Das Schicksal" (1793), which is about a three-stage dialectic model of human history: the golden age of prehistoric times—here also called "Elysium" and "Arcadia," or in the Bible, the Garden of Eden and Paradise—was replaced by the "era of necessity," or destiny. Although this is accompanied by the loss of peace and carefree safety in nature, the "iron necessity" (*eherne Notwendigkeit*) functions as the "mother of heroes" (*Mutter der Heroen*). Unrest drives mankind to perfection, to fight for a new golden age at a higher level. In the last three verses of the poem, the general observations change into the first person. The "I" speaks directly to the goddess of destiny (Pepromene), and sets its own youth parallel to the golden age, the "flame of the noon" (*Mittags Flamme*) of its adult life, and the heroic struggle for "the last sun" (*der Sonnen letzte*), thus the renewed Elysium. Hölderlin also pursued this concept of history philosophically, developing together with his friends Schelling and Hegel the program of German idealism. It became the core idea of this philosophical school, which was essentially influenced by Hegel in particular, and whose immense effect was later reflected also in Marxism.

The following years, the Homburg period, are central to Hölderlin's work. Wilhelm Michel (1967) states in his biography of Hölderlin:

> It is in the spiritual growth of these Homburg months that in his own, as well as in his historical life, the part of destiny and the part of man are more clearly separated from each other. . . . It leads to a purification that resembles the contemplation at the end of the Attic tragedy, and when Hölderlin in Homburg learns to see the schematic course in the tragic-dramatic work of art more and more genuinely, as it were inaugurated, then his own experiences of life come to fruit and yield. (271)

During this time, it becomes clear to Hölderlin that destiny can take two forms: the immanent and the transcendent. In 1796, he writes: "I will probably get even more accustomed to living with little, and to directing my heart more to the fact that I seek to approach eternal beauty more by my own striving and working than that I expect from destiny something like it."[20] He must emphasize his personality, his immanent destiny—and at the same time, he must try to harmonize his essence with the transcendent will of destiny. This means that his task is to merge with the divine, to become a prophetic man: for him, the poet. The poet carries within him the embodiment of the divine; he is the divine in earthly appearance. The purification of the individual spiritual form to the unique destiny is Hölderlin's service. His aim is to reconcile immanent destiny and transcendent destiny. Hölderlin explains the connection between poetry and religion in the fragmentary essay "Über die Religion"[21]: "all religion is poetic in nature"—meaning the spiritual side of religion. Of course, this implies, conversely, that the lyrical text can, according to Hölderlin, be seen as a religious text. The prophetic aspect of his poetry is most clearly expressed in his late elegiac and hymnlike poetry and in his epistolary novel *Hyperion*, published in two volumes in 1797 and 1799, in which nature is hymnally celebrated as a space filled with god.

When taking a look at the final stage of his life, which for a long time researchers have ignored because he was considered mentally ill, we must explore the poems written in the tower room where he spent the second half of his life in isolation. These poems are characterized by a high formal order and a loss of the poetic "I". This loss of the "I" can be interpreted in two ways: in a passive sense, the loss of one's identity in falling victim to mental illness; or actively, in the conscious abandonment of individuality for the universal. Hölderlin sometimes dates his poems decades or centuries into the past or future; hence both, history and identity, become blurred—in themselves and with each other. Theodor Adorno calls it "the sublimation of primary docility to autonomy." He is one of the few critics who writes about Hölderlin's later poetry, in his essay "Parataxis." The quote continues: "[it] is that supreme passivity that found its formal correlate in the technique of series. The instance Hölderlin now submits to his language" (Adorno 1992, 475). Interestingly, submission was always present in Hölderlin's life; it merely took different forms.

Looking at his biography overall, first submitting to his mother during childhood and early adolescence to his final years when language became the passive authority, it is as if he felt freedom most through experiencing his own finite self. Hölderlin was able—in the spirit of the Romantic poet—to unify two binary opposites, which he explains in a letter in 1799: "I see and feel more and more how we waver between the two extremes, the lack of rules—and the blind submission to old forms and the associated compulsion and misapplication."[22]

One year after Hölderlin's death, Hölderlin's half brother Karl Gok had these lines, taken from the poem "Schicksal," carved on his tombstone:

In heiligsten of the Stürme falle
Zusammen mit meiner Kerkerwand,
Und die freie Wand.
Mein Geist im unbekannten Land!

(Falling in the holiest of the storms
Along with my dungeon wall,
And the free wall.
My spirit in the unknown land!)

This choice seems appropriate: Hölderlin frees himself from his earthly walls and reaches "unknown lands" calling it the "holiest of storms." As discussed earlier, the poem is about a three-stage model of human history; Hölderlin may have, in his own view, now reached the higher level while he became what he wanted to become: a prophetic poet who continues just again nowadays, 250 years after his birth, to inspire through his writing—in a religious sense *writing* that delivers messages from a divine source to the believer, or in other words, one that delivers its universal claim to mankind.

Arendt and Freedom

Compared to Hölderlin, Hannah Arendt deals more with the concept of freedom than with the one of destiny however two works of her discuss the fate of the Jewish people: her essay "We Refugees" that was originally published in January 1943 in a small Jewish journal called *Menorah* and her biography on Rahel Varnhagen, published in 1957. In the latter she writes:

> History becomes more definitive when (and how rarely this happens) it concentrates its whole force upon an individual's destiny: when it encounters a person who has no way of barricading herself behind character traits and talents, who cannot hide under moralities and conventions as if these were an umbrella for rainy weather; when it can impress something of its significance upon the hapless human being, the *shlemihl*, who has anticipated nothing. (Arendt 1997 [1957], 85)

Arendt had told herself in her fragmentary journal that she titled "Shadows" and wrote as a 19-year-old that she "did not belong to anything, anywhere, ever"; Rahel as well was "exiled . . . all alone to a place where nothing could reach her, where she was cut off from all human things, from everything that men have the right to claim." Arendt's goal became to avoid this helpless place in her life as well as in her thinking. Therefore, as Adam Kirsch (2009) rightly puts it in his article for the *New Yorker*, the categorical imperative of her work could be phrased: Thou shalt not be a *shlemihl*.

Important to note, that for Arendt being Jewish is a form of fate. In a letter to Karl Jaspers she writes: "This lecture is only a preliminary work meant to show that on the foundation of being Jewish a certain possibility of existence *can* arise that I have tentatively and for the time being called fatefulness. This fatefulness arises from the very fact of 'foundationlessness' and can occur only in a separation of Judaism" (Arendt 1992, 11).

In "We Refugees," she explains her own destiny and that of other European Jews who were able to save themselves from the national socialist extermination apparatus during World War II. It's written with pain and bitterness but also noticeable optimism, while Arendt makes a radical argument: they are no longer a people that is to be understood as a model of biblical patterns of destiny as the national socialist extermination apparatus exposed the murdered and the living to brutal conditions. Both now have a common history (Arendt 1943).

The idea of a historical necessity that only assigns man the role of the executor of history, who cannot influence the events through his actions, is incompatible with Arendt's concept of freedom. The dissolution of Hegel's contradiction between freedom and necessity represents for her the "most intolerable paradox of all modern thought" (Arendt 1963, 66). Arendt uses history to make a "critical engagement with the present" while she never systematically dealt with it. She was convinced that historiography did not follow any laws that could be systematically explored and that it was therefore unsuitable for describing and analyzing the pathological side of modernity. Hence, she strictly rejects any sense of Hegel's philosophy of history, which states that "freedom is insight into necessity" (*Freiheit ist die Einsicht in die Notwendigkeit*).

For Arendt, freedom means freedom of action; the opposite of freedom is destiny. According to her, real freedom can only exist in the space that arises between people when they live and act together. Therefore, action falls under the category of freedom. All attempts to "hide" freedom in work or labor are hypocritical; what it actually means is "freedom hidden in necessity" and similar tricks. And yet "the meaning of politics is freedom" (Arendt 2014, 265).

The most important aspect here is that speech and action are in the center of the public realm where politics take place. Both can, according to Arendt, never be done by an individual alone yet only *lived* in the togetherness. She may seem to come into conflict with both enlightened and romantic thinkers since they try to maintain the supremacy of the individual, while at the same time subjugating them to a universal whole, however, I argue, that Hölderlin's romantic idea and Arendt's way of thinking are more closely linked than they may appear: To both, Hölderlin and Arendt, the *community* was at the center.

The French Revolution and Messianicity

> The messiah will only come when he is no longer necessary,
> he will come after his arrival,
> he will come, not on the last day, but the very last.[23] —Franz Kafka

Even if, following Kafka's assumption, the messiah comes *after* his arrival, messianic politics was possible for Hannah Arendt and for Hölderlin alike. "The profane task of politics consists in keeping the Messiah's place *empty* before his arrival and refraining from occupying it in a theocratic manner" (Khatib 2013, 4).

Arendt writes in her essay on the founding fathers in 1963: "This is the freedom exp[erienced] in revolutions—to be free to begin something new. And this side of human existence is being discovered and we hope preserved in revolutionary times" (Arendt). And in "On Revolution," published in the same year: "Revolutions are the only political events which confront us directly and inevitably with the problem of beginning" (Arendt 1963a).

Almost 200 years earlier, in 1793, Hölderlin declares in a note to his brother:

> We live in a period of time when everything is working towards
> better days. The seeds of enlightenment, these silent desires and
> efforts of individuals to educate the human race will spread and
> intensify, and bear wonderful fruit. Look! dear Karl! this is what
> my heart now clings to. This is the sacred goal of my desires and
> my activity—that in our age I may be the seed of paths which will
> mature in a future. (Hölderlin Bd. 6.1, 92)

In the design of his historical model of the ascending stages, in the hope of a better world after the French Revolution, and in his vocation as a pro-claimer of a better future, one can clearly identify a messianic aspect to it. In both works, Arendt's and Hölderlin's, a messianic notion of revolution resonates while for Hölderlin it was imbedded in the French Revolution: To achieve a better future for the community, not only in France, but all over Europe, was what Hölderlin saw in it. Arendt's assessment in retrospective was a different one, however. For her it was a failure, it was "doomed to end in a cycle of terror and revolutionary wars because of the entry of the masses of the *sans-culottes*, of the disenfranchised, the poor, downtrodden, and sepses into the scene of history" (Benhabib 1996, 157).

Hölderlin observed the political situation in France and was inspired by the ideas of the French Revolution. He was not only informed through news-papers and pamphlets but he was also in direct conversation with eyewit-nesses on the other side of the Rhine. Hölderlin's pathos corresponded to the pathos of the Jacobins (Bertaux 1969, 49). He linked the events in France to the hope that his own country could also change:

> I believe in a future revolution in attitudes and ways of thinking that will make everything shameless so far. And perhaps, Germany can contribute a great deal to this. The quieter a state grows up, the more wonderful it becomes when it reaches maturity. (Hölderlin Bd. 6, 229)

For Hölderlin it was decisive that only in the climate of freedom a more beautiful humanity can grow, so that freedom must be achieved unconditionally, and even fought for if necessary (Bertaux 1969, 113).

Arendt writes in *On Revolution* that freedom means to matter, hence freedom means that every human being has meaning. In this book, she refers above all to the French and American Revolutions. She argues that black Americans had no freedom as they could not participate in public life. In a conversation with Carlo Schmid, Arendt explains:

> This means that you are only free if you have the opportunity to act. And the idea that action itself, as you say, belongs to the dignity of man and not only thinking, and that one can only act in the light of the public, and that it is now a matter of revolutions, which all began with the fact that one claimed the other freedoms, that is, the freedoms that guarantee, against oppression. (Arendt)

During the French Revolution, according to Arendt, necessity took the place of freedom; this marked the beginning of a transformation of future revolutions: they were no longer dedicated to freedom but to the abolition of poverty. To her, the true success of the American Revolution lies in the creation of a new government that the French Revolution failed to do. Arendt continues in her writing about the Hungarian revolution and totalitarian imperialism,

> that both freedom and equality as political principles are determined neither by a transcendent authority before which all men are equal qua men, nor by a general human destiny like death, which one day takes all men equally from this world. Rather, they are inner-worldly principles which grow directly out of the human beings living together and acting together. (Arendt 2012, 104)

How is this idea of "acting together" for freedom linked to the Hölderlian idea of the immanent and transcendent destiny and how does Arendt express it through "poetic language"?

Universalism, Individualism, and the Poetic "I"

In a Marxist sense, Hölderlin opposes the "realm of freedom" to the "realm of necessity." Necessity for Hölderlin is destiny in its rigid, hostile opposition to being human. God then gives him the mission to serve men "who still flee to the mountains, where the air is purer and the sun and stars are nearer, and where one looks cheerfully down into the restlessness of the world, that is, where one has risen to the feelings of godliness, and from this, one contemplates everything that was, is, and will be."[24] These two forces in Hölderlin's life are not surprising: romantic poets imagined themselves as an instrument of god, just like Hölderlin when he became the prophet. Involvement in creation, imagination, compassion and love had a divine aspect to it, while the goal was *unity* and *wholeness*—the sublime. The reason for this assumed separation of the unity arose from the eating from the tree of knowledge of good and evil—or, for that matter, any two binary opposites: masculinity vs. femininity, spirit vs. matter, human vs. divine, individual vs. universal. Through the separation into two binary opposites, mankind became alienated from god, from nature, from others, from themselves as one splits in many ways, also within oneself: private self vs. public self, a feeling self vs. a thinking self, a private self, governed by natural law as opposed to a public self in conventional society following man made law.

For Arendt, these separations become unified through the poetic language, just like Hölderlin's immanent and transcendent destiny. In her essay on Walter Benjamin published in the collection *Men in Dark Times*, Arendt specifically writes about "thinking poetically" (Arendt 1968, 205). In *The Life of the Mind* she dedicates two full chapters to metaphors and explains how they transfer experiences of the external world into the internal world, thus is to say the mind. Through this process ("metapherein") we create a connection between ourselves and the world (Cornelissen 2017, 77). Arendt refers to Ernest Fenollosa (1967), who declares that "the metaphor is the very substance of poetry; without it, there would have been no bridge whereby to cross from the minor truth of the seen to the major truth of the unseen" (25). Benhabib (1996) writes:

> Romantic introspection leads one to lose a sense of reality by losing the boundaries between the private and the public, the intimate and the shared. Romantic introspection compounds the "worldnessness" from which Rahel Varnhagen suffers to the very end. The category of the "world" is the missing link between the "worldless" reality of Rahel Levin Varnhagen and her

contemporaries, and Hannah Arendt's own reach for a recovery of the "public world" through authentic political action in her political philosophy. (11)

Today, as we lose touch with the notion of universalism and instead set our focus on the individual, we find ourselves disconnected from the idea of the "universal I" of romantic poetry. A universal attitude in the spirit of a life for the community rather than one that is based on personal needs has, in a romantic sense, a divine aspect to it; however, it comes with personal sacrifices that we, self-centered as we have become, might not be willing to take. At the same time, only through community, through a united "us,"—if we are willing to step out of our *Bequemlichkeit*—can revolution take place. Leaders like Obama and Clinton, and even more so, of course, Trump, aim at catching people with universal ideas yet actually present rather simple solutions; one can more easily turn to a Messiah figure that promises us a "greater" future than start a movement within our society, within our thinking.

Both lives, Hölderlin's and Arendt's, were tragic in different ways and marked by rebellion not only within their thinking but also within the times they lived. Their admiration for (Greek) poetry, their search for truth, their struggle not only for freedom but also with their destiny, as well as their optimism for "he who has won a lot can understand life without grieving,"[25] is where they show parallels. It is not surprising that Arendt was drawn to Hölderlin's poetry, that she incorporated some of his ideas into her concepts. She writes explicitly about the separation of the public and the private, while living her own life in a tension between thinking without borders, her identity as a Jew, the feeling of infinity and that of loneliness and statelessness. In this interspace, we can understand her connection to the poet, the "unifier," Hölderlin. What he achieved as a Romantic poet, she achieved as a writer:

> The metaphor, bridging the abyss between inward and invisible mental activities and the world of appearances, was certainly the greatest gift language could bestow on thinking and hence on philosophy, but the metaphor itself is poetic rather than philosophical in origin. It is therefore hardly surprising the poets and writers attuned to poetry rather than to philosophy should have been aware of its essential function. (Arendt 1977, 106)

Arendt filled the interspace with poetic language, connected *inside* and the *outside,* or, thought and action; in a Hölderlian way, she unified two opposites, the human being as the reconciling force.

Untitled Poem by Hannah Arendt (1943)

Aufgestiegen aus dem stehenden Teich der Vergangenheit
Sind der Erinn'rungen viele.
Nebelgestalten ziehen die sehnsüchtigen Kreise meiner Gefangenheit
Vergangen, verlockend, am Ziele.

Tote, was wollt Ihr? Habt Ihr im Orkus nicht Heimat und Stätte?
Endlich den Frieden der Tiefe?
Wasser und Erde, Feuer und Luft sind Euch ergeben, als hätte
Mächtig ein Gott Euch. Und riefe

Euch aus stehenden Wässern, aus Sümpfen, Mooren und Teichen
Sammelnd geeinigt herbei.
Schimmernd im Zwielicht bedeckt Ihr mit Nebel der Lebenden Reiche,
Spottend des dunklen Vorbei.

Spielen wollen auch wir; ergreifen und lachen und haschen
Träume vergangener Zeit.
Müde wurden auch wir der Strassen, der Städte, des raschen
Wechsels der Einsamkeit.

Unter die rudernden Boote mit liebenden Paaren geschmückt auf
Stehenden Teichen im Wald
Könnten auch wir uns mischen—leise, versteckt und entrückt auf
Nebelwolken, die bald

Sachte die Erde bekleiden, das Ufer, den Busch und den Baum,
Wartend des kommenden Sturms.
Wartend des aus dem Nebel, aus Luftschloss, Narrheit und Traum
Steigenden wirbelnden Sturms.

(Rising up from the still pond of the past
Are so many memories.
Fog-figures draw wistful circles of my imprisonment
Elapsing, enticing, arriving at the finish.

Dead ones, what do you want? Have you not found a home and place
    in Orkus?
The final peace of the deep?
Water and earth, fire and air are yours devotedly, as if
A god possessed you with might. And summoned

You up from a still water, out of the mires, moors and ponds
Collected, merged here.
Shimmering in the twilight you cover the living realm with fog,
Mocking the dark past.

We too want to play, to take hold of and laugh and catch
Dreams of times past.
We too became tired of the streets, the cities and the rapid
Change of loneliness.

Among the rowboats adorned with loving couples
on still ponds in the woods
We could also merge—quiet, hidden, and lost in reverie in
clouds of fog, which soon

Gently cloak the earth, the shores, the bush and the tree,
Waiting for the coming storm.
Waiting out the fog, daydreams and folly
Rising out of the whirling storm.)[26]

The writing of this essay was made possible by a fellowship from the Friedrich Ebert Foundation, Germany. I am grateful to the Hannah Arendt Center at Bard College, which I am honored to be a part of as a visiting fellow. Special thanks to Dr. Samantha Rose Hill for her time and support.

Works Cited

Adorno, Theodor W. 2003 [1961]. "Parataxis: Zur späten Lyrik Hölderlins." In *Noten zur Literatur* (1958–74), *Gesammelte Schriften*, vol. 11. Edited by Rolf Tiedemann. Frankfurt am Main: Suhrkamp.

Arendt, Hannah. 1929. *Der Liebesbegriff bei Augustin: Versuch einer philosophischen Interpretation*. Berlin: J. Springer. English translation (1996): *Love and Saint Augustine*.

———. 1943. "We Refugees." *Menorah Journal* 31, no. 1 (January): 69–77.

———. 1958. *The Human Condition*. Chicago: University of Chicago Press.

———. 1961. *Between Past and Future*. New York: Viking Press.

———. 1963a. *On Revolution*. New York: Viking Press.

———. 1963b. "Founding Fathers." Bd. 7, nr. 1. In *Zeitschrift für politisches Denken*. Transcribed, edited, and with notes by Ursula Ludz.

———. 1964. "Was bleibt? Es bleibt die Muttersprache?" Interview with Günther Gaus. Recorded 16 September; broadcast on the ZDF TV program *Zur Person* on 26 October.

———. 1965. "The Right to Revolution." Transcript of a conversation with Carlo Schmid, broadcast on the television channel Norddeutscher Rundfunk (Northern German Broadcasting) on 19 October 1965.

———. 1968. *Men in Dark Times*. New York: Harcourt Brace.

———. 1977 [1971]. *The Life of the Mind*. Vol. 1: *Thinking*. 2nd ed. New York: Harcourt Brace Jovanovich.

———. 1997. *Hannah Arendt / Karl Jaspers: Correspondence, 1926–1969*. Edited by Lotte Kohler and Hans Saner. Translated by Robert and Rita Kimber. New York: Harcourt Brace Jovanovich.

———. 1997 [1957]. *Rahel Varnhagen: The Life of a Jewess*. First Complete Edition. Edited and with an introduction by Liliane Weissberg. Translated by Richard and Clara Winston. Baltimore: John Hopkins University Press.

———. 2003. *Denktagebuch*. Bd. 1: *1950–1973*. Edited by Ursula Ludz and Ingeborg Nordmann. Munich: Piper. Hereafter DTB.

———. 2012. "Die Ungarische Revolution und der totalitäre Imperialismus." In *In der Gegenwart: Übungen im politischen Denken II*, 73–126. Edited by Ursula Ludz. Munich: Piper.

———. 2014. "Was ist Politik?" In *Texte zur Politischen Philosophie*, 261–72. Edited by Marcel van Ackeren. Stuttgart: Reclam.

———. 2015. *Ich selbst, auch ich tanze: Die Gedichte*. Munich: Piper.

Benhabib, Seyla. 1996. *The Reluctant Modernism of Hannah Arendt: Modernity and Political Thought*. Vol. 10. Thousand Oaks: SAGE.

Berkowitz, Roger. 2017. "Reconciling Oneself to the Impossibility of Reconciliation: Judgment and Worldliness in Hannah Arendt's Politics." In *Artifacts of Thinking: Reading Hannah Arendt's "Denktagebuch,"* 9–36. Edited by Roger Berkowitz and Ian Storey. New York: Fordham University Press.

Bertaux, Pierre. 1969. *Hölderlin und die Französische Revolution*. Edition Suhrkamp, vol. 344. Frankfurt: Suhrkamp Verlag.

Bertheau, Anne. 2016. "Das Mädchen aus der Fremde": Hannah Arendt und die Dichtung. Rezeption—Reflexion—Produktion. Bielefeld. Transcript.

Cornelissen, Wout. 2017. "Thinking in Metaphors." In *Artifacts of Thinking: Reading Hannah Arendt's "Denktagebuch,"* 73–87. Edited by Roger Berkowitz and Ian Storey. New York: Fordham University Press.

Fenollosa, Ernest. 1967. "The Chinese Written Character as a Medium for Poetry" (1920). Edited by Ezra Pound. In *Instigations of Ezra Pound; Together with an Essay on the Chinese Written Character*. Freeport: Books for Libraries Press.

Grunenberg, Antonia. 2006. *Hannah Arendt und Martin Heidegger: Geschichte einer Liebe*. Munich: Piper.

Hölderlin, Friedrich. 1943–85. *Sämtliche Werke*. Edited by Friedrich Beißner and Adolf Beck. 8 vols. in 15 parts. Stuttgart: Cotta. Hereafter SW.

Kafka, Franz. 1992. *Nachgelassene Schriften und Fragmente*. Edited by Jost Schillemeit. Vol. 2. Frankfurt am Main: Fischer.

Keedus, Liisi. 2014. "Thinking beyond Philosophy: Hannah Arendt and the Weimar Hermeneutic Connections." *Trames* 18 (December): 307–25.

Khatib, Sami. 2013. "The Messianic without Messianism: Walter Benjamin's Materialist Theology." *Anthropology & Materialism* (1): 1–31.

Kirsch, Adam. 2009. "Beware of Pity: Hannah Arendt and the Power of the Impersonal." *New Yorker*, 12 January.

Kristeva, Julia. 2003. *Hannah Arendt*. Translated by Ross Guberman. New York: Columbia University Press.

Michel, Wilhelm. 1967. *Das Leben Friedrich Hölderlins*. Frankfurt am Main: Insel.

Starobinski, Jean. 1971. "The Style of Autobiography." In *Literary Style: A Symposium*. Edited by Seymour Chatman. New York: Oxford University Press.

Weigel, Sigrid. 2012. "Sounding Through—Poetic Difference—Self-Translation: Hannah Arendt's Thoughts and Writings between Different Languages, Cultures, and Fields." In *"Escape to Life": German Intellectuals in New York—A Compendium on Exile after 1933*, 55–79. Edited by Eckart Goebel and Sigird Weigel. Berlin: De Gruyter.

---

1. Letter, Hannah Arendt to Heinrich Blücher. 14 February 1950. Arendt Papers, Container I.
2. In English in the original interview.
3. Arendt's *Denktagebuch* (1950–73) comprises twenty-eight journals that are less a diary (diary—German: *Tagebuch*) than experiments of thoughts, or results of her thinking (to think—German: *denken*); primarily in German but partly in English and Greek. See Arendt (2003) in "Works Cited."
4. XXVI.30, 728. Translated by Wout Cornelissen.
5. (German) romanticism as an intellectual movement versus Romanticism as a political one; focus on the aesthetics first (romanticism), then increasingly political, especially nationalistic after 1806.
6. Of course, Arendt's interest in Greece and Greek poetry is closely linked to the Romantics, as they themselves were highly influenced by Greek mythology.
7. I.1.3: "Das Unrechte, das man getan hat, ist die Last auf den Schultern, etwas, was man trägt, weil man es sich aufgeladen hat." Translated in Berkowitz (2017), 9.
8. The correspondence, which is collected in *Letters, 1925–1975* (New York: Houghton Mifflin Harcourt, 2004), is revealing—first of all, in its incompleteness: Arendt kept all of Heidegger's letters from the very beginning; he kept few of hers, and none from the early years.
9. "*Zu den wenigen Büchern auf meinem 'Schreibtisch' gehört Hölderlins Hyperion. Das mag Dir sagen, das Du und Deine Liebe mir zur Arbeit und Existenz gehören. Und ich wünsche, das heiligste Erinnerung so oft Dir naht wie mir. Sie wird mir dann immer zur Mahnung, würdiger zu werden dieses Lebens mit Dir*" (One of the few books on my "desk" is Hölderlin's Hyperion. This may tell you that you and your love belong to my work and existence. And I wish that the holiest memory approaches you as often as it does me. It is then always a warning to me to become more worthy of this life with you) (Letter 28, 46).
   And also: "*Ich schrieb Dir schon, dass ich den Hyperion lese. Ich fange an, langsam zu verstehen. Du musst es an jeder Zeile spüren, Liebstes, wie es in mir stürmt und ich nur zusehen muss, in der rechten Weise damit fertig zu werden*" (Letter 29, 48). Heidegger here sees himself in Hyperion and Arendt in Diotima: Hyperion lives in the infinite feeling that Diotima gives him, she combines the divine and the human; when he loses her, he retreats into solitude, just like Heidegger into the mountains.

10. Letter, Hannah Arendt to Mary McCarthy, New York, 31 May 1971, 426. In *Between Friends: The Correspondence of Hannah Arendt and Mary McCarthy, 1949–1975* (New York: Houghton Mifflin Harcourt, 1995), 426.

11. Arendt writes about Jarell in her collection of portraits entitled *Men in Dark Times* after his death in 1965: "He opened up for me a whole new world of sound and meter, and he taught me the specific gravity of English words, whose specific relative weight, as in all languages, is ultimately determined by poetic usage and standards. Whatever I know of English poetry, and perhaps of the genius of the language, I owe him" (Arendt 1968, 264).

12. Carl Viëtor, *Hölderlin: Die Briefe der Diotima* (Leipzig: Janus Press, 1923).

13. I, 469.

14. For further reading on "reconciliation" in Arendt's work, see Berkowitz (2017).

15. I.I, 4. Translated by Roger Berkowitz.

16. *SW* VI.1, Letters, 1784–1788, 9. All subsequent quotes are taken from the same German edition of Hölderlin's collected works (see "Works Cited") and, unless otherwise stated, translated into English by the author.

17. Ibid., 13.

18. Ibid., 18: "Überall ist mir so leer—bin dann ich nur allein so? Der ewige, ewige Grillenfänger!"

19. Ibid.

20. Ibid., 199.

21. IV.1, 416. The Stuttgart edition contains its own dating proposal ("The dating is difficult"), but places the text in a thematic context with the so-called "Werden im Vergehen."

22. *SW* VI.1, Letters, 1799, 499.

23. "*Der Messias wird erst kommen, wenn er nicht mehr nötig sein wird, er wird nach seiner Ankunft kommen, er wird nicht am letzten Tag kommen, sondern am allerletzten*" (Kafka 1992, 56).

24. *SW* VI.1, Letters, 1798–1800, 297.

25. VIII.18, 191 (1952)—Reflection from: Hölderlin, Friedrich: Sämtliche Werke [Hyperion] (ed. Beißner, Friedrich), vol. 4, Stuttgart 1961, 235.

26. Translated by Samantha Hill.

Toward a Poetic Reading of Arendt and Baldwin on Love

Peter W. Brown

Introduction: Arendt Pushes Baldwin on the Love Question

November 21, 1962
Dear Mr. Baldwin:

Your article in the New Yorker is a political event of a very high order, I think; it certainly is an event in my understanding of what is involved in the Negro question. And since this is a question which concerns us all, I feel I am entitled to raise objections.

What frightened me in your essay was the gospel of love which you begin to preach at the end. In politics, love is a stranger, and when it intrudes upon it nothing is being achieved except hypocrisy. All the characteristics you stress in the Negro people: their beauty, their capacity for joy, their warmth, and their humanity, are well-known characteristics of all oppressed people. They grow out of suffering and they are the proudest possession of all pariahs. Unfortunately, they have never survived the hour of liberation by even five minutes. Hatred and love belong together, and they are both destructive; you can afford them only in the private and, as a people, only so long as you are not free.

In sincere admiration,
cordially (that is, in case you remember that we know each other slightly) yours,
Hannah Arendt[1]

In response to James Baldwin's 1962 essay "Down at the Cross: Letter from a Region in My Mind," Hannah Arendt wrote him a letter to express her disagreement with his supposedly political invocation of "love." Arendt considers love to be "a stranger" to the political realm—it thus belongs with "hatred" insofar as both are "destructive." In *The Human Condition* she describes it as a "passion" that "destroys the in-between,"[2] the space that separates two people and thus makes political action possible. Baldwin, on the other hand, speaks of love as something that "takes off the masks that we fear we cannot live without and know we cannot live within": it is love, "in the tough and universal sense of quest and daring and growth."[3] For Baldwin, love is synonymous with destroying the ideology of whiteness and creating other modalities of living together. On its surface, Arendt's letter seems to be an ungenerous reading of Baldwin's work; instead of attempting to understand his logic, she steamrolls over it with her own paradigm.

Arendt's objection to Baldwin's invocation of "love" as political, I argue, misses out on their mutual preoccupation with poetry and poetic possibility. In her work, Arendt treats poetry not just as an object of study but also as a tool of thinking. In her oft-quoted essay on Walter Benjamin she describes his "gift of thinking poetically," something she nearly reveals to be her own hermeneutic. Arendt writes that "thought-fragments" of the past could "crystallize" over time and become the "rich and strange" material out of which we imagine politics differently—using "Ariel's Song" in Shakespeare's *The Tempest* as her poetic guide.[4] Benjamin's poetic thinking, for Arendt, operates primarily through metaphors, a link she revisits in *The Life of the Mind*, where she writes that "the metaphor, bridging the abyss between inward and invisible mental activities and the world of appearances, was certainly the greatest gift language could bestow on thinking."[5] Arendt understands metaphor to be the thing that invigorates thought and in turn allows thought to affect the world. Metaphor allows for thinking and the world to be compatible, creating the conditions within which human plurality can exist and thrive.

In this essay I hope to accomplish two things: (1) narrate a genealogy of Arendt's thought that links poetry, love, and thinking in solitude as separate from but indispensable to a politics of plurality—that is, as "worldless" things that ideally usher us back into the "world"; and (2) draw a distinction between a politics of collective warmness and Baldwin's idea of love. In all, I argue that Arendt fundamentally misinterprets Baldwin's essay. Her disavowal of love in politics would better apply to Baldwin's critique of the religious groups he encounters in his *New Yorker* essay, which is to say, groups that claim love as an insider's privilege and use it as a means of social cohesion. If we take Arendt's letter to be referencing the language of her remarks on Lessing, wherein she claims that "under the pressure of persecution the persecuted have moved so closely together that the interspace which we have called the world . . . has simply disappeared," then she clearly does not understand how Baldwin is thinking about love.[6] Arendt understands love to be a power of the universe that humans experience as an ephemeral phenomenon. The basic problem of love in politics, therefore, is that it cannot be *used*—love is not a thing subject to our will. Baldwin, similarly, shows a deep reverence for the power of love *over* us; for him, the key is to allow love to do its work in a country whose politics is trying to destroy love. For example, at the end of Baldwin's essay, he writes that we (i.e., "the relatively conscious whites and the relatively conscious blacks") "must, *like* lovers, insist on, or create, the consciousness of others."[7] Love in this sentence appears as a simile, signaling his knowledge that turning love into a public mandate would not work. Rather, he is interested in consciousness, which is to say, a knowledge of self and a willingness to be affected by the other. Baldwin is not calling on us to create a political order of love but rather a political order that allows for love in the first place. That distinction may seem minor, but, as I follow poetic strains of thought in both Arendt and Baldwin, my hope is to rethink the convergences in their thinking. Ultimately, the difference between them is not that one thinks love is antipolitical and the other does not. Rather, Baldwin is willing to take the risk of saving love from an American politics tied up in racism and hatred, and Arendt is not. Her attachment to the idea of a stable public sphere prevents her from accepting such a risk.

Love, Solitude, and Poetry vis-à-vis Politics

George Kateb distinguishes love in Arendt's thought from action insofar as "love abolishes distance between people," whereas "action not only connects people, it connects people in a way that also keeps them distinct, separate."[8] Here we are presented with a basic spatial problem: we cannot have politics if there is nothing we hold in common. Kateb goes on to characterize love, influenced by *The Human Condition*: "Love is great; it is rare; it is too easily mistaken for romance; but whatever it is, it is antipolitical."[9] Love takes on a kind of mystical quality in Kateb's characterization; whatever love is, we are not sure, but what we are sure of is that it cannot be political. Whereas Kateb might not have much more to say about what love is or does, Arendt dwells on it, especially in her *Denktagebuch*. Arendt is clear on the point that love is antipolitical, but she continues to think about different forms of love and distinguishes between its misinterpretations and her own understanding of it. Arendt's preoccupation with certain a- or anti-political concepts suggests that she wants to theorize the conditions under which they can simultaneously be far away from politics and yet supportive of it. Plurality, for example, is essential to Arendtian politics. Plurality, also, comes about through the production and destruction of people and ideas. By turning to Arendt's thinking about love alongside poetry, we see the importance of alternative worlds—or the worldless spaces of thinking and poetics—in returning us to the world of politics with new ideas and a sense of continuous beginning.

To be clear: poetry, solitude, and love are all necessary *precursors* to Arendtian politics even as they cannot be political as such. This point is apparent in Arendt's German writing, especially in her *Denktagebuch*. Arendt's idea of love as worldless arises, unsurprisingly, in close proximity to her thinking on poetry—not exclusively but perhaps most notably with the poetry of Rainer Maria Rilke.

In 1930, Arendt and her first husband, Günter Anders, published an essay on Rilke's *Duino Elegies* in the *Neue Schweize Rundschau*.[0] The essay has no unified argument, for, as they remark, the poetry is unclear about "the extent to which it wants to be understood."[11] One thing they focus on, however, is the poem's treatment of *Einsamkeit* (solitude) and *Verlassenheit* (abandonment or loneliness). In the *Duino Elegies*, solitude arises from a "double abandonment," wherein "things abandon us" and "we abandon things." Arendt and Anders come to the conclusion that Rilke's love "is principally love of the abandoned."[12] Here we see a play on the duality in the phrase *Liebe der Verlassenen*. It remains unclear whether it means love of (as in directed toward) the abandoned or, in the German possessive, love of (as in love that belongs to) the abandoned. In the world of this poem, love sucks all into abandonment, such that there is no place that lovers can properly inhabit; they exist within a liminal space between our world and the world of the divine. For Arendt and Anders, Rilke dramatizes the situation of "objectless being-in-love," where "the beloved person is forgotten [by the lover] and surpassed in favor of a transcendence."[13] This kind of love can only exist within the homelessness of mere being, and, as Arendt and Anders summarize at the end of the article, Rilke depicts the condition of "*being* human, insofar as a being of this kind is not at home in the world and finds no entrance into it."[14] This is because of the poem's central problem of *Gottverlassenheit*, or God's abandonment of humanity. In Arendt's later *Denktagebuch* entries she invokes Rilke in ways that on their surface seem to be poetic citations of convenience; they say just the right-sounding thing when pulled out of context. But I am interested in Arendt's continued thinking with Rilke's *Duino Elegies* as taking seriously what it means for love to exist within a world order of abandonment, and what it means to call on poetry to evoke the depths of that alternative world.

Two entries in Arendt's *Denktagebuch* follow the line of thinking she and Anders start in their 1930 essay. The first is an entry on love from 1951 wherein she describes the problem of transforming "love into feeling" (here we see echoes of the phrase "objectless being-in-love" from the earlier essay). For Arendt, love-as-feeling "loses its 'object'" and "destroys the original togetherness of those who are stricken together by their love for each other."[15] Turning love into feeling deceptively prioritizes transcendence over solitude, which she clarifies in a parenthetical as *sovereignty*. Unlike Rilke's solitude (meaning double abandonment), Arendt here means solitude as the two-in-one experience of thinking or talking with one's self that she most notably describes in the final pages of *Origins of Totalitarianism*, published the same year.[16] In Rilke's world of *Gottverlassenheit*, the condition of being in love exceeds the human at the expense of the world, which Arendt captures with a single line from Rilke's second elegy: "For our own heart always exceeds [übersteigt] us."[17] In an abandoned world, love rises above, into "higher ranks," and leaves its objects—the lovers—behind and beneath. Just before the poetic line Arendt cites, Rilke writes: "If only we too could discover a pure, contained, / human place, our own strip of fruit-bearing soil / between river and rock."[18] Arendt is clearly interested in a kind of love that is compatible with solitude and sovereignty. Rilke tells us that we cannot wield the power of love without giving up on inhabiting our own "human place."

The second entry that continues her thinking from 1930 is, of all things, on the topic of logic. In short, logic (or "logicality," as she calls it in *Origins of Totalitarianism*)[19] references deductive reasoning that starts from a premise of truth, foreclosing the possibility that such thinking would deviate from its original claim. Arendt calls this "abandoned thought."[20] Solitude, on the other hand, is a dialogue with one's self; it is a two-in-one experience that produces doubt and prompts further thought. Thinking in solitude, unlike logical thinking, is a crucial precursor to public life because it relies on external thought to start a two-in-one dialogue and prompts the thinker to return to the world with new ideas. For Arendt, the only thing exempt from this interplay between solitude and the common world is love, which is "free from" both: "The speech of lovers is therefore 'poetic' in its own right. . . . It is, as if in that kind of speech people first become what they appear to be as poets: they speak not, and they talk not, but rather they resonate, make sound."[21] If the primary characteristic of solitary thought is a duality within, and that of talking with others is a duality without, then the "poetic" speech of lovers is an expression of a momentarily shared existence. Duality collapses into unity; within and without simply become "with." At the expense of the world, love turns to poetry, which, as we know from Rilke's verse, exists within a space of expansive creative possibility, if also volatility.

However, as I suggested earlier, Arendt is interested in a form of love that is compatible with solitude rather than abandonment, which is to say, one that is momentarily "exempt" from solitude and the world. As Arendt writes, pulling several thoughts together,

> The idea that 'love cannot endure in the world' is the same as the idea that 'solitude cannot endure.' Just as all solitude prompts from its conflicting nature—really its "split-in-two-ness," from which doubt then arises—the wish of being-with-others in order to become one through the other, so do the pure sounds of love again and again prompt communication [*Mit-teilen*]: one divides/ shares [*teilt*] a common thread with the other. The 'you' of 'I' becomes the other—if it goes well, the neighbor.[22]

Even though love is initially a break from solitude and the common world, it reaffirms both. That is because love and solitude share an investment in the self through others. Both solitude (an internal dialogue) and love (a collapsing of two people into one) are permitting conditions for communication. Their shared withdrawal from the common world, for Arendt, is precisely what allows for the common world to continue renewing itself. In *The Human Condition*, Arendt points to the most literal form of renewal—a child[23]—but here we get the neighbor (as in, "Love thy neighbor as thyself"). Poetic love, in its best form, is what Arendt elsewhere calls *welt-schöpferisch*, or world-creating;[24] the unity of love ideally produces something else that ushers the lovers back into the world from which they came.

Baldwin's Poetic Critique of Love

Having established Arendt's stake in a form of love that does not threaten the world, I now turn again to her misreading of Baldwin and his critique of love. I argue that his thinking on love is more compatible with Arendt's than might otherwise be apparent, but I will come short of claiming that they are in agreement.

When Arendt writes about the problem of love in politics, she echoes the language of her Lessing speech, where she critiques a politics based on "fraternity" and "humanity," as exemplified by the French Revolution. In the speech she says that "the humanity of the insulted and injured has never yet survived the hour of liberation by so much as a minute."[25] To be fair, in the letter she gives a generous *five* minutes. Arendt understands the value of that warmth and closeness as a tool of survival, but she stops at politics. Baldwin, however, identifies the complexities of love and power in his essay, especially when he writes about his childhood experience of getting involved in the black church. In Arendt's letter she tells Baldwin that "hatred and love belong together," a point he gets at when he writes that "the passion with which we loved the Lord was a measure of how deeply we feared and distrusted and . . . hated almost all strangers . . . and avoided and despised ourselves."[26] The sense of love that bound Baldwin's church together—love of God—was tied to a hatred of the world and a hatred of the self. And yet, for Baldwin, "there was in the life I fled a zest and a joy and a capacity for facing and surviving disaster that are very moving and very rare": in short, "we sometimes achieved with each other a freedom that was close to love."[27] Baldwin points to the "zest" and "joy" of "surviving disaster," with full knowledge that it was unsustainable. The sense of warmth and worldlessness of the church, for Baldwin, was disastrous and thrilling; it was *close to* love insofar as this love was deceptive. Baldwin concurs with Arendt that using love as a binding agent for a group of people is not only a perversion of politics but also a perversion of love.

Baldwin's essay, as I understand it, is primarily a corrective on love. As a child, Baldwin conflates "God" and "safety," thereby mistaking love *for* safety;[28] as an adult, he points to love as both "constant" and a site of "quest and daring and growth"—the constant of risking everything.[29] Political theorist Susan McWilliams rightly points out that, for Baldwin, "horror is the fact, and safety is the illusion," such that "the fact of our horror and depravity is our *common* fact. It is, along with our births and deaths and capacities for love and laughter, what makes us human and what gives truth to that old proposition that all people are created equal."[30] What Arendt does not understand but Baldwin does is that America's problem with love has intimate ties to its political problems. In other words, Baldwin understands the political stakes of our shared unlovability, and that it keeps us from achieving a fully human and pluralistic body politic.

What Arendt misses out on, therefore, is the opportunity to understand love in America as something that has lost its world-creating [*welt-schöpferish*] capacity. In his essay "Nothing Personal," Baldwin pinpoints this problem precisely, speaking to the entanglement between lovelessness, loneliness, and an unpoetic world:

> You will search in vain for lovers. I have not heard anyone singing in the streets of New York for more than twenty years. By singing, I mean singing for joy, for the hell of it. I don't mean the drunken, lonely, 4-AM keening which is simply the sound of some poor soul trying to vomit up his anguish and gagging on it. Where the people can sing, the poet can live—and it is worth saying it the other way around, too: where the poet can sing, the people can live. When a civilization treats its poets with the disdain with which we treat ours, it cannot be far from disaster; it cannot be far from the slaughter of the innocents.[31]

Baldwin is more outwardly a theorist of love than Arendt. As a poet, he risks "fool[ing] us" (as Arendt warns us with regard to romance in poetry)[32] by overstating the importance of love. But Baldwin is not naive, nor is his mind stuck in a poetic world. Baldwin, like Arendt, knows the importance of the mystifying yet creative forces of poetry, thinking, and love—without which we would surely be doomed. Whereas Arendt takes politics as her object of study, driving her to imagine the conditions under which we could cultivate a pluralistic world, Baldwin focuses on love, something to which he sees American politics as an apocalyptic threat. Baldwin and Arendt are interested in a world that accommodates for the worldless—one in which we understand the mutuality of Baldwin's declaration that "where the poet can sing, the people can live."

By way of conclusion, I want to consider Baldwin's use of poetic citation at the end of his *New Yorker* essay. He declares that, should we not "end the racial nightmare," then the American experiment will expire in accordance with apocalyptic Biblical prophecy: "*God gave Noah the rainbow sign, No more water, the fire next time!*" Baldwin carefully notes, however, that the poetic line is not the prophecy itself, but prophecy "re-created from the Bible in song by a slave."[33] The line is at once a confirmation of the prophecy's possibility and a call to imagine an alternative, precisely because it comes from the mouths of those who are already in the midst of that fire—those who have the greatest knowledge about living within apocalyptic prophecy. Pulling prophetic certainty into the realm of the poetic, the slave song risks being right about the fulfillment of the promise for "fire next time," just as it creates the possibility of something else. The contingency that love, thinking, and poetry produce is powerful and dangerous; if only Arendt could see that she and Baldwin shared an interest in protecting them from the world so that, perhaps by chance, the world might eventually benefit from their capacity to create.

---

1. Hannah Arendt, "The Meaning of Love in Politics: A Letter by Hannah Arendt to James Baldwin," *HannahArendt.net Journal for Political Thinking* 2, no. 1 (2006 [1962]): https://bit.ly/2nMWTM4.

2. Hannah Arendt, *The Human Condition* (Chicago: University of Chicago Press, 2005), 242.

3. James Baldwin, "Down at the Cross: Letter from a Region in My Mind," in *James Baldwin: Collected Essays*, ed. Toni Morrison (New York: Library of America, 1998), 341.

4. Hannah Arendt, *Men in Dark Times* (New York: Harcourt Brace & Co., 1968), 205–6.

5. Hannah Arendt, "One: Thinking," in *The Life of the Mind*, ed. Mary McCarthy (New York: Harcourt), 105.

6. Arendt, *Men in Dark Times*, 13.

7. Baldwin, "Down at the Cross," 346. Italics mine.

8. George Kateb, *Hannah Arendt: Politics, Conscience, Evil*, Philosophy and Society (Totowa: Rowman & Allanheld, 1984), 26.

9. Ibid.

10. Hannah Arendt and Günther Stern [Anders], "Rilkes 'Duineser Elegien,'" *Neue Schweize Rundschau*, no. 11 (1930): 855–71. https://bit.ly/2HNLI42.

11. Arendt and Stern [Anders], "Rilke's Duino Elegies," trans. Colin Benert, in *Reflections on Literature and Culture*, ed. Susannah Young-Ah Gottlieb (Stanford: Stanford University Press, 2007), 1.

12. Ibid., 12–13.

13. Ibid., 15.

14. Ibid., 23.

15. Hannah Arendt, *Denktagebuch. Bd. 1: 1950–1973. Bd. 2: 1973-1975*, ed. Ursula Ludz and Ingrid Normann (Munich: Piper, 2002), IV.2.83 [journal/*Heft*, entry, page]. Translations are my own, with proofreading and suggested revisions from Friederike von Schwerin-High. See Appendix for complete versions of the referenced entries in both English and German.

16. See Hannah Arendt, *Origins of Totalitarianism* (New York: Harcourt, 1951), 468–79.

17. Arendt, *Denktagebuch*, IV.2.83. For the English translation of Rilke, see Rainer Maria Rilke, *Duino Elegies & The Sonnets to Orpheus*, ed. and trans. Stephen Mitchell, First Vintage International Edition (New York: Vintage, 2009), 15.

18. Rilke, *Duino Elegies*, 15.

19. See note 16.

20. Arendt, *Denktagebuch*, IX.19.214.

21. Ibid.

22. Ibid., 215.

23. Arendt, *The Human Condition*, 242.

24. Arendt, *Denktagebuch*, XVI.3.373.

25. Arendt, *Men in Dark Times*, 16.

26. Baldwin, "Down at the Cross," 310.

27. Ibid.

28. Ibid., 296.

29. Ibid., 339, 341.

30. Susan J. McWilliams, "Introduction," in *A Political Companion to James Baldwin* (Lexington: University of Kentucky Press, 2017), 8.

31. James Baldwin, "Nothing Personal," in *Collected Essays*, 695

32. Arendt, *The Human Condition*, 242n81.

33. Baldwin, "Down at the Cross," 346–47.

In the Archive with Hannah Arendt

Samantha Hill

> The question is: Is there a form of thinking that is not tyrannical?[1]
> —Hannah Arendt

When Hannah Arendt arrived at the German Literature Archive in Marbach, Germany, in June 1975 to organize Karl Jasper's papers, she stood up in the cafeteria and began reciting Friedrich Schiller by heart. She was fond of "Das Mädchen aus der Fremde," but this is pure speculation. As Arendt said to Günter Gaus in her last interview, she carried German poems around in her *Hinterkopf*.[2] I'd wager she knew more than one.

The German Literature Archive is an expansive brutalist building designed by Jörg and Elisabeth Kiefner, set next to the Friedrich Schiller Museum. Built in the early 1970s, it houses papers from some of the world's most famous writers: Friedrich Schiller, Rainer Maria Rilke, Hermann Hesse, Erich Kästner, Franz Kafka, Siegfried Kracauer, Martin Heidegger, Karl Jaspers, and Hannah Arendt. While most of Arendt's papers are at The Library of Congress in Washington, D.C., the archive in Marbach holds her *Denktagebuch*, or thinking journals, alongside her correspondence with Heidegger, Jaspers, Hilde Domin, and Hermann Broch, among others. I went to visit her journals.

Hannah Arendt kept her thinking journals between 1950 and 1971.[3] The twenty-eight notebooks are 5 by 8 inches, mottled reddish-brown. Arendt favored the Champion Line Wiremaster, ruled, 45 sheets, 15 or 20 cents apiece. She ordered the journals with roman numerals on the covers, and numbered the inner left- and right-hand corners respectively. She writes with blue and black ink and edits with pencil.

Arendt's journals were delivered to me in two bursting blue folders, out of order, pulled from a museum exhibition. Unlike the two heavy volumes published by Piper as the *Denktagebuch* in 2002, which appears as two thick black tomes, I was struck by how thin and colorful Arendt's journals were. Worn corners, coffee rings on the covers. Journal XXVI looks waterlogged. They appear as intimate artifacts of daily existence. Somehow, naming them *Denktagebuch* had crystallized the journals in my imagination as a single, consistent work spread out over time. Much to my surprise, they were not one work but many.[4]

In his 1936 essay "Art in the Age of Mechanical Reproducibility" Walter Benjamin talks about "aura." Aura is the element eliminated from the original when we encounter a reproduction. The plurality of copies that appear readily available lose their unique quality, which can only be retained in the original. Arendt writes about this phenomenon in her essay "Culture and Politics," though she worries more about the socialization of texts than aura:

> It is not the entertainment industry that is a sign of what we call 'mass culture,' and what should more precisely be called the deterioration of culture. And it is not that this deterioration begins when everyone can buy the dialogues of Plato for pocket change. Rather, it begins when these products are changed to such an extent as to facilitate their mass retailing—a mass retailing that would otherwise be impossible.[5]

Mass retailing requires loss, and reproduction forces a kind of conformity that loses uniqueness. This cuts against Arendt's definition of plurality as that which is distinct. And while there is much to be said for the experience of aura itself, opening those blue folders I was struck by how the form of encountering Arendt's journals changed my experience of the text. The thinking journals appeared to me as an entirely new work.

How we experience a text depends on form as much as content. Seeing the originals changes the experience of reading and gives one a sense of context, a sense of tone, a sense of how a text might have been written—which is not to claim that we can ever know the thoughts or feelings of another, but it is to say that there is something different we gain from the tactile experience of handling original papers. This experience expands our imagination of the text, and so too our capacity for engaging with it. I was struck most by how essential space is to reading Arendt's thinking journals, and how much this sense of space and time is lost in the reproduction of the text.

Space and time are essential to how Arendt is using her thinking journals. Benjamin discusses how even the most perfect reproduction still lacks one element, "its presence in time and space." And certainly Arendt's journals bear this historical quality of time and space as well, but in the journals time and space appear across the page as a form of thinking itself. The relationship between *theoria* (theory) and *poiesis* (making) that Arendt talks about in *The Human Condition* is visible in the ordering of the entries. Arendt is wrestling with concepts spatially, putting thoughts into conversation with one another.

In *The Life of the Mind* Arendt asks, where are we when we think? Her answer is spatial and temporal. We are caught in the gap between the forces of past and future that press upon us. We absent ourselves from the realm of appearances in order to retreat into a space of solitude where thinking is possible, where we can re-present our experiences in the world to ourselves in our imagination and engage with them in self-reflective thinking. And for Arendt there is always a space between the process of thinking that unfolds in the mind and the way our thoughts appear in the world. Arendt's thinking journals appear as a medium, carrying thoughts to a physical space where she can engage and reengage them. It's not surprising in this sense that many of the entries are poems, aphorisms, sayings, and passages from texts that she finds illuminating.

Arendt writes in German, English, French, Hebrew, Greek, and Latin—perhaps one reason why the thinking journals have not appeared in an English translation. It would be a shame to lose their linguistic richness, where language is a material for her thinking. The multilingual journals are testament to Arendt's life: the philosophical tradition she emerged out of, learning Greek at an early age, memorizing Homer, her attachment to her mother tongue, German, and her lived experiences as a refugee learning French and English to survive. Arendt did not live in one language; she lived in many.

Arendt also asks how thinking appears in *The Life of the Mind*. Thinking appears in her journals in the spacing of the entries, in the way we see a thought carried out in a single stroke of a pen, in the way she stacks letters and contrasts quotes to create new meaning. There's something of a Brechtian and Benjaminian spirit alive on the page. Her thinking journals illustrate constellated thinking, the ways in which we make connections and think relationally. The way the passages are placed on the page indicates that she is writing them out intentionally and thinking about them in conversation with one another. A Nietzsche quote in German sits above a Pascal quote in French. They are talking with each other.

On one page, Arendt places Wordsworth on top of Hölderlin on top of Melville:

> Imagination, which, in truth,
> Is but another name for absolute power
> And clearest insight, amplitude of mind,
> And Reason in her most exalted mood. —William Wordsworth

> *Denn der hat viel gewonnen, der das Leben verstehen kann ohne zu trauern* (Because he had won a lot, he could understand life without mourning). —Hölderlin, *Philosophical Aphorisms*

> 'Tis dream to think that Reason can govern the reasoning creature, man. —Melville

Each passage deals with thinking and reason. Seen this way on the page, the languages play with one another, sounds and words echoing. Arendt is illustrating her method of constellated thinking, which refuses rational or reductive forms of logic. These passages are about mourning, imagination, and the dream of Reason. Each reflects a different angle of Arendt's work on thinking, which uplifts the power imagination over reason. The lines from Wordsworth's *Prelude* elevate imagination as the internal power of the mind, enabling creation, allowing us to begin again. For Hölderlin, mourning becomes a form of poetic contemplation, a way of thinking that is interruptive and unexpected. This echoes Melville's *dream* that Reason could govern man. To think that Reason might win out over the chaos of mere life is melancholy, and almost laughable.

Arendt is a relational thinker, bringing together ideas through cutting, binding, taping. She was known to write with a large pair of silver scissors and roll of Scotch tape at her desk. These instruments of cut-and-paste give one the impression of collage, or montage. She is creating an image as much as a text, typing up bits of poems and taping them into her journals, along with newspaper clippings and passages from texts. Handwritten notes are tucked between pages. The colors in the original journals enhance the tactile experience of handling them. There's a rhythm created through color. A dash of red pencil, a blot of blue ink, the thickness and shade of black. A sense of how her hand moves. The force of the pen or pencil is visible in the grain of writing, which is lost on the screen or printed page.

This sense of space that Arendt is playing with is emphasized by the tempo of the journals. Arendt is not keeping a daily journal; often there is only one entry per month. Arendt's great axiom from *The Human Condition*, to *stop and think what we are doing*, appears in the journals this way. There is no sense of urgency in her handwriting; there is a great sense of space. There is a pause giving room for each entry to breathe. Often she leaves the bottom of a page blank to begin a new thought at the top of the next page. She breaks up entries with long hash marks that resemble equal signs, upward slashes, and she indicates breath with one dash or two. There are no sprinting thoughts. Many entries are full sentences with indented paragraphs written out as notes for books or essays she is working on.

The relationship between space and time in thinking is most apparent in the way Arendt writes out poems. Almost every poem is given its own page. The first poem that Arendt copies out from Emily Dickinson is draped down the lines. Arendt sets letters down as she's writing them. The final line in "Up Life's Hill": "Homelessness, for Home" stands out and echoes as you encounter it. (She copied the poem in 1950, the same year she first returned to Germany after the war.) Arendt has a bit of Dickinson's penchant for painting with the hand, stretching out *und*, for example, layering *und* on *und*, creating an undulating wave, like Dickinson writing out "The Sea, The Sea, The Sea." At moments, Arendt's *und* becomes a line in itself; a great connector of *inter-esse*.

The difference between the printed *Denktagebuch* and Arendt's thinking journals illustrates the difference between knowing and understanding. The typed-up words, ordered, numbered, lose all texture, and become crystallized artifacts. Printed words appear on the page as carriers of semantic meaning, to be deciphered through reading. We are confronted with a fixed image that has been made from an original, and in this way we are confronted with frozen words. But to see the words on the page, in the stroke of her hand, to see the ink spread out, is to begin to understand the process of thinking. The clean, ordered, numbered pages of the *Denktagebuch* stand in stark contrast with Arendt's handwriting, with the cuts of poetry typed up and taped in, with the juxtaposition of ink and pencil that turns words into images to be encountered, not simply read. The idea of the word changes in form as we see it. Similar to Benjamin's *Passagenwerk*, which documents the passage of time through text and image, Arendt's thinking journals document the dialogic nature of thinking interior to the life of the mind.

Arendt began keeping her thinking journals in 1950, when she returned from visiting Germany for the first time after the war, and she stopped keeping them when her husband Heinrich Blücher died in 1971. The first entry in the last thinking journal dated 1971 reads:

1971, *Ohne Heinrich. Frei — wie ein Blatt im Wind.* (1971, Without Friedrich. Free — like a leaf in the wind.)

The last two pages are travel itineraries dated 1972 and 1973.

In 1971 Arendt switched to keeping day planners, a practice she maintained until her death in 1975. The small black "Diary and Memo" books are less organized, more utilitarian. Grocery lists, reminders, appointments, phone numbers, travel itineraries. They reveal a different side of thinking, a kind of routinization: haircuts, manicures, lists for entertaining, opera tickets, shopping, travel expenses. A way of keeping track of daily life. The pleasurable, the irritating, the necessary.

The year 1971 is also when Arendt begins writing *The Life of the Mind*. Moving from her thinking journals to what was to be her three-part masterpiece on thinking, willing, and judging. From her earliest days in Marburg studying thinking with Heidegger, Arendt was passionate about the life of the mind, about the process of thinking itself, and driven by a need to understand. Her thinking journals illustrate her process of thinking materially, making visible part of that two-in-one dialogue she carried on with herself and others in silence. And as much as Arendt heard Homer echoing in her head, I hear Arendt echoing in mine: there is no end in thinking, we must always begin again.

---

1. Hannah Arendt, Thinking Journal II, December 1950. The German entry reads: "*Die Frage ist: Gibt es ein Denken, das nicht tyrannisch ist?*"
2. Ulrich von Bulow related this story to me. Elisabeth Young-Bruehl talks about the four grueling weeks Arendt spent sorting through Jasper's papers in *For the Love of the World*.

3. Arendt's correspondence with Martin Heidegger, Hilde Domin, Hermann Broch, and Karl Jaspers, among others, is also kept in Marbach. (The rest of Arendt's papers are at the Library of Congress in Washington, D.C.) Arendt's estate is spread across at least four different locations: her papers are kept at the Library of Congress, and digitally accessible at the New School for Social Research in New York City and the German Literary Archive in Marbach, Germany; her personal library is housed at Bard College's Stevenson Library, in Annandale-on-Hudson, New York; her *Denktagebuch* (thinking journal) and correspondence with Martin Heidegger are kept at the German Literary Archive in Marbach; and it is rumored with certainty that a private collector holds a number of her papers in New York City. I haven't seen those.

4. Looking at the thinking journals, it's difficult to imagine how much work went into publishing those two thick Piper bands. The journals themselves were typed up by Arendt's assistant Lotte Kohler, and published from her notes and transcriptions.

5. Arendt, *Thinking without a Banister*, 163.

Twilight of the Gods: Walter Benjamin's Project of a Political Metaphysics in Secular Times—and Hannah Arendt's Answer

Antonia Grunenberg

In the following essay I will talk about elements of a political metaphysics in the thought and writings of Walter Benjamin and Hannah Arendt.[1]

Let me make two preliminary remarks: I am using the concept of metaphysics in asking about the transcendental dimension in the concept of the political in the writings of both Benjamin and Arendt. I am not using it in the sense of a "system," like Hegel's or Kant's metaphysical systems. Benjamin and Arendt did not rely on philosophical "systems." Rather, their discourse evolved out of criticizing traditional systemic philosophy.

A further remark focuses on the methodological aspect: Arendt and Benjamin chose different paths to the process of thinking: they both worked on interrelating categorical thinking and the world of a multitude of experience in order to understand how human existence and political life refer to each other. Benjamin had experienced World War I and its dramatic political aftereffects. He wanted to intertwine philosophical, theological, and revolutionary thinking.

However, when World War I broke out, Arendt was still a child. Of course she experienced the consequences of the Great War. In fact, she witnessed the revolutionary activities among the political and military ranks in her Königsberg surroundings. Later on, she was confronted with National Socialism as an adult. For her, being confronted with totalitarian rule became a quite existential experience insofar as she, being a Jew, was forced to flee from Germany. However, she continued working on the question of what this experience meant for political thinking.

In the following years, Arendt theoretically reacted by fundamentally criticizing the category-based perception of the world by philosophers. At the same level, she started criticizing the intellectual elite in Europe flirting with National Socialism as well as with Fascism because of their estrangement of the "real" world.

After having arrived in the United States, she worked constantly at relinking (or superseding) philosophy to the world by political thinking. What she meant was not just any political discourse but referring to the republican discourse that originated in Greek and Roman philosophy.

However, Benjamin's search for a political metaphysics came clearly out of political romanticism followed by the trauma of World War I and the political dynamics following the war. On this background they both kept reflecting about the refounding of "the political."

I am using the concept of "the political" as being different from the notion of "politics." Politics is the ensemble of processes in which decisions are made. Politics happens within the clash of interests. However, political action is embedded both in politics and in the dimension of the political. Again, I keep the concept of the political quite formal. I am not giving it a normative definition because I intend to open up the different dimensions of the access to the political provided by Benjamin and Arendt.

I.

Whoever enters the realm of the political in Benjamin's and Arendt's thinking is confronted with vast landscapes, not very easy to analyze.

Let me go on with giving more historical background.

Benjamin and Arendt had slightly different family backgrounds. Benjamin was born in 1892, Arendt in 1906, a difference of fourteen years, which means almost a generation. Benjamin grew up in a liberal-bourgeois Jewish family in Berlin, the capital of the German Reich. The family seemed to be quite assimilated. However, Arendt grew up in the provincial town of Königsberg within a family of liberal Jews standing in the tradition of a double identity: being German citizens in the first place and Jews in faith, which meant in private. Her family was not wealthy but got along mainly because one of the grandfathers, being the head of the liberal Jewish community in Königsberg, owned a tea company.

When Benjamin became inflamed by the Russian Revolution, Arendt had finished school and started studying philosophy at the University of Marburg. She was interested in the revolutionary events of her time but was not familiar with the current political discourses.

In 1940, when Benjamin took his life in a little Spanish harbor town, Arendt had just escaped from the Gurs internment camp in Southern France and fled to Lisbon waiting to board a ship to the United States. At this time Fascist and National Socialist governments had taken over Europe. However, the genocide of the European Jews was still more of a rumor going around than a brutal fact.

Both of them referred to experiences they personally had had. They equally shared the conclusion that traditional systems of legitimation and sense giving to life were disrupted from reality.

One may conclude that the loss of tradition in the context of World War I has influenced two generations of philosophers—the generation of Benjamin quite directly, and the generation of Arendt more indirectly. To name just a few others within this context: Martin Heidegger, Hans Kelsen, Ernst Cassirer,

Carl Schmitt, Bertolt Brecht of the older generation, and Herbert Marcuse, Hans Jonas, and others of the younger generation.

Whoever wants to understand the notion "breach of tradition" must understand that it was not only World War I causing it. Long before World War I broke out there were developments in industry, science, and the arts causing the tradition to erode; there was the workers' movement too, questioning the old monarchic or otherwise semiauthoritarian rule. Throughout the nineteenth century the "breach of tradition" was anticipated and desired on many levels of society. However, it was always linked to the belief that the erosion of old customs and habits would make place for new ideas, new customs, giving new sense to social and political life.

The generation of philosophers and thinkers born between the 1880s and 1900 intended to find new answers for basic questions of legitimation, or in other words, to find substitutes for the traditional system of legitimation.

However, in World War I the confidence of young philosophers and intellectuals vanished in the mass slaughtering of the battlefields. They still believed that they would renew the world by solving the problems of the society at the same time. However, they understood that problem solving had to be even more radical than before. Toward the end of the war the Russian Revolution broke out. In what followed it seemed clear for most Western intellectuals that only a political revolution could redeem the world. Only a radical turnaround of the world would answer fundamental questions such as: What is the sense of human existence? Who or what is sense giving for our life? What is a good life? What is good politics?

Benjamin belonged to those working on these questions. Arendt belonged to those growing up among those questions. Both of them were deeply convinced that politics at that time—meaning parliamentarism as well as political parties, and compromise embedded in formally democratic institutions—would give no answers, nor would those democratic institutions provide "solutions" for basic questions.

II.

In Benjamin's writings there are a lot of approaches to the phenomenon of the political, beginning with essays like "Critique of Violence" or his "Theological-political Fragment" (1921), ending with his manifesto "On the Concept of History" (1940).

Looking back, there are some characteristic traces that Benjamin was following during this period. One of the traces is the German youth movement and its cultural elitism in Benjamin's early writings. For a couple of years he had belonged to a progressive educational movement in Germany. He was convinced that German-Jewish culture was chosen to lead the future development of Europe.

However when large parts of the youth movement—Jews and non-Jews—went over to the nationalist camp convinced that the upcoming war was fought for a new, German-dominated European culture, Benjamin immediately broke up with the movement. In the following years he opened up toward new political discourses like revolutionary or progressive political theories among German intellectuals and politicians. They either propagated a radical-leftist break with the bourgeois system or they intended to install a rigid conservative moral order. Their common denominator was their explicit antiliberalism.

To better understand Benjamin's antiliberal approach to the political realm one should look at texts that influenced him at that time. I name just two authors by whom he was impressed at this time: Georges Sorel and Erich Unger. Sorel's most influential book was *Reflections on Violence* from 1908; the one by Erich Unger was *Politics and Metaphysics* from 1921.

Georges Sorel, following Henri Bergson intended to regain a new immediacy within the realm of the political. Any mediation between the political powers (checks and balances) should be refused, all politics of parliamentarianism and compromising should be ended. All traditional historic institutions—including the institutions of the worker's movement—should be destroyed. At the place of a rule based on parliamentary customs a worker's revolution should take place. Only on this ground—like on a tabula rasa—would it be possible to build a new classless society. Within this framework, violence became an important impact being the mediation center of a collective cathartic process. By collectively revolting the oppressed class, workers mainly, should empower themselves to be the avant-garde of a new society self-managing the new order without any political institutions.[2]

Another influential impact in Benjamin's approach to the political realm at this time—like in *Critique of Violence*—was Erich Unger's monumental work *Politics and Metaphysics* (1921). Unger's point was that a new political system would have to be embedded in a "metapolitical universe." Here, too, we find a fundamental criticism of bourgeois politics. In Unger's view democracy with her layers of secular legitimation (division of power, parliamentary rule, law-based system, etc.) would not provide enough spiritual sense.[3] Only a system rooted in an overarching transcendental reference would be able to dissolve the antagonistic opposition between body and mind.

Unger's reflections led to the utopian concept of redefining all basic notions of the political realm, such as people, nation, state, and politics. For him, all concepts should be restructured by referring them to the universe: neither experience nor acting should be the reference but rather the universe as the only sense-giving dimension. In order to be receptive to the aura of the universe one should verbally appeal to it, transforming one's own self into an ecstatic state of mind in which the universe and the human world would flow into each other.

Benjamin was fascinated by Unger but did not share the esoteric dimension of his theories. However he, too, was convinced that the classical concept of the subject was outdated. Thinking had to start from anew, beyond any restriction given by classical philosophy.

Criticizing Sorel, Benjamin argues that all violence refers to the goal of instituting and safeguarding the law. Benjamin uses Sorel's syndicalist as well as anarchist concept to underline his thesis that all relations within a society were based on violence. In his view it was basically violence enabling societies to be established. Therefore violence would not be the absolute opposite to law. However, it enables the law. Vice versa, instituting law would not abolish violence but define its borders. So violence was not supposed to be the antipode of the law and its institutions but rather its precondition. Without it, neither law nor institutions could exist. Therefore, instituting law meant to limit violence, not to abolish it.

In a sophisticated manner Benjamin attacked the tendency among liberal political theorists to establish a rationalistic as well as positivistic legitimation for social relations and political action. He repudiated any attempt by the positivists to claim evidence for their concepts.

For me it is not accidental that within this discourse one finds a lot of direct and indirect connections between Benjamin's discourse and that of Carl Schmitt. Both kept criticizing liberalism of the Weimar Republic.[4]

In those times—I am talking about the '20s and early '30s of the last century—Schmitt belonged to the same intellectual discourse as Benjamin and others. But Schmitt ended up pleading for a concept of the political that consists of decision-making by a leader, eventually in a coup d'état. However, Benjamin at that time was occupied by reflecting on the mythical or the theological dimensions of the political realm. There he again met Schmitt, who wanted to create a political theology. Schmitt's theology is different from Benjamin's. Yet Benjamin feels near to Schmitt when he refers to Schmitt's concept of sovereignty in his essay "On Violence." However, he ends up with different conclusions. Those one can see in his manuscript "*Ursprung des deutschen Trauerspiels*" (Origin of the German Tragedy) of the mid 1920s.

In a rather short essay under the title "Theological-political Fragment"[5] Benjamin focuses on another basic concept of the political. For him, the promise of happiness is one of the basic notions of the political realm. However, neither the Christian concept of redemption nor the concept of a theocratic political imperium would be able to fulfill the promise of happiness. This promise could only be fulfilled in the precarious space between present and past. Happiness would then be the ability to gain the "Messianic moment" from the profane world.

In 1923 Benjamin studied the Hungarian philosopher Georg Lukács's famous book *History and Class Consciousness*.[6] In the following year, the Latvian theater director and actor Asja Lacis told him about her fascination for the

Russian Revolution and for the Russian theater. Both Lukács and Lacis reignited Benjamin's interest in a different understanding of the political realm, namely as a space in which revolutionary action takes place. In the following years Benjamin focused on the concept of violence and action. He kept reflecting on the idea of a primal revolutionary act of violence enabling "the masses" to take action, thus making a new world possible. Here again he refers to Sorel giving the political sphere a kind of metaphysical grounding.

At the end of the 1920s, Benjamin met with the poet and theater director Bertolt Brecht. The contact with Brecht opened Benjamin's mind to a further metamorphosis. From then on, "the political" becomes an educational project: education for revolution.

Many scholars have interpreted Benjamin's manifesto "On the Concept of History" being his ultimate heritage regarding his understanding of the political realm. I agree with that. First, because Benjamin said so. Second, when Benjamin ended his life, "On the Concept of History" was the last text on which he was working.

In it, Benjamin sums up his political philosophy. Between the lines, the post-WWI history appears: the breakdown of the prewar bourgeois society, the catastrophic peace treaty of Versailles effecting not peace but civil war in Europe, the Russian Revolution and the establishment of a regime based on violence, the erosion of the political order called the "Weimar Republic," the betraying of the proletarian revolution by Social Democrats, the breakdown of European democracies, and so on.

The text reflects, too, his own situation: being forced into exile and experiencing the endangered life of a refugee, being a nobody without any "right to have rights."

Anyway, in this text Benjamin's thoughts on the political are classified. Whoever wants to fully understand its complex meaning has to reflect Benjamin's adaption of romanticist philosophy being transferred into Marxism in order to end in a theological interpretation of dialectical materialism.

It is impossible to decide when exactly Benjamin started working on this text. He often worked on several texts at the same time, for years, putting them aside while working on others. In all his writings he kept spinning the red thread and condensing what had already been written. The manifesto "On the Concept of History," for example, goes back to his 1937 essay on the great collector and historian Eduard Fuchs—a text on which he had worked since 1935.[7] The "manifesto" is equally rooted in Benjamin's notes on the concept of history, which he put down in his notebooks beginning in the 1920s. There you can follow his process of thinking by choosing different perspectives from literary as well as from scientific sources on history. It was in these notes that he started reflecting on the concept of progress. It was equally in these notes that he developed his distinct concept of history, following his own understanding of historic materialism. By then, his materialism basically differed from the Marxist/leftist/communist concept.

As he did with other texts he provided complex commentaries for the readers of "On the Concept of History." At the beginning of the year 1940 he wrote to Gretel Adorno, wife of his friend and mentor Theodor W. Adorno: "The advent of war [World War II] and the constellation which made it happen have motivated me to formulate a couple of reflections. I can say that I worked on them for twenty years, I even hided them from me over the time."[8] And then he proposed that she first read the manifesto's XVIIth thesis as a kind of summary.

In his text he harshly criticized the politics of appeasement by Western governments toward Fascism and National Socialism. He condemned equally liberalism and Social Democratic politics whose weaknesses would have led to the victory of Fascism/National Socialism. At the roots of the break down of Western civilization he diagnosed the concept of linear time and politics of progress. In criticizing the Western rationale he elaborated a concept of understanding the world differently. Following Benjamin, *present* is only recognizable when it is understood as *past*, too.

Phrases like "There is never a document of culture without being a document of barbarism"[9] will only be understood if one follows Benjamin's paradoxical concept of time. It is a new way to understand the past as still present and, vice versa, the present as encompassing the past. This way of thinking had little to do with the Social Democratic understanding of politics and even less with Communist doctrine—not to mention liberalism.

Looking for Benjamin's conclusions regarding his concept of the political realm it is obvious that for him political action in the revolutionary sense is only possible with a new reference to history and time. Action does not come out of the so-called means-to-an-end relation like in the maxim "I am using all means to achieve the purpose." Rather, action occurs in confronting present and past, blowing up time, putting a halt to all historic events—with a "tiger's jump into the past."

Another metaphor for what is meant by Benjamin's concept of time and history is the image he quotes from the French Revolution of 1830. It was then that revolutionaries in a collective act shot the clocks of towers and churches in Paris—in order to destroy the clocks and to mark the revolutionary breach. In Benjamin's conceptual thinking this act symbolized that a breach of time was occurring. The shootings effected a pause, and time came—symbolically—to a halt. At this point of reflection Benjamin brings in the "Messianic moment" that is now is possible, as action is possible too.

In this extraordinary situation an unknown perspective should be rising, namely the perspective of salvation. Benjamin could not give any hint that salvation would surely come—how could he have done that anyway? However, he insisted that salvation was possible in the form of a miraculous event within the breach of time.

"On the Concept of History"is sketchy and programmatic at the same time. Benjamin's style of writing is almost authoritarian. Before the decay of the European world his voice rises like a biblical announcement. The author who had stayed hidden behind his texts for a very long time was now coming to the forefront to declare who he was and what he stood for. He declared himself to be somebody summarizing his ultimate reflections on the world.

Let me end my sketchy overview about Benjamin's understanding of "the political." I will come back to it at the very end of this essay.

III.

Quite similarly to Benjamin, Hannah Arendt critically reflected the political realm referring both to the history of political thought and to historic experience.

In her analysis she followed her teacher Martin Heidegger. But unlike Heidegger her reflections referred directly to the experience of the double catastrophe of World War II and the genocide of the European Jews. Therefore the conclusions she drew are a bit different.

Like Benjamin, she refused to return to the traditional instruments of morals and ethics. She declared that after those events that should never have happened mankind had to start reflecting the human condition from anew. In front of unimaginable mass murdering and total destruction, for her, the conclusion was not to return to the status quo ante but to the roots of what "the political" originally was when the Greeks and Romans created it.

For us, it seems quite paradoxical to suppose that the survivors, the witnesses, and the victims of the catastrophe should be able to establish freedom. However, Arendt argues, there is no choice, there is no one else who could do it for us. In this context she quotes the French poet René Char saying, "*Notre héritage n'est précédé d'aucun testament*"—our heritage was left to us by no testament.[10] As the catastrophe was unprecedented, the new beginning was unprecedented too.

In her understanding that meant: human mankind can no more rely upon traditions that were destroyed by mankind itself. So political community had to be built from the start. But where to start and how to begin? Arendt's references to the political realm are widespread throughout her essays. You can find elements of her work on political concepts in texts ranging from "Vita Activa" to "On Revolution," including her lectures and essays such as "Religion and Politics," "What Is Authority?," and "Truth in Politics." In short, one could say that Arendt spun the red thread of her reflections on the political in all her writings—closing with an analysis of the basic concepts of thinking at the end of her life.

If you look at her writings chronologically, her discourse on the political starts with a paradoxical image. At the end of her first major work, *The Origins of Totalitarianism* (1951), Arendt compares totalitarian rule with "devastating sandstorms" raging all over Europa. Surprisingly, she then quotes St. Augustine: *"Initium ut esset creatus est homo"*—that a beginning be made, man was created.[11] That quote was not at all in the logic of her discourse in the book, which ends with the description of practices of mass murdering. Obviously she wanted to point out that there would not be a return to the times before because of the fundamental breach. Only a new beginning could help. Indeed, in her next essay, "The Human Condition," she lays out the conditions of a new beginning, and—paradoxically enough—starts with a critique of modern mass society destroying the political realm.

In fact, reading "The Human Condition" you may think that this essay continues discussing the question Arendt brought up at the end of *The Origins of Totalitarianism*: how does one start from the beginning? She ends up analyzing how modern mass societies destroy the realm of the political and how one has to rethink the concept of a political beginning. It is there that the reader realizes how Arendt reflects on the political. It is a realm in which action takes place, a space defined by "the human condition" and—in the very beginning and at the end—by birth and by death. This realm enables action and restricts action at the same time. All conditions mark the space in which the world of life and action takes place.

Here, Arendt defines a further condition of the political: following the Greek understanding of freedom, she argues that freedom and free action are only possible in a realm where the necessities of life do not play any role and there is no domination. Only then can freedom be enacted—freedom understood as the human capacity to build the realm of the political.

One can interpret this thesis as a foundational idea of the political: having found the benchmark for the world enables us to establish the world of the political.

However, in a world centered on the reproduction of life and laboring or using things there is little place left for political action and discourse. The common understanding of "public happiness" vanishes behind the overarching activities of labor and production. However, if labor and production are the only legitimation of life, then the dimension of freedom goes missing.

If I were to summarize the basic elements of Arendt's concept of the political, I would have to name the principles of public space, of the conditionality of life and action, and the concept of plurality, meaning the common capacity to institute freedom and to create political power. These are elements, paradoxically enough, of a political metaphysics.

At first glance, the reflections of both Walter Benjamin and Hannah Arendt have little to do with our modern concepts of freedom and politics. Arendt was well aware of that fact. However, she insisted that in order to regenerate the political sphere one had to go back to its roots, that is, to the Greek *polis* and the Roman *civitas*. In the cultural splendor of the *polis*, public action taken by free men showed what freedom meant. Who somebody was was revealed by his actions, in his narrative about these actions, in the consultations about laws in warfare, and in sports.

Arendt knew very well that the separation of the public political sphere from "the social sphere" had vanished in modern times. She also knew that the political sphere was overlapped by laboring and using. And yet she maintained "that the measure can neither be the driving necessity of biological life and labor nor the utilitarian instrumentalism of fabrication and usage."[12]

In the end, she maintained that, first, political action and speaking are only possible in a common space. Second, political action is directed toward the fellow citizens and not toward a fixed end. Therefore, action cannot be identified with laboring or using. Rather, it aims at mutual understanding about the "common good." One result can be—like in the American Revolution—a constitution.

IV.

Throughout their lives, both Arendt and Benjamin were reflecting on the deep crisis in Western thought and politics. However, they did this from slightly different perspectives. Benjamin looked upon the crisis from a time period in between two catastrophes: the primal catastrophe of World War I and the impending disaster of World War II. He evoked the hope that mankind would be saved. At the same time, he himself did not believe in his own salvation.

However, Arendt, having personally escaped the catastrophe of war and genocide, evoked the human ability to start from anew. She took this possibility from the human ability to create new life. For her, the fact of a new life created the possibility of starting anew politically.

The fundamental difference between them comes from their different methodological approaches to the question of the political. On his part Benjamin merged elements of Jewish theology with the reference to a political metaphysics. Regarding his discourse on the political, we have to keep in mind that many of his texts circle around the notion of revelation. His thoughts kind of encircle the moment when the Messiah should appear—the Messiah taken as a metaphor for a sudden and even miraculous event that enables salvation.

It is Benjamin's project to merge historical materialism and theology in order to provide the concept of the revolution with a theological legitimation. For him, revolution is the only possibility to evoke the moment in which everything is possible. But only revelation can transfer the messianic moment into the political realm. That is basically his late concept of the political.

However, Arendt starts on a different path. As a survivor of the catastrophe, she had also experienced the totalitarian potential of the revolution. Moreover, she was convinced that the event of totalitarian rule had basically ruined all analytical concepts. Benjamin, however, followed the idea that false concepts can be changed by giving them different connotations. On the other hand, Arendt was kind of forced to go beyond the contemporaneous concepts, ending at the roots of political thinking in antiquity. Methodologically, she takes a step that separates her from the entire academic and scientific world. She dissolves the classical concept of the traditional subject, though not in the way Benjamin does: she transfers it into a new concept of freedom as being a capacity of man. Instead of coming up with a new essential definition, she opens up the concept of plurality, which is something quite different from Benjamin's concept of the collective subject. Benjamin, on his side, relies heavily on the concept of collective subjectivity ("class" combined with "mass" linked to a quite obscure concept of an elite).

Notwithstanding basic differences between them, Arendt refers to a metaphysical moment in the concept of the political. She shares Benjamin's point of view that it is the sudden event that can turn the world around. Another hint to Arendt's "political metaphysics" is her reference to the Pilgrims of the *Mayflower* concluding a mutual covenant between themselves in order to create a political community reliant upon its citizens.[13] However, they did that in reference to their God.

We all know that there was no new beginning in the Arendtian sense. Likewise, the promise of a secular redemption in the discourse of Benjamin has vanished from the public discourse. But this was what they thought to be an alternative to liberalism.

Last but not least, for us, the basic question always remains: what/who occupies the empty space of the metaphysical reference of "the political"? This remains an unsolvable dilemma in modernity.

Let me summarize by quoting Ernst-Wolfgang Böckenförde, former judge at the German Supreme Court and constitutional theorist: "The modern liberal secular state exists of preconditions he cannot guarantee."[14] One may assume that both Arendt and Benjamin have tried to encounter the dilemma of modernity, namely by creating—paradoxically enough—a kind of "secular political metaphysics."

Works Cited

Walter Benjamin. *Gesammelte Briefe*. 6 vols. Edited by Christoph Gödde and Helmuth Lonitz. Frankfurt am Main: Suhrkamp, 1995–2000. Hereafter GB.

———. *Gesammelte Schriften: Werkausgabe*. 17 vols. Edited by Rolf Tiedemann et al. Frankfurt am Main: Suhrkamp, 1972–91. Hereafter GS.

———. *Kritische Gesamtausgabe*. Edited by Christoph Gödde and Henri Lonitz. Frankfurt am Main: Suhrkamp, 2008– . Hereafter KGA.

1. This paper was given at the Hannah Arendt Center on 29 November 2019. It refers to my book *Götterdämmerung Aufstieg und Fall der deutschen Intelligenz 1900–1940: Walter Benjamin und seine Zeit* (Freiburg: Herder, 2018).

2. See Georges Sorel, *Über die Gewalt* (Reflections on Violence) (Berlin, 1928), 143f.

3. See Erich Unger, *Politik und Metaphysik* (Politics and Metaphysics) (Berlin, 1921), 48.

4. See Walter Benjamin, letter to Carl Schmitt, 9 December 1930, in GB III, S. 558.

5. See Walter Benjamin, "Theologisch-politisches" (fragment), in GS II.1, 203ff.

6. See Georg Lukács, *Geschichte und Klassenbewusstsein* (Berlin: Malik, 1923).

7. See Walter Benjamin, "Eduard Fuchs, der Sammler und der Historiker," in GS II.2, 465ff.

8. Walter Benjamin, letter to Gretel Adorno, April/May 1940, in *Walter Benjamin / Gretel Adorno: Briefwechsel 1930–1940,* ed. Christoph Gödde and Henri Lonitz (Frankfurt am Main: Suhrkamp, 2005), S. 410 (my translation); regarding the connection of these reflections to his Baudelaire project, see also Benjamin, letter to Adorno, 7 May 1940, in GB VI, S. 447.

9. Walter Benjamin, "Thesen über die Geschichte," in KGA, vol. 19 (2010), 97 (my translation).

10. René Char, in Hannah Arendt, *Between Past and Future* (New York: Viking Press, 1961), 3.

11. Hannah Arendt, *The Origins of Totalitarianism*, new ed. with added prefaces (San Diego: Harcourt Brace Jovanovich, 1979), 479.

12. Hannah Arendt, *The Human Condition* (Chicago: University of Chicago Press, 1958), 174.

13. I am reminded here of the beautiful book *Exodus und Revolution* by Michael Walzer (Berlin: Rotbuch-Verlag, 1988).

14. Wolfgang Boeckenfoerde, "Die Entstehung des Staates als Vorgang der Saekularisation," in Sergius Buve, *Saekularisation und Utopie: Ernst Forsthoff zum 65*, Ebracher Studien (Stuttgart: Kohlhammer, 1967), 75–94.

"Der Holzweg": Heidegger's Dead End

Philippe Nonet

To what end should thinking be devoted? How and why did the question of being become a dead end for thought? What is to take its place as the key concern of thinking? What did Heidegger say regarding this matter? Such are the leading questions that will presently occupy us.

The notes Heidegger wrote to himself while working on *das Ereignis* have now been published in the edition of his collected writings. There, Heidegger comments upon his earlier publication of *Holzwege*[1] (Tracks in the Woods):

> *Man hat diesen Titel nicht ernst genommen. Man hat nicht beachtet, daß die unter diesem Titel gesammelten Abhandlungen in die Entfaltung der Seinsfrage gehören. Man hat nicht gedacht, daß diese Entfaltung und die Seinsfrage selbst—der Holzweg des Denkens sind.*[2]

(One has not taken this title seriously. One has not noticed that the essays gathered under this title belong in the unfolding of the question of being. One did not think that this unfolding and the question of being itself—are **der** Holzweg, *the* dead end, of thinking.)

Often "tracks in the woods" lead nowhere: they are "dead ends," so much so that in German "*Holzweg*" is understood as "*Irrweg*," a "wrong track." To Heidegger, the question of being had been *the* dead-end that prevented thinking from moving in proper direction.

Recall now that *die Seinsfrage* (the question of being) had long been regarded by Heidegger as **die** *Sache des Denkens* (*the* matter for thought), namely, what called upon man to think, *das Geheiß* (the call), and what determined the task of thinking, *die Aufgabe des Denkens*. Since it had been a dead end, *das Sein* had to be abandoned as *die Sache des Denkens*. Thinking had now to devote itself to another task.

This was to be *das Ereignis*, which was no longer to be understood in its ordinary sense as "event," derived from "*Er-äugnen*," but was instead constructed as a formation of "*eignen*," to be translated as "appropriation." The decision to elevate *Ereignis* to the position *das Sein* occupies as *die Sache des Denkens* is not publicly made until later in a difficult lecture, "*Zeit und Sein*" ("Time and Being," 1962), to be published even later (in 1969) in a short collection under the title *Zur Sache des Denkens*[3] (On the Matter for Thought).

The decision entailed a change in Heidegger's account of the relation between *Sein* and *Ereignis*. Until then, since about 1936, Heidegger spoke and wrote of "*das Sein als Ereignis*" (being as event), an ambiguous phrase, apt to suggest a certain equivalence of the two thoughts. With "*Zeit und Sein*," *Ereignis* comes to define the "*es*" employed in the phrases "*es gibt Sein*" and "*es gibt Zeit*"; *Ereignis* gives being, and *Ereignis* gives time. The "gifts" of both being and time, and their mutual relation, are now to be thought of as "resting," *beruhen*, in *das Ereignis*.[4] "*Sein verschwindet im Ereignis*"[5] (being vanishes into appropriation).

One may well wonder how seriously Heidegger could have meant that the *Seinsfrage* had been a *Holzweg*, given that the question of being had guided nearly the whole of his work until then. The assertions in his notebooks[6] are unqualified and seem unambiguous. It remains, however, that before the *Gesamtausgabe* (complete edition) of his works Heidegger did not publish any statement that could be construed as such a repudiation. On the other hand, Heidegger approached publication itself with a healthy measure of distrust. No discussion of *das Ereignis* appears in print until 1954,[7] more than twenty years after Heidegger began writing about it in his notebooks. He feared that, with publication, his most essential thoughts would fall into the domain of scholarly chatter, and thus lose their ability to serve as pointers to what is worthy of thought.

We must examine the grounds upon which he first embraced, and then repudiated, *das Sein* as *die Sache des Denkens* (being as the matter for thought). Heidegger justified his embrace on grounds of the "difference" between *das Sein* and *das Seiende*. English is unable to state a distinction between "*sein*" and "*seiend*" because it employs the same grammatical form, namely "being," for both the participle, "*seiend*," and the gerund, "*das Sein*." We shall therefore always employ the untranslated German words. A concise and quite common way of restoring a difference between *sein* and *seiend* in translation is to capitalize "Being" when it renders the gerund, *das Sein*. Convenience dictates that we follow that rather mechanical practice in the text that follows, hoping with little hope that the capital will not be read as attributing divinity or sanctity to Being.

The distinction between *Sein* and *Seiende* has ancient foundations in earlier philosophy, but Heidegger was the first to call it by a formal name: the "ontological difference." His later repudiation of *das Sein* rested in turn upon his finding that *das Ereignis* made it necessary to abandon the ontological difference, "*die ontologische Differenz zu erlassen*."[8]

Our task accordingly divides itself into two parts. The first is to explain the sense of the ontological difference, and the reason why Heidegger held on to it for so long. The second is to show how the thought of *Ereignis* eventually required "abandoning" this ancient principle and founding a radically new thinking.

I. The Ontological Difference

The principle of the ontological difference asserts that a "difference" separates *das Sein* from *das Seiende*. The principle is first stated by Heidegger himself in *Sein und Zeit* (Being and Time), twice in paragraph 1 and again in paragraph 2:

> *"Sein" kann in der Tat nicht als Seiendes begriffen werden.* . . .
> *"Sein" ist nicht so etwas wie Seiendes.* . . . *Das Sein des Seienden*
> *ist nicht selbst ein Seiendes* ("Being" cannot be conceived as a
> being. . . . "Being" is not something like a being. . . . The
> Being of beings is not itself a being).[9]

Notice that the difference is asserted here as quite unproblematic. It is not put into question. No attention is paid even to the manifest grammatical ambiguities of the statements. Does not the naming of *"das Sein"* as a *nomen* instead of a *verbum* entail conceiving it already as something that "is," *ein Seiendes*? Does not the participle, *"seiend,"* have a verbal as well as a nominal sense?

The difference is not given its formal name until shortly thereafter in *"Vom Wesen des Grundes"* (On the essence of ground).[10] It is called "ontological" because it constitutes the indispensable premise of all "ontology." Ontology, in turn, is that part of philosophy which concerns the λόγος τοῦ ὄντος (in Latin, the *ratio entium*). In German it is *"der Grund des Seienden"* (the ground of what is). Its fundamental principle is that *das Sein* itself "is" ground—that is, λόγος, *ratio*, of *das Seiende*; hence the necessity of difference as a premise of ontology.

Thus the ontological difference is not just a distinction between concepts. It cannot be thought on the model of logic as a contradiction, the terms of which may then be reconcilable in a Hegelian dialectic. It concerns a phenomenon in the broad sense of the word, a state of affairs—*ein Sach-Verhalt*—that shows itself in the world.

Heidegger held on to the "ontological difference" for most of his life as a thinker.[11] He asserts it once again in the last major essay that he published, a few months before announcing it would have to be given up. *"Zeit und Sein"* launches its argument from the following starting point:

> *Ist das Sein so wie ein jeweilig Seiendes in der Zeit? Ist das Sein über-*
> *haupt? Würde es sein, dann müßten wir es unweigerlich als etwas*
> *Seiendes anerkennen und demzufolge unter dem übrigen Seienden als*
> *ein solches vorfinden. Dieser Hörsaal ist. Der Hörsaal ist beleuchtet. Den*
> *beleuchteten Hörsaal werden wir ohne weiteres und ohne bedenken als*
> *etwas Seiendes anerkennen. Aber wo im ganzen Hörsaal finden wir das*
> *"ist"? Nirgends unter den Dingen finden wir das Sein. Jedes Ding hat*
> *seine Zeit. Sein aber ist kein Ding, is nicht in der Zeit.* . . . *Sein—eine*
> *Sache, vermutlich die Sache des Denkens . . . aber nichts Seiendes.* . . .

*Vom Seienden sagen wir: es ist. In der Hinsicht auf die Sache "Sein" .
. . bleiben wir vorsichtig. Wir sagen nicht: Sein ist, . . . sondern es gibt
Sein.*[12]

(Is Being like a current being in time? Is Being at all? If it were,
then we would inevitably have to recognize it as a being and con-
sequently find it as such among other beings in time. This auditorium *is*. The auditorium *is* lighted. This lighted auditorium we
shall recognize as a being without further ado and without any
doubt. But where in the whole auditorium do we find the "is"?
Nowhere among things do we find Being. Everything has its
time, but Being is no thing, is not in time. . . . Being—a concern,
presumably *the* concern of thinking . . . but nothing that is. . . . Of
a being we say: it *is*. With respect to this concern "Being" . . . we
remain prudent. We do not say: Being is . . . but it gives Being.)[13]

The last sentence of that quote makes no sense in English. One wonders:
What is "it"? Whence this "giving"? And looks in vain for an answer. These
two questions turn out to be key focal points of Heidegger's essay.

There follows an argument the chief conclusion of which is that *"im
Verhältnis von Sein und Zeit"* (in the relation of Being and time),

*zeigt sich ein Zueignen, ein Übereignen, nämlich von Sein als Anwesenheit
und von Zeit als Bereich des Offenen in ihr Eigenes. Was beide, Zeit und
Sein, in ihr Eigenes, d.h. in ihr Zusammengehören, bestimmt, nennen
wir: das Ereignis* (there shows itself a belonging-to, a conveying,
namely of Being as presence and of time as domain of the open,
in what is proper to them. What determines both time and Being
in what is proper to them, i.e., in their belonging-together, we
call: *das Ereignis*).[14]

Only a few months later does Heidegger announce for the first time in a
published statement that this *Verhältnis*

*ist nicht ohne Schwierigkeit. . . . Die Hauptschwierigkeit liegt darin,
daß vom Ereignis her nötig wird, die ontologische Differenz zu erlassen*
([This relation] is not without difficulty. . . . The chief difficulty
lies in that out of *Ereignis* it becomes necessary to abandon the
ontological difference).[15]

What had held Heidegger attached to the ontological difference? It
enabled him to relate the course of his own thinking to that of his predecessors, while at the same time distinguishing it from theirs. Ever since Aristotle's

Metaphysics, the defining focus of philosophy has been the question regarding the essence of *das Sein*, the ἀεὶ ζητούμενον καὶ ἀεὶ ἀπορούμενον, τί τὸ ὄν, τίς ἡ οὐσία,[16] what is always sought and always unattained: What is a being? What is Being? Heidegger embraced the tradition but found it came up short in one major respect. Philosophy had, from its very beginnings, conceived *das Sein* (Being) as "ground," λόγος, or *ratio* of *das Seiende* (what is), either as origin of all common features of das *Seiende* (τὸ κοινόν, e.g., unity, identity, constancy, etc.), or as ultimate cause of its actuality (τὸ θεῖον). Thus philosophy represented *das Sein* (Being) only for the sake of *das Seiende* (what is), subordinating the ground to the grounded. Heidegger resolved instead to consider *das Sein* *"für sich"* or *"an sich," "als solches"*—Being "for itself" or "in itself," "as such"; that is,

> *ohne die Rücksicht auf eine Begründung des Seins aus dem Seienden,*
> *[durch welche] das Sein gedacht und begriffen wird umwillen des*
> *Seienden, so daß das Sein, unbeschadet seines Grund-seins, unter der*
> *Botmäßigkeit des Seienden steht* (without regard for the grounding
> of Being out of beings, [in which] Being is thought and conceived
> for the sake of beings, so that Being, despite its essence as ground,
> stands under subordination to beings).[17]

This oblivion of *das Sein*, *die Seinsvergessenheit*, the forgottenness of Being, cannot be understood as a consequence of some failure or negligence on the part of the thinkers who founded philosophy. *Das Sein* itself invites it. Even as it opens the clearing in which *das Seiende* comes to manifestness, it keeps itself out of that revelation, as though it would efface itself for the sake of what it reveals. Never does *das Sein* appear as *ein Seiendes*, a being among others. Its own essence is to remain concealed. Of itself it would allow thinking to represent it as merely an empty abstraction.

Neither the thought of *"das Sein als solches"* (Being as such) nor that of the oblivion of *das Sein* can be articulated without a statement of the difference between *das Sein* (Being) and *das Seiende* (what is). Both thoughts were crucial to the determination of Heidegger's intellectual development. How, then, did the ontological difference come to lose its position of virtually unquestionable authority?

II. *Das Ereignis*
The decisive objection to the ontological difference was that it reifies the concepts of both *Sein* and *Seiendes*, Being and what is. The word "reification" does not occur here in Heidegger's own vocabulary; it may nevertheless have the advantage of familiarity to English-speaking readers. At times, but not in this context, Heidegger speaks of a *Verdinglichung* (reification) or *Vergegenständigung* (objectification) of man's humanity.[18] Here, in Heidegger's

own words, the ontological difference is said to represent both *Sein* and *Seiendes* as "*auseinander-gesetzt und für sich selbst gesetzt*"[19] (posed out of each other and posed for itself). Reification speaks of both *Sein* and *Seiendes* as though each could be thought "*als solches*" (as such) independent of its relation to the other:

> *Doch was heißt hier "Sein selbst" —? Meint der Titel das vom Seienden abgelöste "Sein für sich"? Bleibt nicht Sein als es selbst gerade das Anwesenlassen von Anwesendem?* (But what does "Being itself" say here? Does the name mean "Being for itself" detached from what is? Does not Being itself remain precisely the letting-be-present of the present?)[20]

> *Wie vermag es Sein gegen Seiendes zu unterscheiden wenn im "Seienden" schon Sein "liegt"?* (How can one distinguish Being from what is if Being already lies in what is?)[21]

> *Sein ist nie ohne Offenbarkeit von Seiendem zu denken* (Being can never be thought without the manifestness of beings).[22]

> Just as Being cannot be conceived without beings, so can a being itself not be separated from Being; the name itself says it: "*nicht von vereinzelten 'Dingen' ausgehen—was es gar nicht gibt—jedes Ding = ereignetes Geviert*" (not to proceed from singular "things"—there are none—every single thing is appropriated fourfold).[23]

Above all, and by the same token, the ontological difference misrepresents the very difference of which it speaks: It fixes attention upon the "different" at the expense of the differing of their "difference" proper:

> *Man hat sich unversehens auf das Differieren von Seiendem und Sein festgelegt, auf Differentes bei vergessener Differenz; damit fängt die Philosophie an und darin bewegt sich ihre ganze Geschichte als Metaphysik* (One has unwittingly focused on the differing of beings from Being, on the different in the forgotten difference; so does philosophy begin and therein its whole history moves as metaphysics).[24]

The reification of difference was indeed indispensable insofar as philosophy intended to maintain a properly "meta-physical," that is, "transcendental," account of man's relation to Being, *das Sein*, as a rising ("*Übersteigung*") of mind above the realm of sensuous "nature."

Against metaphysics, Heidegger insists that

> *der Unterschied [ist] nicht Trennung als Zerreißen und Zernichtung—sondern Austrag. . . . So ereignet sich die Nähe und hier erst die Ferne des aufeinander Zukommens des je Eigenen und Unverwechselbaren* (difference is not separation as tearing apart and annihilation—but a drawing out. . . . So emerges the nearness and here first the distance of the coming upon one another of what is proper to each and cannot be confused).[25]

"*Unterschied*" is German for the Latin "*differentia*," and says nothing else. Given the reification of "difference" and "different," the doctrine as a whole had to be given up. Judging from Heidegger's notebooks, the sole ground of this necessity was *das Ereignis* itself as *das Zusammengehören des Gegenwendigen* (*Ereignis* itself as the belonging together of opposites). Both "*Gehören*" and "*Gegenwendigkeit*" require closer examination.

Gehören is a formation of *hören* (to hear, to listen, to obey). The thought of obedience, *Hörigkeit*, brings into play that of being in the service (*das Dienen*) of a master. Thus the *Ereignis* of *das Sein* and *das Menschenwesen* (Being and the essence of man) calls upon man to let himself be placed in the service of truth as the unconcealment (*Entbergung*) of Being. Man is to be "used" (*gebraucht*) by *das Sein* for the sake of its own revelation, *Enthüllung*. *Es gibt kein Sein ohne das Menschenwesen* (There is no Being without the essence of man).

The relation between man and Being has the character of a "*Brauch*," a use or employment by virtue of which man becomes a property, *Eigentum*, of the truth of Being. Whence the word "*Ereignis*," a formation of the German verb "*eignen*" (to belong to), various forms of which—for example, *aneignen* (to acquire), *übereignen* (to convey), *zueignen* (to dedicate)—are used to denote aspects of appropriation. *Ereignis* never "is" anything other than a possible fulfillment of the essence of both man and Being; it can never be found as "actual," as a "fact" of which one can say that it "is." It *is* not, nor can one say that "*es gibt das Ereignis*." All that can be said is that "*Ereignis ereignet*," a manifest tautology.

Das Ereignis, as mutual belonging, presupposes a *Zerklüftung*, a cleavage of what it *ereignet* (brings together). This opposition, *Gegenwendigkeit*, has the character of a movement by which the opponents separate from each other in such a way that each becomes more properly its own self. But this separation is no "parting," no *Trennung*. On the contrary, it deepens the mutual belonging—*das Ereignis*—of the opponents. Instead of difference, Heidegger finds the German word "*Unter-Scheiden*," almost always spelled with a hyphen, less suitable to convey the thought of differing than "*Austragen*," a drawing out that would sustain unity in difference.[26]

But what is this *Gegenwendigkeit* (opposition) now that the ontological difference has been ruled out as a possibility? Answer: the *Zwiefalt* of *Sein* and *Seiende*s (the twofold of Being and being) has now given way to a *Vierfalt* (fourfold), produced by the crossing (*die Kreuzung*) of two other primordial differences, the strife (*der Streit*) between sky and earth and the encounter (*die Entgegnung*) of gods and mortals.[27] Of the two differences, the second is a byproduct of the first, which speaks to a primordial experience of human existence: Man finds himself standing on the ground under the open vault of heaven. Since Earth and Sky are primordial divinities, their evidence is at once a revelation of the encounter of gods and mortals. The crossing of the two differences yields a differentiation of four open expanses, *Gegenden*, the unity of which is the world, *die Welt*, ὁ κόσμος.[28]

It would appear that, were a relation (*Verhältnis*) among human beings to be stamped with the character of *Ereignis*, it would bear the name of "friendship," φιλία. Indeed, in notes that Heidegger wrote in the mid 1940s, he goes so far as to call *Ereignis* "*Liebe*" (love), a name he never uses in his published writings.[29]

Not far removed lies a thought—never proposed by Heidegger in the following words—that *Ereignis* constitutes a supreme law of universal harmony, for beings of nature as well as for man. The scope of *Ereignis* is indeed coextensive with being as whole, *das Seiende im Ganzen*. But since, in his later years, *das Sein* no longer stands as *die Sache des Denkens* (the matter for thought), Heidegger will no longer speak of *das Seiende im Ganzen*. In its place—if we may point to such formal equivalences—he prefers "the play of the worlding of world," *das Spiel des Weltens der Welt*. "Harmony" in turn becomes *die Fuge des Verhältnisses von Ding und Welt*, the joining of the relation of thing and world. Indeed, Heidegger expels from his language virtually all of the conceptual vocabulary of philosophy. The harmony of *Ereignis* echoes a theme of ancient Greek thought to which Plato once alluded:

> Φασὶ δ' οἱ σοφοί . . . καὶ οὐρανὸν καὶ γῆν καὶ θεοὺς καὶ ἀνθρώπους τὴν κοινωνίαν συνέχειν καὶ φιλίαν . . . καὶ τὸ ὅλον τοῦτο διὰ ταῦτα κόσμον καλοῦσιν (The wise say . . . that sky and earth and gods and men are held together by community and friendship . . . and that is why they call this whole a world).[30]

In a short series of notes written soon after 1945, Heidegger calls *das Ereignis*

> *die Eschatologie des Seyns, das ist: Daß der Unterschied aus der Vergessenheit zur Sprache kommt, die Sprache heimsucht—[das ist: ein] Sich-Zu-Sagen der Sage* (the eschatology of Being, that is: That difference emerges from oblivion and comes to speech, seeks a home in language—a self-saying of the essence of language, *die Sage*).[31]

Ereignis teaches the "ultimate word," that the belonging of man to the truth of Being promises to bring a "healing" or "saving" (*die Rettung*) of man and thing from the devastation of earth under the sway of technique. The thought of *Ereignis* as salvation will retain its prominence in later work, but then without word of a "last word."

---

1. *Holzwege*, Gesamtausgabe (hereafter GA), Bd. 5 (1950; Frankfurt am Main: Klostermann, 1977).

2. *Zum Ereignis-Denken*, GA Bd. 73 (2013), 1285–86.

3. *Zur Sache des Denkens* (Tübingen: Max Niemayer Verlag, 1969), GA Bd. 14 (2007), 3–30.

4. Ibid., 24–25.

5. Ibid., 27.

6. See, e.g., GA Bd. 73, 1221, 1225, 1261, 1270, 1280, 1281, 1287.

7. *Vorträge und Aufsätze* (Neske: Pfullingen, 1954), GA Bd. 7, 33, 69, 77, 98, 134, 142, 175, 179, 180ff., 283, 285.

8. Martin Heidegger, "Protokoll zu einem Seminar über dem Vortrag 'Zeit und Sein,'" in *Zur Sache des Denkens*, GA Bd. 14, 46.

9. GA Bd. 2 (1927, 1977), 4 and 8.

10. In *Festschrift Edmund Husserl zum 70: Geburtstag gewidmet* (1929); reprinted as an offprint by Vittorio Klostermann, Frankfurt (1949), 7. Auflage (1983), 14.

11. That is not to say that Heidegger never had any reservations about it; see, e.g., *Beiträge zur Philosophie*, GA Bd. 65 (1936–38, 1989), sect. 132, 250; sect. 151, 273; sect. 268, 465. But they never reached the level at which it became necessary to abandon *das Sein* as *die Sache des Denkens*.

12. GA Bd. 14, 7–9.

13. "*Es gibt*" cannot readily be translated into English. It is commonly rendered as "there is," but here its negative point is precisely to avoid asserting that *das Sein* "is." The French phrase "*il y a*" poses the same problems.

14. Ibid., 24.

15. "Protokoll," 46.

16. *Met.* VII, 1, 1028b1.

17. "Protokoll," 41.

18. See, e.g., *Zollikoner Seminare*, ed. Medard Boss, 2nd ed. (Frankfurt am Main: Klostermann, 1994), 271.

19. GA Bd. 73, 1331.

20. Ibid., 1313.

21. Ibid., 984.

22. Ibid., 975.

23. Ibid., 1343.

24. Ibid., 976.

25. Ibid., 905.

26. "*Differenz*," from the Latin "*differre*" (i.e., dis-ferre: "to carry away from"), is said in German as "Aus-trag," in Greek as δια-φορά. Heidegger's attempt to distinguish *Austrag* and διαφορά from *Differenz* has no etymological or semantic support.

27. These two differences, if not the fourfold itself, are a manifest echo of ancient Greek mythology. See particularly Hesiod's *Theogony* and the marriage of Earth and Sky. One finds an allusion to them in Plato, "Gorgias," 507e5–508a1.

28. The fourfold is spelled out by Heidegger when he first articulates the thought of *Ereignis* in the mid to late 1930s, thus long before the ontological difference is "abandoned." See *Beiträge zur Philosophie*, GA Bd. 65 (1936–38, 1989), sect. 10, 30; *Besinnung*, GA Bd. 66 (1938–39, 1997), sect. 8, 15.

29. GA Bd. 73, 916–17.

30. *Gorgias*, 507 E 5–508 A 1.

31. *Zum Ereignis-Denken*, GA Bd. 73, 1174–84. The word "eschatology" is also used, without explicit reference to *das Ereignis*, in "Der Spruch des Anaximander" (1946), *Holzwege*, GA Bd. 5, 6.

Woman as Witness, Beginner, Philosopher

Jana V. Schmidt

In "Regarding the Cave," the Italian feminist philosopher Adriana Cavarero offers a reading of Plato's allegory of the cave that expands on an interpretation of that same narrative by Hannah Arendt. Cavarero is perhaps the first to notice how Arendt's remarks in "Tradition and the Modern Age," "What Is Authority?," and *The Human Condition* connect, how together they form a spirited critique of Western philosophy, and how indispensable they are for a feminist reckoning with what might be called masculinist ontology. This last project is further developed by Cavarero in her 1995 monograph *In Spite of Plato: A Feminist Rewriting of Ancient Philosophy*, which presents Arendtian natality alongside the philosophy of sexual difference to bend ancient myths toward their slighted female heroines. In her discussion, the question of whether Hannah Arendt was a feminist is immaterial to Cavarero, and yet in reading Cavarero and Arendt together I am left with the sense that any feminism worth arguing for would be centrally concerned with the possibility of women-as-philosophers, and with their dialogue. In this spirit, I want to follow feminist readers of Arendt in engaging her in a dialogue with two female philosophers—Cavarero and the French philosopher Catherine Malabou—as all three wrestle with the legacy of the philosophical universal.

> No doubt woman will never become impenetrable, inviolable. That's why it is necessary to imagine the possibility of woman starting from the structural impossibility she experiences of not being violated, in herself and outside, everywhere. An impossibility that echoes the impossibility of her welcome in philosophy. (Malabou 2011, 140)

In her book *Changing Difference*, Catherine Malabou underscores that the impossibility of a woman philosopher—"there is no woman philosopher"—is foundational to the *possibility* of philosophy, because only the long exclusion of women has rendered the thinking of its concepts "pure." If women were to challenge philosophy as they have challenged art and literature, Malabou claims, they would "change the given rules" rather than continuing to receive the same old questions (102). Because the feminine is split between its actual, ontological, and metaphorical repression by philosophy, which renders it a modality of being that is always yet to arrive, *and* its simultaneous boundedness to an essential position, which forever ties it back to established dichotomies, Malabou turns to a reconsideration of the concept of essence as "plastic."

In the female body she locates an "essence" that resists the immateriality of the trace (121).

Malabou's insistence on embodiment joins her approach with most varieties of feminist critique—a shared emphasis that stems from the fundamental fact that women have not recognized themselves in the mirror that representations by men hold up to them. Women find themselves the "object, not the subject, of the other's thought" (Cavarero 1995, 2), such that a mere reference by a woman to herself and to her sexed body can have a disruptive effect on the assumptions of neutrality and universality that come with the notion of "man" (or its contemporary replacement, the supposedly even more disinterested "guys"). "Man," this Arendt knew, is a dangerous abstraction—not, to be sure, because she was interested in the overwriting of sexual difference. Rather, Arendt's critique of the concept of man aims at the philosophical solipsism of thinking man as *one*. But—and this I would call Arendt's feminism—the two criticisms are inextricably linked; feminism is necessarily a tearing down of individualism. Thus, much like thinkers of sexual difference, Arendt announces that the new political philosophy would have to begin with two, not one. And again like feminist interpreters, she underlines that the *two* of difference describes, at its most basic level, the distinction between male and female: "'Male and female created He *them*'" (Arendt 1998, 8). Thus, the *given* is plural; "in its elementary form" it is the difference that marks "them."

In this light, the important question for feminists should not be whether Hannah Arendt is a fellow traveler but in what sense she is a "woman philosopher." Does Arendt challenge the rules of the game of philosophy in Malabou's sense? Are her questions different from those posed by a long line of (male) philosophers? Does she allow us to posit a different notion of "woman"? To ask this last question is to advance a definition of "woman" that is neither essentialist—as some critics have understood Arendt's frequently cited admission of a "rather old-fashioned" attitude toward the woman question and the "problem as such" (Arendt 2013, 4)—nor entirely "empty" (i.e., completely exhausted by its social function) but rather tries to open the signifier "woman" to its more than binary possibilities. Arguably, Arendt begins to do so herself when she defines her position as "*feminini generis*" in her acceptance speech upon receiving the Sonning Prize in 1975. There she speaks of her femininity as phenomenologically tied, from the get-go, to other qualities of being: "I am, as you know, a Jew, *feminini generis* as you can see, born and educated in Germany as, no doubt, you can hear" (Arendt 2003, 4). Vis-à-vis the binary options of being either female or male, another logic operates here: Jewish as you know, female as you can see, German as you can hear. Thus, if Arendt offers a change in perspective it is because she begins to rewrite political philosophy by taking "the structural impossibility" of not being divided as her premise.[1]

Cavarero notes that it is Arendt who, before similar poststructuralist critiques became commonplace, queries the philosophical tradition for its institution of the logic of binary oppositions. In Plato Arendt locates "a first turning-about which institutes the philosophical tradition 'in terms of opposites' and acts as a model for all successive overturnings which populate the history of philosophy" (Cavarero 1996, 2, 3). As her early essay "Tradition and the Modern Age" (1954) and its drafts show, Arendt's recognition of plurality thus flows from another "structural" insight: the oppositions and turns of Western philosophy are "predetermined by the conceptual structure" set by Plato's cave allegory. Though dichotomous thinking does not yet rule Socrates's dialogues, it begins to take shape in the "turnings-about" of the allegory. For Arendt, the story of the cave is a story of three turns, each of which implicates a "loss of sense":

> The story of the cave unfolds in three stages: The first turning around takes place in the cave itself when the cave-inhabitant frees himself from the chains which keep him and his outlook glued to the screen on which the [sh]adows and images of things appear and turns around to the rear of the cave where an artificial fire illuminates the things in the cave as they really are. There is second the turning from the cave to the clear sky where the ideas appear as true and eternal essences of the things in the cave, because they are illuminated by the sun, the idea of ideas, which makes it possible for man to see and for the ideas to appear. There is third the necessity of returning to the cave, of leaving the realm of eternal essences and mov[ing] again in the realm of perishable things and mortal men. Each of these turnings is accompanied by a loss of sense and orientation: the eyes used to the shadowy appearance on the screen are blinded by the fire in the cave; the eyes then adjusted to the dim light of the artificial fire are blinded by the light that illuminates the ideas; finally, the eyes adjusted to the light of the sun must re-adjust to the dimness of the cave. (Arendt 2018, 478)

A story about truth thus proceeds by blinding vision, disorienting the senses, and cleaving the soul from the measures of the body. As in the *Phaedo*, the task of philosophy must be to "untie the soul from the body" (Gallop 1975, 84a), to free it for contemplation and, ultimately, for death. Though the cave-dwelling philosopher must return to the cave of ignorance—armed with the criteria he gathered on his second turn—his deprivation actually sets him apart from the others, who continue to trust their impressions. Unlike them, his soul has learned "not [to] return to prior pleasures and pains, nor deliver itself to their chains"; it has realigned itself exclusively toward "discourse [*logismos*] and always keeping within it, by contemplating truth, the divine and what is not appearance" (Gallop 1975, 84a–b).

In "Tradition and the Modern Age," Arendt's provocative thesis is that Western dichotomies are established and "predetermined by the conceptual structure itself," a structure that Plato advances for polemical effect—"solely for political purposes" (Arendt 2018, 499)—against Homer and the world-embracing, sense-based ethos of literature. As a result, Plato's ideas are transcendent mainly with respect to the common world of the polis, which appears to him as a version of Hades. The "yardsticks" he seeks to set in stone transcend only that to which they are applied, the ever relative "realm where everything seems to dissolve into relationships and to be relative by definition" (481). Most of all, these measures resist being relatable to a human scale. Their transcendence lies in their "speechlessness." Nevertheless, the Platonic abstractions are enthroned as universals, and only those who are permitted to recognize themselves in their blinding light, only those who are similarly abstracted—disembodied, unsexed, unworldly—are fit to apply them to those who are not. It is through the depreciation of the polis as fakery that a novel mode of thinking gains traction: this is the mode of thinking in order to "unrelate."

In her gloss of Plato's and Arendt's texts, Cavarero concentrates on the persistent strangeness of the image of the cave. No explanation illuminates that dark hollow for her, since the political world "hardly resembles the cave imagined by Plato, with all of its tricks, traps, and devices" (Cavarero 1996, 10). Rather than presenting us with an analogue of the polis ("a shared scene in which 'human affairs' have the unforeseeable character of action and men themselves are shown to be a plurality of unique beings"), Plato's construction presents men as hypnotized "puppets . . . without any relation" (10) and the realm of ordinary life as if it "were a collective hypnosis or a cinema which always shows the same film" (14). For Cavarero, "the cave remains an image which is not adaptable to any notion of politics" (10). According to her reading, the reasons for what she calls the "bizarre" imagery of the allegory derive from the narrative doubling that allows Plato, the narrator, to escape Socrates's fate. While the "original" philosopher—who dwells very much among the living and whose philosophy consists in talking to ordinary people—is killed off, along with Homer's alluring stories, Plato escapes scot-free. In turn, the allegory also offers a visual substitute and persiflage, "a world centered around coerced visions where no one is looked at or spoken to" (19), to the oral, communicative fascination of the voice. It marks the regime change from Socratic dialogue to Platonic solitude. Contemplator: last man standing.

Clichés aside, the problem with Plato's survival (or "*Selbstbehauptung*"), as Arendt shows in *The Modern Challenge to Tradition*, is that the plural political realm begins to be ruled by the singular criteria of the philosopher. From then on, the subject of politics becomes the object of rule. Hannah Arendt's decisive contribution to a rethinking of Western political theory and to feminism is the insistent reminder that the subject of politics is *not one*. One of the most interesting questions for her work grows out of this density: how, from the insight that "plurality is *the* condition . . . of political life" (Arendt 1998, 7), does Arendt arrive at the contention that "natality . . . may be the central category of political, as distinguished from metaphysical, thought" (9)?

Never indivisible, never not violable, but also—and surely this is as important—more than one in her openness, "woman" complicates the very dualities she has been so firmly embedded in. Though this alternative ontology must ward off essentialist idealizations of pregnancy or motherhood, the long exclusion of pregnancy from masculine ontologies appears conspicuous—a strange gap in our accounts of being. Wouldn't a phenomenology of being have to begin with the beginning of being? Wouldn't it have to reckon with the simple fact that each one of us came not from "nowhere" but was born to a mother, who was also the first witness, the first other, the body and consciousness from whose divisibility issues a "new beginning"? Unlike the cave dwellers' static regard, seeing here does not imply a kind of passivity. The mother watches and brings her child into appearance. Unless prevented from doing so—and here we might speculate on the organization of childbirth in Western societies, replete with a theater of cutouts and sheets, screens, and anesthesia—her gaze accords recognition and thus *reality* to the newcomer. "Nothing and nobody exists in this world whose very being does not presuppose a *spectator*" (Arendt 1978, 19). Arendt here repeats what she had asserted almost twenty years earlier, at this time explicitly in the context of birth: "In other words, nothing that is, insofar as it appears, exists in the singular; everything that is is meant to be perceived by somebody. *Not Man but men inhabit this planet*. Plurality is the law of the earth" (19; my italics).[2]

If "men, not Man, live on the earth and inhabit the world," as Arendt had first argued in *The Human Condition* (7), this means that as beings who are born we are never alone. Acknowledging our "bornness" also implies something else, something that she stresses in *The Life of the Mind*: we are born on a particular planet called earth ("this planet"), and thus are "predetermined" in at least one way: our judgments and actions are "earthly," embodied and "born" judgments and actions. For feminist critics such as Cavarero or the Bulgarian-French philosopher Julia Kristeva, this does not mean that our existence is fixed, or that the parameters for action have already been staked out, but that the specificity of our appearance and the special, *born* and *birthing* form of our being-in-the-world can only be rendered neutral, isolated and unilateral through an enormous expenditure of habitual and largely unexceptional, daily violence.

Philosophically, the separation of birth from being enables a vision of being as suppressing mere "existence" (as "*Dasein*" and "*Mitsein*"). By assuming a deeper truth behind all appearances and ascribing to the "ground" a "higher rank of reality than what merely appeared" (Arendt 1978, 24), everything that appears takes on the attribute of that which is to be repressed, denied, and questioned. And yet as "ground," each manifestation of "being" is already shaped by the phenomenon of appearance. It follows that birth might be seen as that unique interface of two levels that never otherwise touch: the level of "expressiveness" that expresses nothing but itself and the level of the life process that exists "for the appearances" but does not itself appear.

The constitution of philosophy is bound up with the simultaneous exclusion of the maternal body and the political sphere of action. Hence, there is no woman philosopher. Except there are: in reading women philosophers like Cavarero, Malabou, Kristeva, and Arendt, philosophy and ontology appear in a new light to us—as violable, divisible, (inter)dependent, "plastic," disruptive, as beginning from the other.

Works Cited

Arendt, Hannah. 1978. *The Life of the Mind*. New York: Harcourt.

———. 1998. *The Human Condition*. Chicago: University of Chicago Press.

———. 2003. *Responsibility and Judgment*. Ed. Jerome Kohn. New York: Schocken Books.

———. 2013. *The Last Interview and Other Conversations*. Trans. Joan Stambaugh. New York: Melville House.

———. 2018. *The Modern Challenge to Tradition: Fragmente eines Buchs*. Complete Works, vol. 6. Goettingen: Wallstein Verlag.

Cavarero, Adriana. 1995. *In Spite of Plato: A Feminist Rewriting of Ancient Philosophy*. Cambridge (UK): Polity Books.

———. 1996. "Regarding the Cave." *Qui Parle* 10, no. 1 (Fall/Winter): 1–20.

Gallop, David, trans. 1975. *Plato: Phaedo*. Clarendon Plato Series. Oxford: Clarendon Press.

Malabou, Catherine. 2011. *Changing Difference*. Cambridge (UK): Polity Books.

---

1. My argument takes inspiration from Peg Birmingham's reading of *Love and Saint Augustine*, which posits that "through the feminine (the *principium* of the alien and the singular) one is able to love the neighbor in his or her singularity. Through Adam, human beings are united universally in their common humanity. Through Eve, each is related to the other in his or her 'absolute isolation'—namely, in his or her alienness, foreignness, and uniqueness." *Hannah Arendt and Human Rights: The Predicament of Common Responsibility* (Bloomington: Indiana University Press, 2006), 82.

2. Cavarero and other feminist scholars have criticized that Arendt hollows out the experience of birth from a relational event to a mere vehicle for the new beginning. For Cavarero, Arendt's newcomer "evokes an inhuman loneliness"; a loneliness Cavarero believes Arendt has to insist on in order to secure the ontological basis for action. Only if the newborn is made to appear as entirely independent from the mother (a fiction, since human babies obviously rely on a caretaker for much longer than most other species) can action thus appear as the spontaneous, free act of beginning. "Her reasoning works only if the scene of birth is used to represent the concept of beginning, which comes at the expense of a phenomenology of natality that would offer the chance to insist on something different: not only and not so much an anti-individualistic rational ontology, but above all a relationality marked by deep asymmetry and by originary dependency." See Cavarero, "'A Child Has Been Born unto Us,'" in *Inclinations: A Critique of Rectitude* (Palo Alto: Stanford University Press, 2016), 119. I think that the phenomenology of appearance as Arendt presents it in her final project, *The Life of the Mind*, complicates this reading.

Book Review

Arendt on the Political by David Arndt. Cambridge: Cambridge University Press, 2019

Review by Ellen M. Rigsby

David Arndt's (henceforth David A.) *Arendt on the Political* is an account of Hannah Arendt's theory of politics. Instead of understanding politics from a philosophical perspective, we should choose to understand what the "non-theoretical forms of thought that prevail in politics" tell us (85). He asks us to largely bracket political theorizing and come down from the realm of philosophy to consider the world of action. And his subject is Arendt because she is the only thinker to try to uncover the aspects of politics that are effaced by our philosophical approaches to it. One may well ask, is this not what political theorists have been doing with Arendt's work since at least George Kateb's *Hannah Arendt: Politics, Conscience, Evil* was published in 1983?[1] But David A. argues that political philosophy elides Arendt's fundamental account of politics with political theorizing, that is, with what he calls "concerns with the eternal, the necessary and the general" (84). It is philosophy's method of distillation from the specific to the general that causes us to misunderstand what politics means for the life of action, and instead explains what it is for the life of the mind. His introduction ends with a quote from page 20 of Arendt's *Essay in Understanding* "Every thought is an afterthought, that is, a reflection on some matter or event." The purpose of this book, then, is to elucidate Arendt's understanding of politics so that we can eliminate the confusions about politics that come from not just Arendt's life, but from our contemporary life.

The reason for engaging in this process is that "her work is an effort to understand the deepest differences between democratic politics and the anti-politics of totalitarianism" (32). And while he does not explicitly say so, the confusions he elaborates on, largely from Arendt's *The Human Condition*, are also laid at the door of contemporary politics. It is not only that Arendt's understanding of politics elucidates how political theory misses seeing the life of action, but also that that mistake sends us on the way to the antipolitics of totalitarianism, and that our particular political moment is enacting this confusion. Conceptually speaking, our confusion of philosophizing with understanding politics obfuscates several fundamental aspects of politics that he distills from Arendt's work. Specifically: because our political discourse tends to make everything political, we lose the genuine sense of politics; because we speak of politics in Social Darwinist or other discursive formats that control its aims and purposes, we mistake its aims and purposes; because we reduce politics to other spheres and discourses, we bring assumptions from those other spheres into politics; and because we approach it as a means to other ends, we forget that politics is a sphere with a dignity and purpose of its own, that it is an end in itself. Thus we forget and misunderstand the experience of politics by philosophizing about it.

The correction for this mistake requires an articulation of Arendt's method, something she rarely discusses explicitly in her writing, but which David A. gleans from her biography and letters. He begins chapter 1 by talking about Arendt the person, and the experiences that led her to write about politics. This intimacy with Arendt herself is bound to make those of us used to more distance from the person of the author to feel some possibly undesired voyeurism, especially because Arendt was not inclined to speak personally about herself; but the intimacy of this text with the historical Arendt lays the groundwork for its reliance on her version of Heidegger's articulation of phenomenology in *Being and Time* to understand politics, which requires experience as its basis. It may be possible to do this work without engaging with biography so directly, but David A. goes this route in the name of clarity and simplicity. If we are to talk about the experience of the political life, we ought to understand her experience of the rise of National Socialism in Germany and across Europe. The text's truth claims about the life of Hannah Arendt may raise concerns, and are ancillary to his main argument.

Chapter 2 of *Arendt on the Political* lays out the phases of Arendt's method systematically, and connects it explicitly to Heidegger's *Destruktion/Reduktion/Konstruktion* components of phenomenology in *Being and Time*. The method sketches out the structure for the rest of the book: David A. traces the genealogy of the inherited terms through which we understand politics, so we understand the authentic experiences from which they are born through Arendt's work. In the second phase of *Reduktion*, he articulates Arendt's particular example of the phenomenon of politics as understood by the ancient Greeks and, to a lesser extent, the ancient Romans; and in the third, he returns to the traditional concepts of politics, to understand their limits, and to add in the insights derived from the earlier two processes. This chapter may be the most interesting and surprising because Arendt does not write about her method. David A. notes that Arendt distinguishes her work from Heidegger's when she abandons the aims of philosophy in the contemplative life to properly encounter the active life of politics, which Heidegger never did, but her method here is understood as Heidegger's early phenomenology. In other words, the way to recover the active life of the political sphere is to follow Arendt through the Greeks and Romans, the "Western tradition," to discern the nontheoretical aspects of politics that we miss when theorizing about them.

The middle of the book traces the genealogies of political concepts Arendt writes about in the body of her work. There is a general footnote to several contemporary classicist historians who wrote about the polis and the ancient Greeks that indicate the sweep of the project, and its engagement with the literature that confirms Arendt's claims about the ancient world. (It is also a reference to the space limits for secondary literature in the footnotes. At a talk I attended by the author, he handed out copies of some of the footnotes he was asked to delete by his editor.) Nonetheless, there is a serious effort to demonstrate that Arendt's interpretations, especially of Greek and Roman thought, are born out by expert studies in classics. And as he moves forward into an analysis of the legacy of our misapprehension of what he calls the classical legacy, he remains deeply engaged with the literature of political theory. If we look at a specific instance of the genealogy in this interpretation, we can see how it works with respect to an aspect of the concept of law. The ancients did not worry about legitimacy, because laws (nomos) were understood to be of human making, and opposed to nature. Once law is understood to be a divine command, as in the Old Testament, which enters the tradition along with Christianity, we come to understand law not as something of human origin but as something that must be grounded by the divine. When we come to realize this change, we can revise our understanding of law, and can accept the idea implicit in the American Revolution that the ground of democratic law can be human-based consent. Of course, this conception does not come without friction because we do not choose the community into which we are born, but it does make clear that the Greeks had access to an understanding of law that bypasses the concern with legitimacy that is taken up in Arendt's discussion of the Revolution. David A.'s book follows suit with the other major concepts of politics that Arendt analyzes in her body of work. The attempt to lay out as clearly as possible what Arendt's sense of the political life succeeds to great effect, and is the book's greatest contribution.

There are tensions in the book that come out of its stylistic choices. The text emphasizes clarity of analysis so much that it eliminates some rhetorical niceties, such as transitions between ideas, and instead substitutes direct questions to move the narrative along. It also seems unnecessary to claim that we need to know Arendt's experience and intention to understand her explanation of political life. In a 2003 review of then recent monographs on Arendt, Mark Reinhardt asks whether "it is still possible, then, to do useful work on Arendt while staying close to Arendt's own thinking?"[2] He decides that it is, but that truth claims about intention needlessly problematize the epistemological field in which one is working. Reinhardt is concerned with the conflicting needs to claim that one is getting Arendt correct while claiming that adaptations of Arendt can stray from her simple and straightforward purpose. David A. addresses this problem well because he claims that Arendt's purpose, her elucidation of aspects of political life that political philosophy obscures, is all that he wants us to see, because it is the appropriate remedy to our own political moment. It is somewhat jarring nonetheless. In the end, though, there is a unity of purpose to *Arendt on the Political*. Understanding the practical aspects of political life always offers the possibility of beginning that life again. "While it is not a substitute for action, it illuminates and makes meaningful the sphere in which effective action is possible" (265). David A. seeks to remind us how to engage in political life in a moment where such life can be hard to find.

---

1. George Kateb, *Hannah Arendt: Politics, Conscience, Evil* (Towata: Rowman & Allenheld, 1983).
2. Mark Reinhardt, "What's New in Arendt?" *Political Theory* 31, no. 3 (June 2003): 443–60. DOI: 10.1177/0090591703251910.

Contributors

Contributors

David Arndt studied literature and philosophy as an undergraduate at Deep Springs College and Yale University, and earned a PhD in comparative literature at the University of California, Irvine, where he studied with Jean-François Lyotard and Jacques Derrida.

Peter Baehr is a research professor in social theory at Lingnan University, Hong Kong.

Etienne Balibar is emeritus professor of philosophy at the University of Paris–Nanterre and Anniversary Chair of Contemporary European Philosophy at Kingston University, London.

Seyla Benhabib is Eugene Meyer Professor of Political Science and Philosophy at Yale University and a former director of the university's Program on Ethics, Politics and Economics (2002–8).

Roger Berkowitz is the academic director of the Hannah Arendt Center for Politics and Humanities at Bard College.

Peter Brown is a PhD student in English language and literature at the University of California, Berkeley.

Raymond Geuss is emeritus professor in the Faculty of Philosophy, University of Cambridge.

Antonia Grunenberg is director of the Hannah Arendt Center at the University of Oldenburg.

Nacira Guénif-Souilamas is a professor of sociology and anthropology at University Paris 8 Vincennes–Saint-Denis.

Samantha Hill is the assistant director of the Hannah Arendt Center for Politics and Humanities and visiting assistant professor of political studies at Bard College, and associate faculty at the Brooklyn Institute for Social Research in New York City. She is the author of two forthcoming books: *Hannah Arendt*, a biography, and *Hannah Arendt's Poems*.

Martin E. Jay is Sidney Hellman Ehrman Professor Emeritus at the University of California, Berkeley. He is the author of 14 books, including *The Dialectical Imagination: A History of the Frankfurt School and the Institute of Social Research, 1923–50*.

Eric Kaufmann is professor and assistant dean of politics at Birkbeck College, University of London.

Jana Marlene Madar is a PhD candidate and scholarship holder in the Department for German Literature at the University of Munich. She is also a fellow at the Hannah Arendt Center for Politics and Humanities at Bard College and works as an author and translator.

Marwan Mohammed is a sociologist and research fellow at the French National Centre for Scientific Research (CNRS), and a visiting scholar at the John Jay College of Criminal Justice, City University of New York.

Philippe Nonet was a lecturer at the Catholic University of Louvain from 1966 to 1970 and a visiting professor at Bremen University in 1981. He is the author of *Administrative Justice* and *Law and Society in Transition*.

Ellen Rigsby is an associate professor at Saint Mary's College of California, where she teaches in the Communication Department, and has published works on Ursula Le Guin and Hannah Arendt.

Jana V. Schmidt is a writer, teacher, and translator living in Los Angeles. She is an associate fellow at the Hannah Arendt Center for Politics and Humanities at Bard College and the author of *Hannah Arendt und die Folgen* and a forthcoming book on Jewish-German exiles and black politics.

Adam Shatz is a contributing editor at the *London Review of Books* and a contributor to the *New York Times Magazine*, the *New York Review of Books*, the *New Yorker*, and other publications.

Natan Sznaider is a professor of sociology at the Academic College of Tel Aviv–Yaffo.

Eric K. Ward is executive director of the Western States Center.

John McWhorter is associate professor of English and comparative literature at Columbia University, teaching linguistics, Western civilization, and music history.

Marc Weitzmann is the author of 12 books, including *Hate: The Rising Tide of Anti-Semitism in France*.

Thomas Chatterton Williams is the author of a memoir, *Losing My Cool*, and a contributing writer at the *New York Times Magazine*. His writing has appeared in the *New Yorker*, *Harper's*, and the *London Review of Books*, among others.

About Bard College

Founded in 1860, Bard College in Annandale-on-Hudson, New York, is an independent, residential, coeducational college offering a four-year BA program in the liberal arts and sciences and a five-year BA/BS degree in economics and finance. The Bard College Conservatory of Music offers a five-year program in which students pursue a dual degree—a BMus and a BA in a field other than music. Bard offers MMus degrees in conjunction with the Conservatory and The Orchestra Now, and at Longy School of Music of Bard College in Cambridge, Massachusetts. Bard and its affiliated institutions also grant the following degrees: AA at Bard High School Early College, a public school with campuses in New York City, Baltimore, Cleveland, Newark, New Jersey, and Washington, D.C.; AA and BA at Bard College at Simon's Rock: The Early College, in Great Barrington, Massachusetts, and through the Bard Prison Initiative at six correctional institutions in New York State; MA in curatorial studies, MS and MA in economic theory and policy, and MS in environmental policy and in climate science and policy at the Annandale campus; MFA and MAT at multiple campuses; MBA in sustainability in New York City; and MA, MPhil, and PhD in the decorative arts, design history, and material culture at the Bard Graduate Center in Manhattan. Internationally, Bard confers BA and MAT degrees at Al-Quds University in East Jerusalem and American University of Central Asia in Kyrgyzstan; BA degrees at Bard College Berlin: A Liberal Arts University; and BA and MA degrees at the Faculty of Liberal Arts and Sciences, St. Petersburg State University, Russia (Smolny).

Bard offers nearly 50 academic programs in four divisions. Total enrollment for Bard College and its affiliates is approximately 6,000 students. The undergraduate College has an enrollment of about 1,800 and a student-to-faculty ratio of 9:1. In 2016, Bard acquired the Montgomery Place estate, bringing the size of the campus to nearly 1,000 acres. For more information about Bard College, visit bard.edu.

JOURNALS

VOLUME 1/2012

Truthtelling: Democracy in an Age without Facts

Human Being in an Inhuman Age

VOLUME 2/2014

Does the President Matter?

A Conference on the American Age of Political Disrepair

VOLUME 3/2015

The Unmaking of Americans:

Are There Still American Values Worth Fighting For?

Failing Fast: The Educated Citizen in Crisis

VOLUME 4/2016

Why Privacy Matters

VOLUME 5/2017

Real Talk: Difficult Questions about Race, Sex, and Religion

VOLUME 6/2018

Crises of Democracy: Thinking in Dark Times

VOLUME 7/2019

Racism and Antisemitism

hac.bard.edu

Made in the USA
Middletown, DE
25 September 2020